IN FOREIGN FIELDS

How Not To Move To France

Susie Kelly

blackbird

A CIP catalogue record for this book is available from the British Library
ISBN-9781916426825

© Susie Kelly 2018
A revised edition of *Two Steps Backwards* by Susie Kelly, first published by Bantam, Transworld Publishers in 2004 as a UK paperback. This is the first digital, and first worldwide, edition.
Published by Blackbird Digital Books
www.blackbird-books.com
The moral right of the author has been asserted.
Cover design by First Impressions Inc
Cover Image by David Lewis, www.davidlewiscartoons.com
Photographs © Susie Kelly

Don't buy this book thinking it's going to be all about Parisian chic, chilled Burgundy, peculiar French people and lolling around the swimming pool. That's a different France. In this book there is no Parisian chic, there is no swimming pool, most of the peculiar people aren't French and there is very little decent wine. If that is what you are looking for you will be sorely disappointed, so look away now.

Chapter One

My love affair with France began in the schoolroom in Kenya in 1963, when our French teacher showed a silent black and white film of Edith Piaf's funeral procession through the streets of Paris.

Funerals didn't excite me and I'd never heard of Edith Piaf, but when Madame put on a record (vinyl – cassettes hadn't arrived yet), and the Little Sparrow belted out *Non Je Ne Regrette Rien*, *La Vie en Rose*, *Milord* and *Les Trois Cloches* with her excessively rrrrrrolling 'r's, a chill ran up my spine. I thought, I want to live in the country where they sing like that.

Chapter Two

Among the stacks of magazines about France that we had collected over the years, a British estate agent regularly advertised properties costing less than £5,000 in the region in southwest France, which at the time was called the Poitou-Charentes and which was where we decided to buy our house. Not too far south where the weather would be too hot; not too far east where the winters would be too cold, and not too far north where it rained a lot. Much later the Poitou-Charentes would merge with two adjacent regions to become part of Nouvelle Aquitaine.

On a brief visit searching for somewhere to buy, we viewed twenty-four properties, most of which were nothing like what we were looking for. One property was inaccessible due to a great tangle of barbed wire across the doors. Several others had internal walls made from polystyrene sheets held up with tape and reinforced with floral wallpaper. In the primitive kitchen of one abandoned house, the sink was still filled with dirty dishes.

Time was running out and we hadn't seen anything even remotely habitable, let alone like the charming £5,000 watermill featured in the estate agent's advertisements. There were two more places to view. From the smudgy grey photocopied sheet of sparse details, the first property resembled the aftermath of a nuclear strike. There was something about it, though, and the nearer we approached, the more strongly I felt that this was the house with our name on it. A narrow track led from a minor road, across a small stone bridge spanning a seep (which in times of heavy rain became a trickle) and into a huddle of a dozen houses.

Scraggy chickens scattered as we halted beside an old stone well where the track ended. Our guide, Valérie, a pretty dark-haired girl with doe eyes, gestured triumphantly, like a magician producing an elephant from a top hat: *'Et voila! C'est superbe, n'est-ce pas?'*

The farmhouse dated back to 'about the eighteenth century,' Valérie said somewhat vaguely. It was a long, rectangular building in three equal parts. One third comprised the two rooms making up the living part. The main room was 20 feet by 12, with a beamed timber ceiling and two in-built cupboards stuffed with spiders' webs. Suspended from a lump of wood nailed to a beam, dangling incongruously three feet above the floor, a length of fraying flex bore a single light bulb topped by a rusty tin shade. Around the edges, the wooden floorboards had long since collapsed onto the earth below.

Originally this room had served as kitchen, dining and living room to the family of seven, as well as the bedroom of the mother and father. The walls were smothered in a weird, almost luminous, shiny green paint. When I peeled it off in little curls, it revealed cracked grey plaster beneath. I was pleased the previous owners had not followed the French fashion of the time and covered every wall, door and ceiling in floral wallpaper. The kitchen part of the room had consisted of a wood-burning stove standing beside the fireplace, its pipe running into a large hole knocked into the chimney breast. The stove had gone, but the hole remained, rather spoiling the charm of the traditional stone mantelpiece. In one corner of the room was the shallow stone sink beneath a small oval *oeil de boeuf* window – a typical feature of the area. A battered door led into the garden.

A second door led to an adjoining room 8 feet by 12 that had been the bedroom for the family's five children. The entire floor had subsided onto the dirt, and fungi were thriving on the walls. Ancient shutters clung with lost hope to cracked windows. Those two rooms were the full extent of the living accommodation. Above them was an empty loft space where tobacco and hams once hung to dry. There was no sanitation and no water supply inside the house.

The adjacent two thirds of the building was a dirt-floored barn divided into two by a rough stone wall, with one section for storage of hay and straw, the other for the animals during the winter. This part of the building was separated from the living part by a three-foot-thick stone wall, embedded in which were two large rectangular hatches covered with primitive wooden shutters that could be slid open to allow the warmth from the animals into the living room.

The sky peered in through gaps between the roof tiles.

Until four years previously, the mother of the five children had lived here. Old age had transported her into a nursing home, leaving her son to sell the house. I thought wistfully that if a family of seven had managed to live and grow in such basic conditions, it was a shame I didn't feel I was going to be able to manage without a fridge/freezer, a washing machine, hot and cold running water and a modern electrical supply. The current dangling bulb and single wall socket had been installed in 1934 when electricity first arrived in the hamlet, and hadn't been updated since. Piped water had arrived thirty years later but hadn't yet reached the interior of the house.

All the properties in the hamlet would have been built by itinerant builders, moving around the country constructing buildings from local materials. The thick walls were comprised of flints and limestones, pockets of earth, desiccated animal manure and colonies of scurrying wildlife. I wondered how long it had taken to collect the hundreds of thousands of stones necessary to build these places, how the massive beams had been hoisted into place, and what those ancient builders would think if they could see modern construction techniques that can erect a house in just a few days.

As well as the farmhouse, there was a collection of quaint and crumbling outbuildings – two small stone sheds, formerly accommodation for goats or pigs; one large, open-fronted barn housing some agricultural machinery and bales of hay; one decrepit building that had been a house and was now acting as a garage; one tiny, murky hovel with a rough cobblestoned floor and caved-in ceiling, with the old wooden shelf that used to store food out of reach of rodents still hanging from a beam. The stone sink and outline of a fireplace showed that this too had once been a dwelling. More recently, when the property was still a working farm, it had been used to stable the working mare.

The mellow stones and mossy pantiles of the roofs blended softly into the landscape. Two massive lime trees and a colossal oak – estimated to be 400 years old – dominated the acre and a half of land, which was roughly fenced and hedged, and maintained in good order by a small flock of sheep. A leaning fence post supported a rakish scarecrow dressed in black trousers and shirt. Small volcanoes of crumbly earth indicated the presence of moles, and battalions of infant sloe bushes were creeping stealthily across the field from the hedge.

Looking around and soaking up the atmosphere of peace and the sweet birdsong, my head and heart started a debate.

Heart said it felt perfect for us, despite the fearsome amount of work needed to make this place habitable. Head replied that it was far too big a project for people with no money, no experience of building and no particular skills. While they were arguing, the peace was ripped asunder by the most horrible noise I've ever heard. I imagined it was what a human sacrifice would sound like during the event: a repeated wail of pure terror and unspeakable pain.

'Whatever is making that terrible noise?' I asked Valérie.

'Probably,' she shrugged in the prosaic manner of a country girl, 'they are killing the turkeys.'

I couldn't live anywhere, even in the kingdom of the perennial money tree and eternal youth, if creatures were being slaughtered on our doorstep. I turned to leave, but Valérie kept steering us determinedly around the property, helping herself along the way to handfuls of purple plums. 'I'm very greedy,' she laughed, rolling her eyes and reaching for another helping. She pointed out the walnut, apples, pears, plums, greengages, and the unspoilt view, while I made a loud humming noise to try to dampen the tortured screams. We explored the hamlet, drawing nearer to the barn from where the agonised yells came. The appalling noise reached an impossible crescendo, a long drawn out screech of agony. I stopped and turned away.

Valérie took my arm and pointed to where a Moluccan cockatoo was perched majestically within an ornate wrought-iron cage, his flamboyant crest raised and his clever boot-button black eyes studying us. Encouraged by our attention, he swayed rhythmically from side to side like a feathery pendulum, escalating the volume until it went right off the scale.

My heart shot up again and I stopped the humming noise. We wandered around the property some more, brushing through the herb-scented grass, under the baleful eyes of the sheep.

Head was estimating the time and work, and the money that we didn't have, which would be needed to make this place habitable. Heart, determined to win, said slyly: 'It's ridiculously cheap. We won't find anything else at this price. We will never again find anywhere that feels so right for us, and we'll end up regretting it for the rest of our lives if we miss this opportunity.'

Do you believe that every house has a spirit that you feel immediately as you walk in? I remembered the strangeness of a newly-built house we had bought twenty years previously. What had instantly struck me was that there was no atmosphere, just empty space smelling of fresh paint.

This house, with its crumbling walls and floorboards had a kind spirit. It felt protective, safe.

'OK,' said Head, giving in just as I knew it would. 'Let's do it!'

Terry and I looked at each other; I nodded at him, and he nodded back.

'*Oui,*' we agreed with Valérie, '*c'est vraiment superbe.*'

We'd read about the pitfalls of buying property in France, the cardinal rule being: DO NOT IN ANY CIRCUMSTANCES SIGN ANYTHING WITHOUT FIRST TAKING PROFESSIONAL ADVICE FROM AN ENGLISH SOLICITOR. Disastrous purchases were made in haste: a rash signature on a *compromis* – a binding agreement to purchase – and you were landed with nothing but trouble: boundary disputes that were impossible to settle, neighbours who had the right to drive their tractors through your bathroom, houses that it was illegal to inhabit and you couldn't sell. You could never be too careful.

We knocked on the door of the vendor, who lived fifty yards away in a neat white cottage. M. Royer was one of the children born in 'our' house, a gentle, shy bachelor in his late sixties. I asked him whether he was sad to be selling the property.

He smiled and shook his head. 'No, not at all. It's a lot of work to maintain so many old buildings.'

I'd remember his words in years to come.

'Please tell your mother,' I said, 'that we will love her house very much.'

He smiled and tilted his head in acknowledgement, inviting us to sit at his kitchen table while he opened a bottle of vintage cider to celebrate our deal. Prompted by Valérie, we wrote on nine successive pages of a *compromis,* of which we could understand hardly a word, '*Lu et approuvé*' ('read and approved') followed by our initials. We had taken an irrevocable step towards buying a French farmhouse.

That was in August. An organisation called SAFER who control land development in rural areas has the pre-emptive right to purchase agricultural property. I could not imagine that they would not covet our little field, and expected daily to hear that they had swiped it from under us, but by early November all the formalities and paperwork had been completed. In the elegant office of a local *notaire,* we signed the *Acte de Vente* and the property was ours. That was in August 1994.

Chapter Three

Eleven months later, on 13th July 1995, we drove away in the small hours of the morning from the cottage that had been our home. In the hired truck were our five dogs, two parrots and a few oddments of furniture. Latter day *Darling Buds of May*. For the time being, our two horses would remain in England.

Although we had said farewell to all our neighbours, it felt furtive as we loaded the animals by torchlight, trying to be as quiet as possible so as not to wake anybody. The truck coughed loudly as the engine rattled into life.

The dogs slept on their beds, the parrots in their cages strapped to the sides of the truck. Once we boarded the ferry, there was no turning back. The dogs could no longer return to England without spending six months in quarantine, which was unthinkable and unaffordable. We had crossed the Rubicon.

At Cherbourg, we disembarked into the rolling green orchards of Normandy, where voluptuous cattle grazed beside quaint thatched cottages. The road was a gentle switchback, rising and dipping, on and on, until the lush northern pastures gave way to the plains of the Touraine. Endless fields of wheat simmered beneath the sun, still high in the early evening air.

The road seemed to reach into infinity; over the modest river Loir, and half an hour later, over his regal sister, the great Loire herself.

By late dusk, we had passed the space-age landscape of Futuroscope on the outskirts of Poitiers, thirty miles from our new home.

Because we were tired, we took a wrong turning and arrived in the centre of a small town. A *gendarme* stepped in front of the truck with an upraised hand. A wave of panic flooded over me. Had we already fallen foul of the law? The *gendarme* stepped towards the truck, smiling, and signalled we should pull over to the side of the road. Around the corner, a procession appeared: frail people leaning on supportive arms, infants in buggies, young, old and those in between, a dozen strutting dogs, all marching down the street behind a brass band, singing merrily and waving candlelit paper lanterns. Somebody banged on the side of the truck, calling: 'Come and join us!' The procession passed and the *gendarme* waved us on. Ten minutes later, we were rolling again, so close now, until we drove into La Petite-Eglise, the last village before our hamlet, and into the heart of another crowd of merry-makers preparing to start the celebration of France's national day.

Apart from several dozen flickering paper lanterns, the only light in the village square – which is actually an oblong – came from the bar with its eccentric 1970s English telephone box inside the doors. Tables and chairs stood on the pavement outside the bar and adjacent restaurant. Children skipped and chased each other around the stone fountain whose jets of water leapt and chuckled in the night air. Huddled around the oblong were the restaurant, bar, bakery, hairdresser, chemist and a manufacturer of a local speciality, *le farci poitevin,* a sort of stuffed cabbage.

Fifty yards away, a tiny 12th century church sat on a bend beside a stone bridge over a little stream, watched over by a 17th century château perched on a steep bluff.

Somebody was trying to marshal the crowd into an orderly line, clapping their hands and shouting to make themselves heard over the chatter and laughter, squeals and clinks of glasses and bottles. It was a quintessentially French scene and we could not have chosen a better moment to arrive if we had tried. A lump appeared in my throat, and Terry said: 'Well, welcome to France!'

Again the local citizenry beckoned to us, calling out that we English should come and share their celebrations. With our eyes burning from tiredness, and the animals still shut in the vehicle, we couldn't stop, but we waved and yelled loudly: '*Vive la France!*' which was met with laughter and applause.

In two miles, we would be home. We drove in silence.

Turning onto the lane into the hamlet, I had a powerful feeling of coming home to where we belonged, to the place that had been waiting for us. At the same time, life was going to be hard because for the foreseeable future Terry and I would be living apart for much of the time, not knowing when or how often we would see each other. It felt strange, exciting and rather frightening.

Terry halted the truck outside the house, switched off the engine and the lights, and for two minutes we sat silently in the dark, savouring the moment. The dogs spilled out of the vehicle ecstatically, in a flurry of legs and tails, snuffling and snorting as they explored, then running back to us to make sure we were still there.

For a few minutes, the only sound was of the crickets creaking, and then rumbles and cracks of exploding fireworks broke the silence. Rockets illuminated the skies, heralding the arrival of *le quatorze juillet,* and unveiling the silhouettes of the buildings and trees. We stood on the grass, warm in shorts and T-shirts, sipping champagne beneath the velvet canopy of night pierced by a hundred million stars.

After we had settled the dogs and parrots in the living room, we dragged a faded sofa-bed in there, and fell on it, too tired to even take off our clothes... but happy.

***

Where the bottom of the living room door had succumbed over the years to damp and wear, a ragged ribbon of moonlight slid beneath. A persistent rattling, scuffling sound pulled me from half-sleep. In the glare, an unwieldy black shape with horns scrunched itself – with difficulty, but determination – through the space and into the room. Terry had heard the noise too and got up quietly to put the stag beetle outside. The beetle forced itself back again beneath the gap and scrabbled around the ancient grimy floorboards for whatever purpose it had in mind.

When the moonlit strip under the door had vanished in favour of early-morning sunshine, we fed the dogs and wheeled the parrots into the shade of a vine overhanging the door, then unloaded and settled the rest of our things.

Beside the sofa bed were cardboard boxes of books and tinned food, some crockery and cutlery and my clothes. Our furniture consisted of a plastic garden table and two plastic chairs which we put in the main room, along with a washing machine and a Porta Potti chemical toilet. Our kitchen equipment consisted of a hideous tomato-red fridge/freezer, a collection of half a dozen old melamine cupboards and a lethal second-hand gas cooker. This shuddered violently whenever it was lit, emitting a great bang and spitting blue flame from the casing joints. For the time being, it was our sole source of hot water and cooked food, which is why we mainly ate salad.

There was nowhere for any of this sorry kitchen to go in the house, as the main barn area had no electricity, the walls were comprised of pieces of rock and flint vaguely held in place by mud and manure, there was no ceiling, we could see daylight through the elderly roof tiles, and the floor had been the livestock's toilet for decades.

Instead we set it up 60 yards away in the open barn at the end of the garden, which also had no electricity, no ceiling, a dirt floor and was accessible to whatever wildlife chose to roam around in it. In retrospect, I can't quite remember the logic, but anyway, there it was at the bottom of the garden. We discovered a working electric power point in the building used as a garage, and installed the fridge/freezer in there.

Although there was no running water inside the house, there was a tap attached to the outside wall. The washing machine stood outside the garage, sharing the power point with the fridge/freezer. It was connected by a piece of hose to the tap 10 yards away, and discharged directly into the earth through a length of drainpipe.

We put the Porta Potti in an old goat shed with a nice view of a flowering cherry tree.

Instead of a bathroom, we had a plastic bucket next to the tap on the wall, and during the scorching summer it was perfectly practicable.

The biggest battle was getting the bed up into the loft which would eventually become the bedroom. It was clean and dry up there, and waterproof, but the only means of access was up an ancient ladder with signs of woodworm, and the second from bottom rung was broken. The base of the bed was in two parts, and by tying ropes around them, with Terry up at the top of the ladder hauling, and me at the bottom shoving, we managed to get them up, but the mattress put up a fight. The ropes slipped off it, it wouldn't fold, it seemed too large to fit through the small loft door. It kept tumbling back down the ladder and onto the dirt of the barn floor. We cursed and laughed and heaved and tugged, and we did so until it finally gave up the fight and squished itself into the loft.

***

M. Royer had cleared every room of any remaining bits and pieces and had swept from the dirt floors any trace of straw, dust and cobwebs, leaving them spotlessly tidy. Many of the outbuildings were inaccessible, blockaded by ivy, brambles and grass that had grown over and around the ancient oak doors with their crude, hand-forged iron hinges and bolts. We laughed at the thought of owning rooms we hadn't even seen. We stroked the trunks of the trees, traced the fossils embedded in the limestones, and picked the wild mint and thyme in the field, crushing it between our fingers and savouring the perfume. The dogs dashed around, their tails wagging with excitement, digging wildly at molehills or chasing butterflies through the long grass. We lunched and dined on cheese and wine accompanied by teeth-cracking baguettes from the local bakery, and we marvelled that this little kingdom really was in our keeping.

Terry had to return to England after two days with the hired vehicle. Climbing into the truck, he blew a kiss and waved as he vanished into the distance. He would have to make a living to support us all. I wondered how anybody could be so eternally, unquenchably positive and optimistic after the events of the previous year. Defeat was not a word in his vocabulary. There was no such thing as a problem – only a situation.

Listening to the sound of the engine growing fainter until it faded into eerie silence, it felt like that moment when you pass your driving test and are suddenly not at all confident that you're ready to drive a car alone. I felt like the first and only human on the moon, uncertain whether I would manage living by myself in a country where I knew no-one. I didn't even know how to wire a plug or change a fuse... but I was soon going to learn.

Sensing my unease, the dogs milled around, pushing their faces at me to say: 'It's OK, Mum, we're here, everything will be fine.' Our canine matriarch was Natalia, a Hungarian Vizsla, a breed that personifies beauty, gentleness and elegance with their smooth russet coats and sincere hazel eyes. She was a faithful companion to us and a doting mother to her children. At 12 years old, she was still in remarkably good condition physically and would live to be 17. However, she was becoming a little fragile in the upper storey, and spent her time wandering around and around with a wrinkled forehead trying to puzzle out why she was doing so. Hecate, her daughter, was an affectionate, strong-willed and independent creature, who did exactly what she wanted to do, where, when and however it pleased her. Grand Wizard (Wizzy) was so handsome and noble in appearance that people who normally didn't like dogs stopped to talk to him. His brother Vulcan was slightly timid with a permanently perplexed and suspicious expression as if he never quite understood what was going on and worried that whatever it was, he may be held responsible.

In contrast with the Vizslas' russet-coated elegance, little Max, an Affenpinscher, looked like a black wig in a gale, radiating charm and high spirits. They reminded me that they were waiting for their breakfast.

Watching them eat, I relaxed. There wasn't much I could do without a car, so it was a perfect excuse to drag one of our two chairs outside and sit enjoying the sun and birdsong. The call of the cuckoo was unmistakable, but the rest was a choir of different voices. Among them, one stood out because it was clearly calling: 'Pleased to meet you! Pleased to meet you! Pleased to meet you!' I wondered what it was.

Apart from the birdsong and the panting of the dogs, it was so quiet. The blue of the sky was unblemished, and a very slight breeze tempered the warmth of the sun. Despite uncertainty about the future, for the time being I bathed in the moment, squeezing every second of pleasure from the day. *Carpe diem*. The book on my lap lay unopened as I passed the hours sitting beneath the vine and practising schoolgirl French.

Chapter Four

All my life I had feared the dark, always keeping a light close by when I was alone at night, but I was not afraid that first night on my own. It may have been the presence of the five dogs, physical and emotional tiredness, or the reassurance that nobody could possibly get into the house through the hefty locked door or thick shutters, but I think it was more a sensation of being completely safe here.

I couldn't sleep upstairs, because that meant climbing the ladder with its broken rung. I'm not good with ladders at the best of times, and that one tilted and rocked precariously, then at the top you had to step off it with nothing to hold on to. If I fell, nobody would know and who would look after the animals? For now, I'd sleep in the living room on the sofa bed. The fly-specked naked bulb with its rusty tin shade dangled a few inches from my face, so I turned it off. It was not dark after all. Blades of moonlight came through the cracks in the shutters, painting bright stripes on the walls and floor.

From heavy sleep, I awoke with a start. Someone was knocking at the door, a voice calling, the dogs barking hysterically. Swathed in a sheet, I opened the door and came face to face with my first Frenchman. He was not wearing a beret, nor a stripey jumper, nor did he have a twirly moustache, and neither was he smoking a Gauloise. Nothing at all like the Frenchman beloved of cartoonists and caricaturists. He was slim, young and clean-shaven, carrying a clipboard and a leather holdall.

'Bonjour, Madame – c'est pour installer votre téléphone.'

I remembered that we were indeed expecting a telephone engineer. I just hadn't expected him at 8.00am.

Unfazed by the dogs sniffing around him, and me wrapped in the sheet like a vestal virgin, he asked where I wanted the telephone. The only suitable place was on the windowsill in the small room adjacent to the living room.

While the engineer worked, I dressed and fed the dogs and parrots. The telephone cable trailed into the room from the outside, passing through the loose-fitting window.

'*C'est fait,*' he called. It's done.

As he gathered up his equipment and handed me the clipboard to sign, I thanked him. The telephone would be working by the end of the week, he said.

'When do you plan to come and live here?' he asked.

I replied that I was living here now.

He looked around at the bare room, the peeling paint, the collapsing floor.

'*Vraiment?*' he asked. Really?

Yes.

He laughed, shook my hand, and left, saying: '*Je vous souhaite très bon courage, Madame.*' I wish you the very best of luck.

***

Straightening my 'bed' I lifted the pillow to plump it up, revealing a large and very flat beetle beneath it. Oh dear, poor beetle. How did it get there? Then I thought: spiders! I read somewhere that the average person (whatever that is) swallows nine spiders in their sleep during their lifetime. I don't know how that conclusion was reached, and by whom. Were there hundreds of thousands of people watching over other people who were sleeping, counting the spiders as they swallowed them? If so, didn't common decency impel them to warn the people in time? I thought it a ridiculous claim, but nevertheless it played on my mind. Finding a beetle crushed beneath the pillow was bad enough, now I was imagining giant spiders down between the cushions. Somewhere in the boxes of foodstuffs there was a drop of Grand Marnier left over from a recipe I made several years ago when we could afford such things. Before I went to bed that night, I'd take a big swig, so if I did inadvertently swallow a spider, the alcohol would kill it and it wouldn't be wandering around in my stomach.

Pushing that unpleasant prospect from my mind, I went to explore.

Fifty yards from our house, outside the barn where the cockatoo had screamed the previous year, stood a battered furniture removal van bearing an English name and address. It looked as if somebody had started to renovate the barn and had changed their mind. Piles of breeze-blocks and sacks of hardened cement, scaffolding poles and old tyres lay all over the place. A rusty cooker peered through the undergrowth. I roamed around, narrowly avoiding falling into a vast pit hidden by shoulder-high stinging nettles. The place was a frightful eyesore, and I was curious to know who it belonged to, but there was nobody around.

The bilious green paint needed to come off the living room walls, so I found a spatula and began scraping. Soon the floor was covered in thick curls of old paint. I amused myself by seeing how big a piece would come off in one go. It's surprising how soothing it could be. As I chipped away at the surface, the adjoining paint broke into a crazed surface of flakes, which I also peeled off, exposing a large area of rough plaster with black stuff growing on it. The black stuff looked like some kind of mould, so I scraped at it. Huge chunks of plaster let go of the wall and tumbled into crumbly heaps on the floor. They left behind inch-deep craters from which trickled cascades of sand and dirt, exposing the stones and flints that formed the main substance of the wall. I prodded around and constructed more craters and cascades: there was something compelling about doing so. I felt I could stay forever digging at the wall with my spatula.

After sweeping up the part of the wall that lay on the floor, I rummaged in the packing cartons and found a box of some kind of plaster powder which I stirred in a bucket with some water until it was thick. Using the spatula, I smeared it into the craters in the wall. It slid back out and landed on the floor. I kept shovelling it back all afternoon, and just when I'd created a nice smooth surface the whole thing would fall out in a sticky, gritty lump and I'd have to start all over again. As the light began to fade, I gave it a final push with the spatula hoping it would stay put. It was still in place next morning and looked like something kindergarten children would create with a flour and water paste.

Not having a bath, shower or even handbasin brought home the reality of life for many millions of people around the world. I had never previously considered how invaluable a bucket can be. Until now, the only uses I'd had for one had been making sandcastles on the beach, and filling them with water for our horses.

My bucket served many purposes: laundry, dish washing, and bathing. When it was hot and sunny, I washed outside, using the tap, with a towel handy in case of unexpected visitors. On cool evenings, I filled the bucket with warm water and took it into the living room. Normally, I placed it on a towel on the floor and stood with one leg in it at a time while I washed. One evening, when every ounce of sense said it was a bad idea, I tried to get both feet into the bucket at the same time. Immediately, I discovered there wasn't room for both, and I lost my balance, fell over, knocked over the bucket, soaked the floor and bruised my elbow. I lay on the floor laughing and watching the water seeping through the cracks in the floorboards onto the earth beneath.

***

On the fourth day, I met my second Frenchman. After a morning of trying to block escape routes for the dogs who were keen to explore further afield, I settled down in the shade of an old goat shed in a patch of the parched earth that was the garden. From the corner of my eye, I caught a moving shadow at the end of the shed. The shadow unmistakably belonged to a person trying to peer round the shed at me without being seen.

I called out '*Bonjour!*' and walked around to find a rather sheepish-looking man wearing a flat cap and wielding a hoe. We shook hands through the fence, and I said, in my stumbling French, how very pleased I was that we were neighbours. From the blank look on his face, I could see he didn't understand. He said something to me that I didn't understand, but I smiled and nodded and made a kind of chirruping noise. I tried again, speaking as clearly as I could, explaining that I was English, and asking how his garden was doing, which is always an excellent way to start a conversation with a Frenchman. He shrugged and replied in French less mangled by dialect, so that I managed to understand that the garden was OK, but very dry. We needed rain. Did he think we'd have some soon? He shook his head. No, not until the wind came from the west. That's where the rain comes from, off the Atlantic. There was just a puff of breeze from the opposite direction – which was why, he explained, we could hear the church bells from a village a few miles away to the east.

He plucked a couple of lettuces and handed them to me over the wire, so I took that as being a good sign. I said *merci* as clearly as I could. M. Meneteau was a retired farmer, a short little man whose out-thrust chest and round eyes reminded me of a pigeon. His wife was one of the five children born in our house, like her brother M. Royer.

Three years previously, M. Meneteau had had five-way heart bypass surgery. He should have been taking life easy, but was always on the go, working in his immaculate vegetable patch, harvesting grapes from his vineyard to brew wine and vinegar, or weaving decorative bowls and baskets from bramble stems, a craft his mother had taught him.

I mentioned the English furniture truck. Did he know who it belonged to? Yes, an Englishman... called Bill, or something like that. He owned the barn and the furniture truck and stopped off here from time to time for a few days to do some work on the property. Sometimes he came in a truck, sometimes in a car. He unloaded things, and didn't always leave in the same vehicle he arrived in. He often got his truck stuck and M. Meneteau had to pull it out with his tractor. M. Meneteau thought he travelled between Spain and England, but he wasn't sure; their conversations were limited as Bill didn't speak any more French than M. Meneteau spoke English. When did he think Bill might be back? He pulled a face and raised his shoulders half an inch. No idea. He came and went about once a month. Maybe he'd be here fairly soon.

From his garden, he had a 360-degree view of the hamlet, and I thought that he probably knew pretty much everything that happened here.

Bill turned up a few days later, with the cockatoo. He came and introduced himself – a pleasant, courteous man who made his living moving furniture between Spain and England, using this place as his halfway point. Contrary to my vision of a big burly man, he was slightly built and not very tall, with a thatch of grey hair and thick-lensed glasses. He looked more like a school teacher than a removal man, apart from his boots, whose steel toecaps glistened where the leather had worn away.

He outlined his plans for his property: the barn would become three houses with stained glass windows and spiral staircases, two for renting out and one for himself. There would be several bungalows for elderly people, and a community bus. Landscaped gardens would feature ponds and fountains. It all sounded charming. The important thing, he emphasised, when renovating these properties, was to do so sympathetically and in keeping with tradition. I nodded, trying to remember where I had last seen a French farmhouse with a stained glass window, but I liked his enthusiasm and ambition.

Over a couple of glasses of wine, Bill mentioned that he had a problem. He was leaving for England the day after tomorrow and couldn't take Sinbad the cockatoo with him because he didn't have the required paperwork. With no way for the bird to get back to Spain, Sinbad was in danger of having to self-cater unless Bill could find somebody to have him 'for a few days'.

As I agreed to look after Sinbad I wondered vaguely what would have happened if I hadn't been here. Bill moved the bird and its titanic cage into the living room alongside our two parrots, then he set off for England. He didn't leave any food for Sinbad.

I hadn't expected to find another English resident in the hamlet. I didn't know whether I was pleased or not. My dream of being the only English person for miles around and totally immersed into French rural life was tarnished. On the other hand, it was comforting to know that there would be, from time to time, somebody with whom it would be possible to hold a conversation that both sides fully understood.

Chapter Five

Saint-Thomas-le-Petit is a sleepy little village with an infants' school, *boulangerie*, a pretty 12th century church, a café/bar/restaurant, a cemetery and an agricultural workshop. The *Mairie* – the mayor's office – also housed the local library and post office, all in one large room with an ornate clock on the wall, a table with maps spread over it, and a single chair.

In almost every account I had read of life in France, the local bakery produced delicious crusty bread. Ours didn't. The loaves, whether *baguettes*, *pain*, *couronnes*, skinny *ficelles* or *pain de campagne* were uniformly encased in a thick, vicious crust which cut your gums and jammed inextricably between your teeth. The interior was a network of large holes linked by a dry white material like polystyrene ceiling tiles. It was exhausting to chew and useless for toasting, as the butter escaped through the network of holes. This was my personal opinion: the local inhabitants liked this bread and were proud of their bakery, but I preferred my bread to be soft and chewy with a fine crust that didn't have the texture of tree bark. I quickly gave up buying bread there, and would soon be glad I had. However, I remained a regular customer for the excellent prune tarts. Prunes are not the subject of bowel movement jokes in France as they are in England.

The baker was a ghostly pale man – maybe because he was permanently coated in flour, or maybe he didn't get out into the sun – and he had a small white terrier.

After our horses arrived – which I will come to in a while – whenever I needed bran, the baker would put aside a large paper sack behind the counter in the little shop. One day he called me to the back, where the ovens were. The air was delicious with the smell of baking, and a pile of fresh loaves was spread out on the floor upon a large sheet. The little white dog was wandering around, and as it passed the pile it cocked its little leg and urinated casually. I was glad the prune tarts were not kept on sheets on the floor.

With no transport, I either walked to the village a mile away, or used the mobile bakery that visited the hamlet three times a week. As well as selling bread, it supplied buttons, cotton for darning stockings, envelopes, tinned fruit, vegetables, cheese, fish and meat, soft drinks and cheap wine, biscuits and fresh cakes, sweets and greetings cards.

One morning, I walked to the village to buy postage stamps, arriving just after 11.00am. There I learned that the post office only opened between 2.00pm and 4.00pm although as the girl who ran it was also the sole waitress at the restaurant, if she was still clearing tables you'd have to wait to buy your stamps.

There was no visible sign of life except the lady behind the counter in the bakery when I bought my prune tart, although I could hear children's voices from the school yard behind the mayor's office.

Having failed to buy stamps in the morning, I set off again in the early afternoon. The heat bounced back from the tarmac and the soles of my shoes stuck to the road. I felt like the filling in a toasted sandwich, when a car drew up and a voice asked in English if I needed a lift. That is when I met my third Frenchman, Jean-Luc, another of our neighbours, who had been born in the hamlet. He spoke perfect English and invited me to let him know if I needed help with anything. I was relieved to have met somebody I could turn to in case of need, something that would happen quite regularly.

If you didn't know better you might have thought nothing happened in Saint-Thomas-le-Petit, but there was an enthusiastic football team, regular tombola and *belote* events (a bit like a whist drive), and the huntsmen's dinner, the fishermen's dinner, the blood donors' dinner, the football team dinner, 14 July celebrations and the re-enactment of the burning of Joan of Arc. There were social activities for retired folk, an organised nocturnal walk, a busy street market once a year, the annual Armistice Day remembrance service and many other activities, all of which were generally accompanied by food and wine.

On sunny days, the elderly residents sat cross-armed and cross-ankled on benches outside their houses, watching the intermittent passing traffic. M. Meneteau talked of a time when there had been a thriving community of busy farms, served by six cafés, two blacksmiths and several builders, joiners and other craftsmen in the village. Over the years, many small farms had been bought by co-operatives who ripped up the hedges to make larger, more convenient fields that could be worked by huge machinery. The arrival of supermarkets in the nearby towns had destroyed all the small shops. Our *boulangerie* was the last man standing.

Occasionally the village burst into life. Cars lined the road, while crowds of villagers and people from the surrounding hamlets stood outside the church in their best clothes, laughing and chatting. This was a sign that a funeral was about to take place. When somebody died, everybody from the commune attended the funeral, unless the deceased hadn't attended their family funerals. If people didn't come to your funeral, you didn't go to theirs. Funerals were more than paying respects to a member of the community; they were also an occasion for people to catch up and exchange news with those they didn't often see.

Life moved at a different speed to the one I had been used to. The local people lived at an unalterably leisurely pace – there's a reason they are affectionately known as *cagouilles* (snails). They were puzzled by English drivers hooting and swerving around in a frenzied attempt to overtake the tractors and combine harvesters that made up a large proportion of the traffic on the narrow lanes, occupying most of the roads' width.

When I was able to get into town, it took me a while to adapt to not rushing everywhere. The day I bought a cookery book at the supermarket the cashier passed it over the bar-code reader and then began flicking through it unhurriedly, pausing at a page with a slight frown. She asked the queue behind me whether they thought 200 grams was too much sugar in a particular recipe. One lady disagreed; the one behind her said she always used brown sugar; another always added a pinch of cinnamon, we learned, but somebody else shook her head disapprovingly: that was not the traditional recipe. Quite a lively discussion built up regarding the recipe and cooking in general, while I shuffled impatiently from one foot to the other, instead of enjoying the event like everybody else, and for absolutely no reason at all. Five more minutes would make no difference to the rest of my life. There was one thing that I found particularly exasperating, again due to the 'hurry-up mentality': if you were in a shop, had paid with cash and the phone rang, the telephone took priority over you. This leaves you in limbo with an outstretched hand awaiting your change during a lengthy and repetitive conversation, almost as if they were doing it deliberately. I'm sure they weren't, but that's how it felt.

'Yes. A hundred and eighty-five francs, including tax. We'll have it on

Wednesday afternoon. Yes, we're open from two fifteen to seven o'clock. Yes, that's right, in the afternoon. On Wednesday. Any time between two fifteen and seven. A hundred and eighty-five francs. Goodbye. No, it won't be here until Wednesday. It's, yes, that's right, including tax. No, we won't have it on Monday, it will be here Wednesday. Goodbye. No, the delivery doesn't come until after lunch… On Wednesdays… a hundred and eighty-five francs…'

Friends sent boxes of provisions, like Red Cross parcels, but local supermarkets stocked dozens of varieties of breakfast cereals, including cornflakes and porridge, as well as the bizarrely named Smacks, Kix and Felties. The fish counter offered kippers, sprats and smoked haddock amongst the *rascasse*, along with oysters, live lobsters and crabs. Indian, Mexican, Chinese and Italian ingredients, ready meals, marmalade, chocolate spread, Guinness, gin and tonic were all readily available. Washing-up liquid came in a wide variety of 'flavours' – green apple, mint, raspberry vinegar, blackcurrant and grapefruit. You could buy garden furniture, car parts, ride-on mowers, clothing, compost, kindling wood, assorted ammunition and, in a refrigerated unit, transparent containers of heaving maggots, writhing worms and other squirming live bait. The only thing I missed was Marmite.

Tuesday was market day. Ladies with wicker baskets on their arms examined cheeses, fish, meats, olives, walnut oil, honey, fruits, vegetables, freshly cooked paella, reinforced pink corsetry, chequered cotton aprons, rubber boots, bread, plants, household goods, pots, pans and rolls of fabric. In fine weather, their husbands stood in groups laughing and sipping glasses of red wine. When it was cold and wet, they sat in the local bars doing the same. For those items not available at the market they came to the supermarkets, which is why Tuesday was the busiest day there, the queues the longest and the chatter the loudest. There was always somebody happy and willing to give advice, to explain how to prepare and use vegetables and products I'd never seen before – vegetables such as the *crosne* which resemble large maggots and in English are known as Japanese artichokes.

Supermarkets were sometimes the setting for impromptu comedies. The day the electricity failed, customers were ordered to immediately stop shopping and queue at the tills. Anxious staff trotted up and down the aisles shooing people away. With the tills out of action, the cashiers were given pencils and pieces of paper to work out each customer's bill with hand-held calculators. It was time-consuming, as each customer laboriously checked their scrappy bills against their purchases, but everyone entered into the spirit of the event, waiting patiently while discussing the likelihood that some people would have taken advantage of the situation to pocket goods, and the improbability that anybody's bill would be accurate.

A week later, we queued outside the same supermarket waiting for it to open, but the doors remained closed. People checked their watches and muttered, and started walking purposefully at the doors, pushing trolleys at them, and waving their arms at the mechanism that made them to slide apart. One man tried unsuccessfully to lever them open.

After we had been standing there for 25 minutes, a woman appeared inside. She slid the doors open just enough to allow her to explain that the tills were out of order and that she had no idea when they would be working again. She closed the doors and vanished. The crowd shrugged philosophically, we replaced our trolleys and drove to another supermarket on the far side of town.

I watched a grubby woman wearing filthy clothes calmly help herself, munching a strawberry tartlet from a packet at the patisserie counter. I also saw two furious women punching, clawing and pulling each other's hair, whilst shrieking something I couldn't understand. A group of customers pulled them apart, and it is a lasting regret that I never learned what they were fighting over.

These incidents enlivened what, to me, is the chore of shopping.

Accustomed in England to shops that were open six and often seven days a week, and didn't close for lunch, mastering the timetables of the local commerce demanded a mental effort akin to taking a degree in nuclear astrophysics. Except for the supermarkets, almost nothing in our local town opened on Mondays, although one of the DIY stores did open in the afternoon. All the banks were closed except for La Poste. The few shops that did open on Mondays, closed on Tuesdays. Of the two supermarkets, one closed for lunch half an hour earlier than the other and opened fifteen minutes earlier in the afternoon. Both supermarkets stayed open all day on Saturdays, although they closed half an hour earlier than on weekdays, and one opened on Sunday mornings in July and August to cater for the summer tourists.

The *Mairie* was open one full day and two half-days per week, and the village restaurant only opened in the evenings by previous arrangement.

Local bakeries had their *hebdo* day off on a rota system that had to be learned by heart. Simple tasks could take an unreasonably long time; maybe we needed a single screw to finish fitting something up, and one of us would drive into town only to arrive at the store one minute after it had closed, or on Monday morning having forgotten it didn't open until the afternoon. The supermarket that was still open probably only sold the screws in boxes of 500, so we would drive back home and wait the two and a half hours before the shop with the single screw we needed had opened again. Just when you were confident that you knew exactly who opened when, you could arrive to find they were enjoying a *'fermeture exceptionelle'* (unexpected, and generally unexplained, closure), closed for stocktaking or some unfathomable bank holiday in celebration of St Bonzo.

It was all part of the challenge of adapting to a new life in a foreign country.

Chapter Six

Bill's 'few days' had stretched into a couple of weeks, and I hadn't heard from him. I wondered whether I'd seen the last of him, and if I could keep Sinbad who was a most entertaining bird.

One afternoon, a large man appeared at the door. His scrubby moustache and thinning hair gave him the appearance of a threadbare teddy bear, so I mentally christened him Fred Bear.

'Are you Sue?' he called.

'Susie,' I corrected.

'I'm a friend of Bill. He said you're an expert on horses and you'd be the person to help me.'

I don't know where Bill had got that idea from as I'd only mentioned that we had left our two retired horses in England.

'No, I'm afraid I'm not an expert at all.'

'Well,' Fred Bear continued, 'it's for me mate in Spain. He's a champion dressage rider. He wins all the cups, and he wants me to find him a new, top-class horse. I don't know anything about horses except one end bites and the other kicks. Bill said you'd know where to find one.'

It seemed quite bizarre, I thought, asking somebody who knew nothing about horses to locate a high-performance animal – like delegating a third party to track down a perfect wife – but being as naive as I was, and because l didn't want to seem unfriendly or unhelpful, I said I'd do my best.

'Don't worry, dearie,' said the threadbare one before he left, 'I'll pay for your phone calls.'

In good and misplaced faith, I set out to try to find a dressage horse for a man I didn't know who lived in Spain. I spent several days phoning people who referred me to other people, who all clearly thought I was quite mad. With a phone bill reflecting calls that had started off local, and from there wended their way to national and then to international, when Fred Bear called round again I reported that I hadn't been able to locate a suitable horse for his friend. I didn't like to mention the phone bill, and apparently neither did he.

Chapter Seven

That first summer was indescribably hot. The tarmac melted and bubbled up through its own cracks. Flies were horrendous – a plague that was everywhere, tangling themselves in my hair. There were clouds of stinging and biting insects. Midges and mosquitoes, biting flies, huge horseflies that really enjoyed a chomp, horrible delta-shaped giant flies called *mouches plates* that almost ate you alive, wasps, bees and a hateful little creature called an *aoutât* (pronounced 'ooter' and which I learned was a harvest mite). It is attracted to parts of the body that you do not wish to be seen scratching, but so intense is the irritation it causes that sometimes there is no choice.

My feet expanded several sizes and wouldn't fit into any of my shoes. I bought a pair of plastic sandals whose soles were studded with hundreds of little spikes. A label said that these massaged your feet and made you feel good. Wearing them was like walking on a bed of nails, but having invested the equivalent of £2 in them I couldn't afford to let them go to waste, so I persevered, and by the end of a week, if I'd had to leave a burning building with only one item, it would have been those sandals.

I could not glow, nor acquire a golden tan as most others seemed to do. I couldn't even perspire like a gentleman. In the overwhelming heat, I sweated like a horse. My skin took on a livid scarlet radiance.

One afternoon in August, the thermometer registered 43°C. Just breathing was a struggle, like inhaling warm treacle. Being in a car, even with all the windows open, was like sitting in an oven. The plums and grapes were ripening, attracting swarms of hornets. The only sensible place to be was indoors, with shutters closed, and doing nothing more energetic than reading. Like the listless, dusty trees and the frazzled brown grass, I was exhausted by the heat, and I craved rain.

Too hot to venture out, I attacked the living room floor with hot soapy water, gritty creams, and noxious foaming chemicals; when they were all used up the floor was no cleaner than when I started, so I used a sander and managed to reveal the wood beneath the decades of grime.

Unfortunately, the sander had lost the little bag that should fit on the side to collect the dust, so all of that spread over the walls, but the old oak floor did look rather nice apart from the collapsed parts around the edges.

My lungs were full of sawdust, my hair brittle with varnish, my clothes and shoes decorated with splashes of paint and plaster and I seemed to have permanently changed shape into a question mark. A strange creature began following me. Its clothes were uncoordinated and ill-fitting. Its disastrous hair was straggly and shapeless, and it wore a frazzled expression. It was either sprinkled with dust, or splashed with mud. I thought it was female, although the shapeless clothing made it difficult to tell. Mostly, I saw it when glancing in mirrors and shop windows. What a dreadful mess it was! I couldn't understand how anybody could let themselves go about looking like that.

Three weeks after our arrival, the first drops of rain fell, preceded by several hours of cracking thunder. Torrents of water from purple clouds smashed into the baked ground, and hail-stones the size of marbles bounced and ricocheted off the roofs. I stood out in it, enjoying its violence and silky warmth, although I could have got almost as wet indoors as it gushed down the chimney, through the broken window panes, under the door, through the ceiling and down the walls.

Because for so much of the time I was alone, and because it was so hot, and because I used the beastly oven as seldom as possible, I ate simply. A typical meal could have been something like a handful of Bourbon biscuits and half a jar of pickled onions. On one of those sweltering days, I sat reading and sipping a glass of wine. While I read, I absent-mindedly smeared a good runny Brie onto some crackers. When it came time to turn over a page, I put down the plate to take a mouthful of wine, and noticed movement. A handful of plump creamy maggots were humping around the rim of the plate. My first optimistic hope was that they had fallen from a nearby bush, or come out of the biscuit tin, but then I saw some of their kith and kin emerging cautiously from the cheese. Wary little maggot faces peeped out to ensure that some great mouth wasn't going to bite them in half, or squash them on a cracker, like those of their brethren that had gone before them. Aieeeeeeeeeeee!

An unpleasant experience for most people, and even worse for a vegetarian. I gargled and swilled out my mouth with vodka, spat, then knocked back the rest of the wine bottle fast. From then on, I kept all the cheese in the fridge, which never allowed it to reach that creamy stage of perfection, but I liked to think that at least if there were things living in it the cold would deal with them.

Chapter Eight

The nearest town was six miles away and there was no public transport. There were still hardy locals who managed with bicycles, but I was not one of them. Unlike in England where second-hand cars were cheap, they were outrageously expensive in France. After scouring all the notices pinned up outside the supermarkets, we saw a card advertising something that sounded perfect – a Citroën 2CV that we could just afford.

These eccentric little cars were conceived during the 1930s, designed to be an affordable and economic vehicle for rural areas, able to carry 120 pounds of potatoes, traverse a ploughed field with a basket of eggs without breaking any, and seat four adults wearing hats. Never mind the aesthetics. They were described as looking like giant snails pieced together out of old biscuit tins. Production was interrupted by WWII, and when they were finally unveiled at the Paris Motor Show in 1948 they were met with ridicule. But people loved them, and the 2CV became a cult car that offered a level of comfort and performance that belied its eccentric design and tiny engine which sounded more suited to driving a sewing machine. At one time, there was a six-year waiting list as demand exceeded production. Used models cost more than new ones.

I phoned the number on the card and spoke to a gentleman who said that yes, the car was in perfect condition and we were welcome to go and see it. He cautioned us not to delay as cars like this were rare and quickly snapped up, especially at such a bargain price. We hastened there.

He and his wife offered us a glass of *pineau* and some little crunchy biscuits, explaining that the car had belonged to Madame when they lived in Paris. It would break their hearts to see it go, but Madame was going to buy a new car and the garage space was needed. We went to their garage and raised a tarpaulin to reveal what looked like a museum piece.

She was sky-blue and absolutely beautiful. Her fabric roof was cracked and torn and her tyres were worn, but beneath a thick layer of dust the bodywork seemed fine.

We handed over the money, to their barely concealed surprise and delight, and Monsieur asked when we would be collecting her.

'We will take her now.'

'NOW?'

'Yes.'

'But she hasn't been driven for four years! She needs new tyres! The battery will be flat!'

Nevertheless, she was coming home with us, even if we had to push or pull her all the way.

After much expostulating and ooh la la'ing, puffing out of cheeks and head-shaking, Monsieur hauled her out of the garage and onto the roadside, and attached jump leads to her battery. It took a while, she shuddered and wailed, but eventually the little car purred into life. Monsieur decanted a few litres of petrol from his car and topped her up. The fuel was free, he explained, a gift.

I had admired a superb wisteria growing over their roof, and before we left Madame gave us a rooted cutting along with the necessary paperwork for my new car. They watched with astonishment as we drove away, Terry at the wheel of the new acquisition which looked like a blue kangaroo bouncing and jumping along, and me following behind. As she picked up speed, the perished fabric roof detached itself from the front and flew into the air like a giant sail, so we removed it completely. It happened that our previous neighbour in England manufactured replacements, but the only colour they could supply was bright red which, married to her blue lower regions, gave Tinkerbelle a distinctive appearance and attracted stares of open-mouthed wonder.

Once we arrived home, we cleaned her up and decided that her tyres could last a while longer. Next morning, we took her out for a run and she hummed into life at the first turn of the key. Mobile and behind Tinkerbelle's steering wheel, with the wind in my hair and the sun on my face, dare I say that I felt just the tiniest bit French?

Much as I loved Tinkerbelle, I didn't have a great deal of confidence in her mechanical competence. Although she bounced along willingly and was well-sprung, she seemed so primitive, so fragile. It was my first experience of driving a car with the steering wheel on the left and driving on the right-hand side of the road, a reversal of what I had been doing for the previous thirty years. Also, I never knew which gear I was in. Tinkerbelle's gearbox configuration was unlike any other gearbox I'd ever used and required simultaneous pulling, twisting and shoving to engage a gear. It was several months before somebody pointed out the diagram etched onto the dashboard to illustrate the location of the gears. In the meantime, each movement was unpredictable as I just moved the knob around every so often and waited to see what would happen.

Shortly, I was bowling along confidently, humming along with Tinkerbelle's soft growling, although it was many months before I was certain of my whereabouts. The countryside is a jigsaw of narrow winding lanes, fields, gentle hills, clusters of trees, copses and scattered hamlets. It all looks very similar. There are two main routes for going to town, and for some weeks I was never certain which one I was on or where I was.

Friends in England cautioned me to be excessively careful when driving, 'because,' they said, 'you know how awful French drivers are.' I didn't, but conducted a small local survey, and here are the results.

More an irritation than a hazard were the botty-sniffers who, like newly introduced dogs, aimed to get their snouts as far up your vehicular backside as possible. They got so close, for reasons you could not understand, that you could smell their breath; they looked hurt and startled if you kept tapping your brakes, and even if you reduced your speed to walking pace they would not overtake, but clung determinedly to your bumpers until you pulled off the road and stopped completely, forcing them to pass, which they did with a reproachful stare.

I didn't often take Tinkerbelle onto motorways because she had no great turn of speed. When I did, I always kept to the slow lane, frustrating lorry drivers who hooted, flashed their lights and sat a hair's breadth from her bumpers before overtaking, when the force of their downdraught lifted Tinkerbelle's front wheels from the road like a small rearing horse.

In a rural area much of the traffic on the roads was agricultural machinery – everything from lovable little snub-nosed tractors with hard metal seats, trundling contentedly along shedding clods of mud and farmyard sludge, to their larger, menacing descendants armed with steel spikes before and multiple rows of ploughshares behind; wagons occupying the entire width of the lanes and occasionally toppling great rolls of hay onto the road; gargantuan combine harvesters as big as villas. Whilst crawling along behind them, you had to remind yourself that the farmers were simply going about their agricultural business, and not purposely obstructing your path.

There were elderly gentlemen, bless them, plump, rosy-cheeked, twinkly-eyed and bereted, who mentally were still travelling in the age of the horse-drawn vehicle. The concept of crossroads, or right of way, was alien to them, and they wore a permanent smile as they drove steadfastly across the paths of other motorists, oblivious to the fact that they had narrowly missed killing or being killed. They neither gave nor responded to signals, but progressed at their own modest speed, and totally unpredictably. In the early afternoon, after lunch, they tended to weave around like slalom skiers.

With no public transport apart from the school bus, for many elderly ladies living alone in scattered hamlets the only way they could maintain their independence was to drive. They zigzagged and weaved, struggled to hold a course, and either had never discovered that the car had more than one forward gear (perhaps like me they'd not noticed the diagram), or had chosen to ignore any gear but first, and ignore their rear-view mirrors too.

I was certain many of them couldn't have reversed a car under pain of death, so must plan their journeys and park accordingly. It was down to those more fortunate drivers among us who still retained some of our faculties to make allowances for these elders, to try to predict their next move, or lack of, and help to ensure the safe continuance of their journeys. Maybe people would do the same for us one day.

The back roads were little wider than one car's width, and passing another vehicle meant having one wheel almost in the ditch to avoid contact. That didn't deter many a driver from using the full width of the road as they hurtled around blind bends.

Having had a few near misses, I always drove expecting somebody to be coming from the opposite direction and on the wrong side of the road. It was not unusual for deer or wild boar to appear from nowhere and spring in front of the car. Every trip was a small adventure.

Along the roads, bunches of plastic flowers marked a spot where a fatal accident had occurred. There were many of them, sometimes several in the same place.

An odd thing I noticed was that in large car parks, no matter how far away from other cars you parked, somebody always parked next to you, even if the car park was almost empty. I don't know why.

Anyway, whether or not the French were particularly dreadful drivers, I couldn't say, and in any case having driven for ten years in Kenya, I'd seen everything there was to see as far as driving goes.

Chapter Nine

Fred Bear, instigator of the abortive horse hunt, was a regular visitor. He had two moods: anger because he thought he had been cheated or overcharged for something, or triumph because he had scored a financial victory in a trivial matter.

Every visit was ostensibly just to see if I was alright, and to ask for 'just a little favour, dearie'. They didn't amount to much – a phone call, a letter translated, an envelope stamped and posted, a fax sent, a few more phone calls. He often brought gifts, things that were of no use to him because they didn't work, like the food mixer that didn't have a lid and couldn't be used without it, which I accepted graciously rather than appearing rude. Then he'd remind me that I owed him something in return.

He wore a pair of ladies' bifocal glasses he had bought from a charity shop for five francs. They looked very strange, being too small for his head so that the arms were bent out awkwardly to fit behind his ears. Fred's moods could change rapidly from belligerent when he wasn't getting what he wanted, to very docile, batting his eyelashes and calling me 'petal' or 'my little flower'. The innocent blue eyes behind the tiny lenses met mine, a helpless, wheedling expression spread over his face as a new 'little favour' issued forth. I stared back at my reflection sure I could see the word MUG stamped on my forehead.

When I mentioned this to Terry his response was that I always attracted strange people (it is true) and scroungers, and I would have to learn to say no, but that is easier to say than to do if you have been brought up to be polite and helpful, and it was something I found next to impossible.

Fred decided to move from where he was living further north. He found the house of his dreams, its sole criterion being that it was cheap, which it was, but he had no intention of paying the full price. As he couldn't speak French he co-opted me as his interpreter, and as he didn't have a phone (not worth the expense, he said), we would use mine.

'Ring the agent, dearie, and tell him I'll give him so much,' he mentioned a figure, 'and he can take it or leave it.'

I phoned the agent and relayed Fred's message. The agent replied that he would call me back once he had spoken to the owners. He didn't phone for a week, and Fred was beside himself.

'What's the matter with these bloody people? Here's me offering them top price for the place, and they can't even be bothered to phone. Ring them for me, dearie, will you, and ask what the hell's going on?'

I phoned the agent again, and he said the house had been sold for the asking price several days previously. Fred ranted and stamped his feet, but a few days later, he arrived waving a fragment of paper over his head, and whooping:

'We've found it! It's the best ever! Can't believe it, perfect for us, and only a mile from here. There's a board outside with a phone number. Ring them for me, dearie, and find out the price.'

He thrust the fragment at me. One of the numbers was in Paris, and the other a mobile phone. The first number didn't reply, but the mobile phone was answered, and I spent the next ten minutes asking questions of the owner and translating the replies to Fred.

They agreed to meet in a week's time at 2.30pm to sign the contract to purchase.

On the day Fred stamped into the house. 'You've given him the wrong bloody address, haven't you? He should have been here by now!'

I pointed out it was midday and the vendor wasn't due for another two and a half hours.

'But I'd have thought he'd want to get here early, being as I'm waving fistfuls of money at him. Give him a ring and find out what's happened.'

With Fred it was easier to just do what he asked rather than waste your time appealing to reason, because he didn't seem to have any.

The vendor was surprised but friendly when I called him.

'Yes,' he said, 'we're on our way to you. Shortly, we will stop for lunch and will meet you as arranged at 2.30.'

Fred muttered and shouted that he'd never known anything like it. People stopping to eat when he was waiting to give them money! I tried to pacify him by pointing out that he'd have his money a little longer.

When the vendor arrived promptly at 2.30pm, we all went to the *notaire's* office where Fred signed the *compromis*, and then the vendor invited us back to his house for coffee. Fred agreed to buy certain furnishings in the house, not, he said, because he needed them, but because they were too cheap to resist. It was 6.00pm before I got home, having devoted six hours to Fred and his house.

Two months later the final papers were ready for signing.

I'd had a horrible morning, because Fred had a banker's draft that he wanted to cash, and the local bank couldn't oblige because he didn't have an account with them.

'Would you tell them, dearie, that in England I wouldn't have this problem?'

(This was a familiar phrase from many new arrivals: 'In England...' Yes, but we were in France.)

'You're not in England.'

'Just bloody tell them that they're a bunch of idiots.'

The lady we were dealing with, whom I knew socially and who had explained very politely and apologetically that she couldn't help, spoke a certain amount of English, and our eyes met.

'I am not going to be rude to these people. It isn't their fault, and you should have organised the money sooner. Please stop shouting.'

He faced the polite lady and yelled: 'You bloody French need to learn how to run a bank properly!' A man came out from an office and asked us to leave.

That afternoon the vendor was waiting with his wife and little girl in the *notaire's* office. The *notaire* waited politely and patiently whilst we exchanged greetings, handshakes and kisses, and enquired as to the traffic on the way. When we were settled, she started reading out the *Acte de Vente*, the document that finalises the sale. I translated for Fred. Once this was finished, the painful moment came for Fred to pay for his new purchase. Now that the time had come to part with his money, he became reluctant to do so.

'Ask her how much it is, dearie.'

'Could you tell me the exact amount, please, madame?'

The *notaire* handed over the final bill for the purchase.

'She's bloody joking! Where the hell did she get that figure from?'

'Please,' I said, 'don't make a scene in here.'

'I want to know where she's got her bloody figure from!'

The *notaire* pointed to the figures on the bill. 'This is the amount for the purchase, less the deposit paid. And this represents our fees for the work we have carried out.'

I explained to Fred, who snorted. 'I'm not paying her that much for a few hours' work! Tell her I don't appreciate being ripped off because I'm English and they're bloody frogs!'

'OK. I'm leaving.' I stood up.

'Now wait a minute, don't you go walking out of here. Just tell her I'm not paying those fees. They're a rip-off.'

'That's fine. Don't pay. You won't get your house. I really don't care. I'm not going to stay here while you make an exhibition of yourself in front of these people.'

'OK. But you just tell her that I know she's cheating me.' Fred was shouting now.

'I'm telling her no such thing. You want to be rude, you learn to speak the language.'

The *notaire* rolled her eyes. The vendors looked flabbergasted.

With much sighing and cursing Fred took out his cheque book and pushed it towards me.

I wrote out the amount, and he signed it angrily. The *notaire* took it, thanked Fred courteously, and stood up to indicate that the meeting was over.

Suddenly, Fred roared: 'Hang on a minute! There's something funny going on here!'

'What on earth is the matter now?'

'Look – this cheque stub's not been filled in! It's blank! Somebody's stolen one of my cheques!'

'Don't be ridiculous. How could anybody steal your cheques? You never let your wallet out of your sight.'

'Well, I'm telling you, someone's had one of my cheques, because the stub isn't filled in, and I want to know what's going on!'

We all sat down again.

'What is the problem?' the *notaire* asked. I explained that there was an empty counterfoil in the cheque book, and she enquired with her eyebrows what it had to do with her.

'I'm not leaving here until I know who's had my cheque. Tell her to give me back my cheque.'

The *notaire* handed him back his cheque, which corresponded with the stub he had just written, but the previous stub was still inexplicably blank.

'Ask her what she thinks that cheque could have been for?'

'The gentleman wonders if you can suggest what the cheque was for?'

I said, trying to keep a straight face.

'But how could I know? I have never met this man until an hour ago. I've no idea what he does with his cheque book!'

Looking at the bewildered faces around me, I was overcome by an attack of giggles, and the more I wondered how I came to be involved in this scene, the more I giggled. I could feel a hint of hysteria.

Then I remembered: 'You cashed a cheque this morning. That's what the cheque was for.'

The mystery was solved and we went our separate ways, Fred waving merrily and promising to pop round to see me very soon, probably daily now that we were neighbours.

Chapter Ten

Terry was managing to visit about once a month and we were slowly making improvements. After two months of sleeping on the sofa bed in the living room, I was keen to return to a proper bed, but to get up to the loft space meant going around the house and into the barn, then climbing the prehistoric, worm-eaten ladder that swayed from side to side. Terry found a way of roping it up to keep it from falling, so that I could use it while he was here. Stepping off the top into the loft was a hairy moment, but the few seconds of anxiety were worth it for the luxury of sleeping comfortably. I still slept downstairs whenever alone. During one of his brief visits, Bill helped us to winch a heavy chest of drawers up the ladder so that my clothes could come out of the boxes.

It would be another year before we were able to buy a staircase. Putting that up between the two of us would have made a very funny short film. Ropes and pulleys, the old ladder, milk crates, broom handles and a great deal of shouting were involved, but at the end of the day I would finally be able to use the bedroom when I was on my own.

Our next purchase was a bathroom suite. There was no bathroom – we still needed to build that and install electricity and water, but at least the fittings were sitting there ready.

We laid a few concrete slabs on the floor in the barn and moved the kitchen units from the barn at the bottom of the garden; a few pieces of wood balanced on breeze blocks formed shelves and a work surface. There was no light except where it squeezed through the cracked roof tiles, so we decided to remove the barn doors, leaving a gaping hole 100ft. square.

When we bought the house, the estate agent had assured us that we would not need any heating.

'It doesn't get cold here, as we are south of the Loire. You may find it rather cool in the evenings, but just wear a jumper and you'll be fine.' I remember how Terry and I grinned with joy at this welcome news.

However, we pinned sheets of plastic over the hole to keep out the wind.

Terry fitted a makeshift electricity supply. The installation resembled a family tree. Into the single two-pin socket in the living room, we plugged a short cable that dangled down into a four-way gang socket connection on the floor, then from each of these four sockets we ran more cables, leading to more multiple sockets. The cables branched all over the floors and up the walls, and would, until such time as we could have the electrics updated, run a fridge, electric kettle, television, bedside lamps, washing machine and computer... but not all at the same time.

Some appliances had English plugs and some had French. I learned that you can plug a two-pin round French plug into a three-pin square English socket if you first poke something into the third hole of the socket – I used a twig because I think if you use something metal you can blow yourself up. There isn't any way that you can get an English three-pin square plug into a French two-pin round socket, though. At least, I couldn't find one.

There were times when it all went pfffffffft and nothing worked, but it was usually just a matter of changing a fuse or re-arranging the family tree.

We also organised some elementary plumbing in the form of a sink that filled from taps, and pipes that removed the water to the outside. The washing machine that had started off in the garden had worked its way into the house at the same time as the kitchen and was linked to the electricity supply.

I had to dig a pit for the water from the kitchen to drain into, and I did my best with a crowbar, creating a hole measuring one cubic yard, which in our stony ground was very hard work. Sadly, the pit was too small. Whenever I used the washing machine, the discharged water soon filled the pit and, having nowhere else to go, started backing up the pipes into the kitchen, bumping into the water that was trying to get out, and erupting from the provisional pipe into which the washing machine outlet was hooked. This flooded the barn with gallons of grey soapy water to a depth of several inches. To prevent this distressing occurrence, I had to drain the used water from the washing machine directly into a bucket, quickly switch off the machine before the bucket overflowed, empty the bucket outside, replace the bucket, switch the machine back on, etc. etc. A complete washing cycle produced forty bucketfuls of water and was ideally a two-person job: one to watch the rising level in the buckets, the other to operate the on/off switch on the machine. Sometimes I wished the machine was still out in the garden. Life and laundry had been simpler then.

To my delight, the despicable cooker blew itself up. However, it was a well-established pattern that if one piece of equipment broke down, another always came out in sympathy at the same time, so it was no surprise when the washing machine chose that same moment when we were at our most financially fragile, to put itself into a wild spin that drove it across the floor totally out of control. With an earth-shattering thunk, it shivered to a standstill and gave up the ghost.

Chapter Eleven

If you watch those television programmes about people moving to France, you may have noticed that the weather is always perfect and the property prices are ridiculously low. We British immigrants (or, as we prefer to call ourselves, expatriates as it sounds less foreign) are spoilt for choice. For the Mediterranean lifestyle, a villa overlooking the bay of St Tropez or Hyères where we can lounge beside the pool, sipping rosé and nibbling olives would have fitted the bill nicely. Inland, quaint, biscuit-tiled farmhouses beckoned us to the rolling hills of Dordogneshire, where beneath the spreading oaks reminiscent of ancient English forests we would be able to collect chestnuts and gather truffles. Anything larger than a cupboard-sized single room apartment in Paris is serious money, but Normandy wouldn't have been too far from the City of Light, property prices there are relatively low, you can pick up a nice little *manoir*, and the generous annual rainfall and cooler climate is ideal for horse lovers.

In many parts of the world, owning a single pair of shoes is a mark of wealth. Elsewhere, it's measured by billions in the bank. If I was asked to describe our status, I would say we would never have been regarded as wealthy, but we had been more than comfortable, with two small businesses, a nice (mortgaged) cottage, a small vintage aircraft, two modest cars and two family ponies living on a nearby farm. We could pay our bills, enjoy our hobbies and take holidays when we wished. To people with no shoes, we were rich beyond their dreams.

For ten years, we'd planned to buy a property in France. We were going to do it. No hurry. There would be plenty of time. And suddenly there wasn't.

The recession of the early 90s swept in like a tsunami, carrying away everything we owned. The signs had been there to see, but we believed we could weather the storm. We held on for too long, until there was nothing left to hold on to. The businesses were gone, and so was our income.

Like Harry Potter's owl, the postman delivered a daily deluge of letters: demands from the bank, the building society, the electricity, the water, the council tax, the house and car insurances, the credit cards, the landlords of our business premises.

We began selling everything we could. When the auctioneers arrived to take away our rather nice antique furniture, our friends were horrified. 'Oh, how awful for you,' they sympathised. As a matter of fact, my main thought was: 'Thank heavens I'll never again have to worry about polishing all that stuff, or scratching it.' They are only things.

The court-appointed bailiff came calling. His job was to remove any of our property he could get his hands on, for the benefit of our creditors. He said that it was not his intention to do so, as he hoped that we would be able to find a way to dig ourselves out of the mire, given time.

'There's nothing to be ashamed of,' he said, leaning over the garden gate and stroking the dogs. 'It's happening all over the country. There are something like a hundred bankruptcies a day at the moment. Keep your chin up.'

The private bailiffs were paid by results and highly motivated. They hooted at the gate or banged on the door for an hour at a time, yelling loudly that we had to pay our debts, so that the neighbours could hear. Posing as delivery men, they bellowed through the letterbox saying they needed a signature for a parcel, or that they had flowers for me.

Final demands arrived, with added penalties for late payments. We must telephone immediately to avoid further action. A threat arrived of legal action being taken for 'forging our own signatures'.

***

There was little work available apart from short-term secretarial contracts, but the cost of running a car to town and the parking fees left almost nothing in my pocket, so instead I decided to do what I most loathe, picked up my bucket and put on my pinny. I became a Mrs Mop, because there was no shortage of job opportunities in the domestic help market.

For four hours, six mornings a week, I cleaned a huge house for elderly millionaires. They kept a daily record of every water and electricity meter reading dating back decades and questioned how long I used the iron each day. I had the strangest relationship with them, as we were members of various associations of which he or she were President. We still received invitations to fundraising and social functions hosted by them, and on those occasions we entered through the front door. However, on the six mornings a week I worked there, I had to go in through the door at the back of the house which would once have been called the tradesmen's entrance but was now referred to as just 'the back door'. The nearest I got to the front door, after my sudden change of fortune was polishing its large brass knob.

There was an angry message on the telephone answering machine one day, as a £5 note left on the hall table for a charity collection had vanished and I was the obvious suspect. However, a subsequent message said that I shouldn't worry, as somebody from the charity had called to let them know that he had picked up the money earlier, when there was nobody around. There was no apology.

On Monday afternoons, I ironed for a giant sportsman, who dried his gigantic clothes on the radiators so that they were as stiff as cardboard and needed drenching to make them manageable.

Tuesday afternoons were spent at a nearby stately home, where I was paid to help clean and move furniture around for various functions, but much of the time was passed chatting, drinking tea and eating ginger biscuits with the kind, titled owners.

Wednesday afternoons, I kept company with an interesting elderly lady who was bed-ridden and wanted somebody to talk to. She had travelled all over the world until she had developed a serious heart condition. She lived with her three adult daughters, but her days dragged as she was confined to her bedroom while they were at work. While I was still visiting her, a new treatment for her condition was introduced, and she made a swift recovery. Within a couple of months, she was up and about and leading a normal life so that she didn't need my visits any more. On my last afternoon as I left, she pressed an envelope into my hand. Inside was a 'thank you' card she had painted, and a large cheque.

Obviously, Tuesday and Wednesday afternoons were the times I enjoyed most, while the rest of my working week was just a mechanism to keep the dogs and us fed, but it was never going to pay off our debts or return us to our previous lifestyle. In my gloomiest moments scraping out plug holes or washing the pots from under the bed, I reminded myself that millions of people around the world worked in dreadful conditions and would be more than grateful for the opportunity to do what I was doing, and what I was earning in an hour they probably didn't earn in a week.

Until we didn't have any, I had never been particularly interested in money. As long as we had enough to pay our bills, that was fine. I never looked at my bank statements. I'd occasionally been short of cash for a month or so, but money had never been a serious preoccupation. Now it was all I could think about.

***

Our closest friends, with whom we had holidayed for many years, socialised with weekly, and to whom we had lent a large sum of money without any guarantee it would be repaid, no longer spoke to us. If they saw us coming, they turned around or crossed the street. When I first realised that we were heading into financial difficulty, I phoned to say we wouldn't be able to go on holiday with them that year, as we were running out of money. She replied: 'Don't tell me that. We couldn't be friends with you if you didn't have any money.'

I laughed, thinking she was joking, as she continued: 'Don't call again,' and hung up.

A short while later we bumped into them. She walked away into a shop, but he hesitated and Terry went up to him and put his hand on his shoulder in a friendly gesture.

'Take your hands off me,' he snapped. 'Don't touch me.'

People who had been casual acquaintances were amazing. Knowing we had no heating fuel, somebody arrived with a great sack of coal because 'he had ordered too much and had nowhere to put it'. Plastic boxes of food appeared at the back door, anonymously.

My greatest concern was for our two horses, long-serving family pets. We could not afford to pay for their keep any more, and they were too old to sell even if we were prepared to do so. If we had to have them put to sleep, it would break my heart. Sandra, the sweet lady who owned the farm where they lived said she would 'foster' them indefinitely. I will never be able to express my gratitude sufficiently.

Because we'd been unable to pay our electricity, we were now on a meter, which gobbled up money alarmingly quickly. We could afford one brief hot shower a week and our meals consisted mostly of sandwiches or packet mashed potato that could be made with a small saucepan of hot milk. We varied it by adding pickle, and on special days some grated cheese. I never turned the oven on.

We learned that you could make perfectly drinkable wine from cheap jam and tinned fruit, and that washed the potato down nicely.

***

There is very little that irritates me more than people saying 'You should have…' It is easy to serve the winning shot at Wimbledon from an armchair, or pot the black, hit the bullseye, clear the wall in the *puissance,* and it's easy to believe we would all do better than anybody else in a given situation, but as they say 'First walk a mile in my shoes,' and honestly, retrospective advice is useless.

That none of us know what it is like to walk in somebody else's shoes was brought home when I was talking to a very dear and longstanding friend who came from a wealthy family and lived handsomely on a trust fund and investments. She had never had to work and was the most generous soul supporting numerous charities for the disadvantaged.

When I told her about our situation, she was aghast. 'How on earth did you do that?' she asked, as if we had achieved something beyond the abilities of mere mortals.

I explained how the recession affected businesses that were dependent on people buying their services or goods, about the rocketing mortgage rate, saying that we had simply run out of money and didn't have any more. She held my hand and looked at me earnestly, then said: 'You must liquidate some of your assets. You cannot lose your home.'

I smiled and replied that we didn't have any assets. She looked completely blank.

'But you must have something,' she said, 'the stock market, offshore, things you put aside for the future.'

'Truly,' I said, 'we are absolutely skint.' We had sold our better car and all our furniture apart from the bed and some garden furniture to keep us going, so there was nothing left to sell.

She sat there gazing blindly at me, shaking her head slowly from side to side, looking into a world that was utterly beyond her comprehension, where educated people who had owned two businesses, two horses and an aeroplane didn't have a penny to their names. Perhaps it may happen to strangers, but not to her friends.

We received a summons to appear in court to declare our assets. I handed the registrar a list of what we had left: a Singer sewing machine bought for £5 from a car boot sale, a canteen of cutlery, a few kitchen appliances, some crockery, our clothes, the bed and bed linen, the garden furniture, some books. A small car.

The solicitor representing one of our creditors said: 'But you also own race horses and valuable show dogs, don't you?'

I laughed at the idea that five family pets with insatiable appetites, and two voracious horses in their mid-twenties who served no useful purpose at all, were seen as assets. To us they were dearly loved liabilities whose welfare was a massive drain on our resources and whose existence was the cause of our inability to find somewhere to live. The solicitor closed her file, secured it with an elastic band and said she doubted very much that in the circumstances her clients would pursue their interest in the animals, shook our hands and wished us the very best of luck.

***

Our most pressing problem was finding somewhere to live, because the building society could not be held at bay indefinitely. Each month that passed, the capital sum due increased as unpaid instalments, penalties and the horrendous interest rates racked up.

Without five dogs and two parrots, it would have been relatively easy to find rented accommodation. With them, it was impossible. People who were not animal lovers had a simple solution: get rid of the dogs and parrots. It was not an option for us. They were part of our family.

We did waver once, very briefly and think we should give up. After months of bailiffs banging on the door, the threats, the lack of hot water, the bills we couldn't pay and not being able to find a way of getting back on our feet again, we were tired. I was sick to death of dusting and polishing and cleaning windows, baths and toilets, ironing mountains of clothes and emptying vacuum cleaners and rubbish bags, all the things I most disliked doing in my own house.

A local business acquaintance had run a successful insurance brokerage. He and his wife lived in a beautiful house and he drove a top-of-the-range car until the tax man caught up with them over irregularities, and they were bankrupted.

We met him in town one day and were commiserating with each other over our changed circumstances.

He said: 'You know what? I suppose I could start again, but I'm 62 and haven't any fight left in me any more. We're happy enough to live simply now. Come and see us.'

They were living in social housing, a small flat in a characterless building with rubbish bins, bikes and prams parked in the communal hallway. Their compact living/dining room was dominated by a large television showing horse racing, which Jack watched while we talked. They had Sky now, he said. Moira kept polishing the table. They agreed that they were content, and very happy to be out of the rat race. The welfare system took care of them, they enjoyed having time to themselves and not having to be in an office at 9.00am every day.

We walked away in silence, knowing that we weren't ready for that kind of existence. We had to find a way out of the mire and move forwards. We were both still on the right side of 60. Just.

We would never be able to buy a property of our own again in England. But… property in France was ridiculously cheap. Could we somehow manage to buy somewhere there?

With the help of a small loan from a friend, that's exactly what we did, and that is how we ended up buying a virtual ruin. It was all we could afford, but it was our own.

I'd move out to France with our animals, while Terry remained in England for the time being to find a way to earn a living and support us all.

I've always believed everything happens for a reason. As a result of our financial predicament, I had achieved two ambitions. I was living in France and on my way to becoming a published author.

Chapter Twelve

Although I had been a Francophile since before I knew what the word meant, for a reason l couldn't rationalise I had my doubts about the efficiency of most things French including the vets. I'd hardly been here any time at all before our dogs provided almost weekly opportunities to put the vets to the test. In England, in the days when money hadn't been a constant worry, they'd never needed veterinary attention, but now, in rapid succession they produced a torn dew-claw, a tumour and a terrible injury caused by entanglement with a barbed-wire fence. These were dealt with so effectively and gently that any doubts I had were quickly forgotten.

Our vet was of medium height with dark, close-cropped hair and large, sad eyes. At first I thought him rather unfriendly, but as my visits became more and more frequent I realised that he was just a little shy and possibly anxious about our ability to communicate properly, as he didn't speak English and my French was still limited.

'How many dogs do you have?' he asked on my second visit.

'Five,' I replied, visualising French franc signs whizzing around in his eyes like cherries on a fruit machine. Over the following years, I came to rely on his generosity and tolerance, as our veterinary bills swallowed up our entire budget. I was continually in debt to the practice, and as soon as we managed to reduce the balance, another more expensive disaster would occur to boost it right up again.

A visit to the surgery was always interesting because of the diversity of the clientèle and medications and appliances on display. In this rural district, most of the clients had originally been farmers, but as household pets became more common the practice was divided between the two, with different tariffs. The rural tariff covered all farm animals and was less expensive than for domestic pets. Neat ladies with trimmed poodles sat in the waiting room, while farmers in mucky rubber boots and muddy overalls came to collect powders for cattle with diarrhoea, treatments for sick rabbits, castration rings and antibiotics for newborn livestock. The articles on display in the cabinets ranged from sinister metal instruments whose function I didn't want to think about, through jewelled collars and hygienic panties for dogs, to ingenious little gadgets designed to remove ticks complete with their heads. They were called Tic Tocs.

Sometimes somebody came in with a creature in a cardboard box, an ailing duck or rabbit that needed to be diagnosed in case it had some rampant disease that might affect all its companions. A man drove up and called the vet outside to examine the carcass of a deer in the boot of his car, that had, so the driver claimed, jumped in front of the vehicle. He wanted to know if it was fit for eating. An old lady came in one day dressed in a cardigan, flowery apron and carpet slippers. She was bent over at the waist at 90 degrees and walked with tremendous difficulty. To talk to anybody, she had to tilt her head to one side, as she couldn't lift it upwards and backwards. Her fingers were terribly swollen and knotted, and ingrained with soil, not only around the nails but deeply in the skin. She sat down next to me and smiled cheerfully.

'It's my sheep,' she explained. 'I've only got the one, now. One of her feet has gone soft, and she's lame. I need some of that blue spray; that'll heal it. Mind you, it's expensive, but all the same, we have to look after our animals.'

I found the French attitude to animals ambivalent. Many hunting dogs spent their lives, apart from when they were out on a hunt, either locked in cages or tied on short chains. Wildlife was trapped, poisoned, shot. Farm animals could live their whole sad lives locked in dark barns. However, I had sat beside a shabby old man with a bowed head, audibly weeping over his tottering and threadbare old dog which was clearly making its final visit to the vet.

In the queue at the supermarket one day, there was a big rough-looking man in grubby clothing in front of me at the checkout, his trolley entirely filled with tins of dog and cat food. I asked him how many animals he owned, and he replied none. In the village where he lived, he told me, there were several stray dogs and great numbers of cats, which nobody else fed.

'I can't stand to see an animal hungry,' he said. 'Nobody else cares about them, but *tant pis*. I buy them food every week and make sure they are all fed.'

A farmer I was talking to one day told me he kept a pet fox he had captured as a cub. 'Ah, what a fantastic pet he is. I really love that animal,' he smiled.

During one of my visits to the surgery, a distraught-looking French woman with a cat box on her lap sat opposite me. Her straggly greying hair formed a crazy halo around her face and she stared fixedly at me with unblinking eyes. I thought her behaviour was due to anxiety over her pet, so I smiled at her and asked what was the matter with the animal. She replied in English, in a croaky voice, that the cat was there for a vaccination. She asked where I lived, which I told her, and then it was my turn to be seen by the vet.

A fortnight later the phone rang. It was the croaky-voiced lady. She said she had got my phone number from another English lady living nearby. She desperately needed help.

'I know you're an animal lover,' she began. 'You must know how cruel the French are to animals. I hate them. All they do is torture animals. There is a dog in my village that the woman owner tortures all the time.'

I was horrified.

'I'm ashamed to be French,' she continued. 'They're such hateful people. Because they know I care about animals they hate me too, and they want to poison me and my dogs. You must help me rescue that terrible woman's poor dog. It's tied up with a huge chain behind her house. You will have to keep her talking, and I will go around and take the dog.'

'You must report it to the *gendarmes*,' I said.

'The *gendarmes*! They're the worst of all! They encourage people to hurt animals; they run them over deliberately. If you won't help me, please help me to find somebody who can.' After she had given me her phone number several times and insisted that I repeated it twice to ensure I had it correctly, she hung up.

I phoned the English woman who had given my number to this strange new acquaintance, and said I'd appreciate it if she wouldn't make a habit of it.

'I'm terribly sorry, but she just wouldn't leave me alone! She rang me to say she'd met an Englishwoman at the vet, who lived in this village, and that it was desperately urgent that she contact you. She was so persistent that I gave in.'

'How did she know you?'

'She started talking to me in the supermarket one day when she saw me buying cat food, and she seemed very friendly so I gave her my number. Then she kept phoning me because she wants me to rescue a dog.'

Over the next few months as I met more English people, they all seemed to know Michelle, and they blanched when her name was mentioned.

'She rings at midnight, or even later, saying that kittens are being murdered, or horses killed, and tries to make you go and snatch them or take photographs. She won't leave you alone. The only way to get rid of her is to find a new English person and dump her on them.'

I couldn't find anybody to pass her on to; everybody I met had already passed her on. Until some new and unsuspecting arrival turned up, I was stuck with her, and few weeks passed without a dramatic phone call with ghastly graphic descriptions of new atrocities. To keep her at bay and stop her phoning day and night, I installed a telephone answering machine. She responded by coming to the house, examining our animals closely to ensure I wasn't mistreating them, and pointing out that our neighbours were probably doing terrible things to their animals.

She was very persistent and clearly a little unbalanced. When I mentioned her to Terry, he replied: 'Another one for your collection.'

M. Meneteau saw her driving away one day, and asked what she was doing here. I said she was worried that animals were being mistreated and wanted me to help her rescue them.

'Be careful of her,' he warned. 'She catches them with food and sells them to laboratories.'

Next time I was at the vet, I mentioned Michelle to the receptionist.

'*Oh, mon dieu!*' she said. 'She is a crazy woman. She asked if we would reduce our charges for all the animals she brings, and when we refused, she threw herself on the floor and screamed.'

***

As well as cars coming around bends on the wrong side of the road, it was common for deer to spring out from the hedges, hares, wild boars, and during the hunting season, gun dogs to run across the road. A journey seldom passed without something of interest happening. I encountered a crowd of camels grazing on the banks of the Charente, a car park filled with llamas and a colourful and noisy muster of peacocks strutting down a lane in the middle of nowhere. Believe it or not, there were confirmed sightings of a kangaroo on the loose not far from our house, and we knew people who had bought a house where a previous owner had been eaten by the pet lions he kept in his barn.

Sometimes I passed Madeleine, the last remaining old lady goatherd in our area. A tiny lady, followed by her sly crouching dog, she pedalled her old bicycle alongside her twenty goats. She and her dog ushered them through the lanes, trotting haughtily on their neat cloven hooves to fields of stubble, where they grazed while she sat on a folding chair, bent over her knitting. On wet days, she shrouded herself in a waterproof cape and green rubber boots; in the summer, she wore a brown cardigan. Her goats were glossy and sleek, and when she steered them home bleating in the evening, their udders bulged with the milk that would be made into one of the regional specialities, goat's cheese. Although she was bent almost double with age, beneath her grey curls, her weather-beaten face was tranquil. When I waved, or pulled over to let her pass, she beamed hugely and raised one knobbly hand, her eyes sparkling like sapphires. When she was gone, nobody would replace her and she would fade into history. There is no romance in modern goat-farming that keeps the animals hock-deep in straw-filled barns for their entire lives, never seeing daylight or grass.

***

The garden teemed with birds: robins, tits, blackbirds, sparrows, wrens in crevices, wagtails strutting bumptiously, redstarts, swallows, martins and clouds of goldfinches. Hoopoes with their pointy crests and striped wings dug insects from the lawn with their long, curved beaks. Crows, jays, magpies and pigeons co-habited in the large oak tree; green and spotted woodpeckers gave themselves away by their high-speed rapping, their laughing call and tell-tale dolphin flight. Herons sailed past on their way to the stream, trailing their long legs behind them like crane flies. The cuckoo's song that had been such a noteworthy event in England became monotonous, sounding repetitively from early morning to last light, when the owls took over with their mournful hooting. In early summer, the nightingales sang through the night.

Climbing up the front of the house were three ancient vines, their trunks twisted and ragged with age. They straggled up to a height of eight feet and branched into festoons of bright green leaves and clumps of grapes. Snuggled into a knot on one of these vines was a nest of flycatchers, screened by the leaves. Three fledglings hung over the edge of the nest with permanently gaping maws, urging their parents to hurry, hurry, hurry, shrieking rudely and bouncing up and down, waving their small feathered arms. The adults worked on the wing from dawn to dusk, snatching morsels from the air and returning to prod them into their offsprings' throats. The mother bird concentrated diligently upon her task, but her mate tended to be easily distracted. One evening as I watched, he returned to the nest with a beakful of bugs for the babies, but just as he was at the point of distributing this feast, a small butterfly bobbed past. He dropped what was in his mouth and winged after that, leaving the infants shrieking angrily with disappointment.

Indignant, panicky bird noise woke me early one morning. Sparsely wrapped in a short, white, semi-transparent kimono, and wearing a pair of battered sandals, I set off to investigate the commotion, which was coming from the rough hedge separating our garden from M. Meneteau's. It was a sad specimen of a hedge – a melée of brambles, ivy and rusting wire netting. Tangled in it, a young blackbird was struggling to escape, while its anxious parents fluttered about on a nearby roof. I went and found a rake, then started pulling away what debris I could, crouching down so I could see what I was doing and making sure I wasn't injuring the bird. After a few moments, I became aware that I was not alone – M. Meneteau was squatting on the other side of the hedge, half-heartedly prodding around with a stick. Protecting what little modesty I had left, I called out 'Good morning', and he stood up.

'What are you doing?' he asked.

'There's a bird trapped – I'm trying to get it out of the hedge.'

'Ah.' He jabbed with his stick, the bird fluttered free and flew off with its parents. I felt we were getting to know each other quite well. Intimately, almost.

M. Meneteau hoed a little, scratched with a fork, turned over some soil, scraped out a few perfectly parallel ridges, sowed a handful of seeds, sprinkled a few drops of water, and very soon neat rows of obedient green seedlings appeared, to shoot up into cabbages, beans, lettuces, tomatoes, sweet peppers, artichokes, leeks, endives, spinach and asparagus, the lines of vegetables prettily divided by clumps of lilies and marguerites. The funny thing was that he hardly ate anything, neither meat nor vegetables; he wasn't interested in food, and most of the vegetables he gave away. He knew precisely the right moment to plant, and the effect of every drop of rain, breath of wind, or blast of sun. He knew exactly what every seed wanted and needed in order to grow into a healthy plant, and never had to look up anything in a book. He pulled up stinging nettles with his bare hands.

He also knew everything there was to know about the local wildlife, the different bird calls and habits. One night, I was woken by a ghastly, bone-chilling noise. It sounded like somebody or something in extremis, almost as bad as the cockatoo and went on for several minutes.

Next morning I asked M. Meneteau if he had heard it and whether he knew what it was.

'Yes, it was the *effraie*, the barn owl. When they scream like that, something terrible is going to happen.'

'What sort of terrible thing?'

'Pff. I don't know,' he shrugged. 'It's just what people say. I don't believe it myself.'

I waited for two or three days for some terrible disaster to occur, but nothing did, so I didn't believe it either.

When I said I'd noticed blackbirds nesting in a hollow cherry tree in the little orchard next to our garden, he shook his head. 'Not blackbirds. They don't nest in hollow trees, they nest in the hedges. They're probably starlings.' I was surprised because they had certainly looked like blackbirds to me, but when I dug out the binoculars for a closer look, I could see that he was right. The starlings nested in the same place each year, struggling to raise their young because of the magpies who lived in the big oak tree and tried to get at their nest. Every year, I built a network of interlocked branches around the nest so that the starlings could get in, but the magpies were kept out.

I mentioned the bird that called 'blublubtweetclicktinkletinkle pleased to meet you. Pleased to meet you. Blublubtweetclicktinkletinkle pleased to meet you' and asked what it was called in French. When I did my best imitation of it, he looked blank and changed the subject, but on the day when we heard it together, I asked what it was.

'*C'est un pinson,*' he said, leaving me none the wiser until I could dig the dictionary out from my box of books whereupon I discovered that it was a chaffinch.

I tried to explain what it was saying in English, but my explanation was lost in translation, as 'blublubtweetclicktinkletinkle pleased to meet you' didn't sound anything like *enchantée*.

M. Meneteau spoke a strong local dialect; some of the words he used were not in the French dictionary. When he mentioned that he'd seen a snake that afternoon, on the *schma*, I asked what a *schma* was. *Le schma*, he said impatiently. *Le schma*.

Later I saw Madame Meneteau and asked her where they had seen the snake, because I couldn't understand her husband and didn't know what a *schma* was. She laughed. '*Le chemin*,' she explained. The path.

I asked M. Meneteau the best place to buy poultry.

At the market, he said. In Hunssay.

I found a local map and searched, but there was no Hunssay to be found. I took him the map and asked him to point it out. There, he said, pointing to Gençay.

They were my nearest neighbours, apart from Bill who was rarely here, and I couldn't have asked to live next to kinder, more interesting people, the last generation of small farmers. M. Meneteau's father had died when he was nine years old, and he had become the man of the family. He had started farming at that young age, helping and looking after his mother.

He had no time for hunters.

'Pff,' he said. 'Why do they want to go out and kill wild animals? It's stupid.'

That didn't mean he was averse to killing animals. The chickens, guinea fowl, pigeons and rabbits that lived in cages in his garden were despatched to feed the family. Madame Meneteau was a soft-hearted lady who loved animals, and she confided that she found it very distressing when they had to kill them, but it was part of farming life.

***

During July and August the holiday season was in top gear, so instead of two cars on the road, there were four; the cafés spilled their tables and chairs onto the pavements, and there were antique fairs, horse fairs, cycle races, street painting competitions, and a display of performing tigers. All around the hamlet, both on the plains behind and on the gentle slopes in front, the land was splashed with geometric ranks of green maize spears, rustling silver-speckled in the sunlight, and outrageous sunflowers, their huge golden faces framed with green collars.

By the middle of September the holiday activity began to melt away, and the countryside returned to its dozy state. The wheat and barley ripened and were reaped, and then the harvesters moved in on the frivolous sunflowers, who were by then hanging their withered heads in mortification; the maize that had been lush green just a few weeks ago was turning to pinky-beige, and the blackberries were ripe for picking.

I sat and wrote lists of all the books I had always wanted to read but had never had the time to. I scoured gardening books and magazines on home renovation, making plans, dreaming dreams and wondering whether, or how, we would ever have sufficient money to accomplish any of them. The future was hazy, but one thing was certain: life here was going to be deliciously peaceful, punctuated by nothing more notable than the transition of one season to the next.

Chapter Thirteen

Because of the time Terry and I spent apart, living at different paces, a lot of adjustment was necessary for his visits to run smoothly. He was always in the fast lane, always under pressure to earn and supply our needs. He drove fast and lived in a country where rushing was the normal pace, while I wallowed in the lethargy of our new home. Consequently, the first few days of each stay were speckled with admonitions from him for me to 'hurry up for heaven's sake', and from me for him to 'please stop rushing around'. The unhurried queues in the supermarket and the casual service in the shops exasperated him; I found my casual routine upheaved by having to produce meals three times a day, and saw red when he commented on the things I hadn't done rather than those I had. After a couple of days, he slowed down and I sped up until we reached a mutually acceptable pace.

I was learning to find my way around whilst looking after our five dogs, two parrots and Sinbad. The weather was glorious, and every day I put all the birds out in the garden in their cages. Unlike our parrots' wheeled, moderately lightweight models, Sinbad's gigantic wrought iron cage weighed about six hundred pounds, and the daily struggle to manoeuvre it in and out through the narrow doorway and over the small step developed muscles in my shoulders and arms that a Sumo wrestler might covet.

Bill lived a nomadic existence shuttling his furniture trucks between Spain and England, stopping off every so often to deliver loads and pick up things to take away with him. His 'house' was a large barn with a corrugated iron roof and a few bits of wall, and it was crammed full of furniture, cartons, crates, tools, building materials, odd wheels, a few breeze blocks, tins and bottles of stuff. Outside there were some caravans in various states of disrepair, speckled with moss and mould. As there was no electricity, running water, floor, doors or windows, when Bill was around he lived in one of the caravans in the back garden. He had many virtues, but reliability was not one of them. If he said he would be back on Tuesday evening, it was more likely he would turn up the following Sunday morning, or not at all for several weeks. I don't recall him ever being where or when he said he would be.

In mid-September, he arrived and began to rearrange the clutter of junk because his wife Gloria was coming from Spain for a visit. She had not yet seen the property, and Bill hoped she would move here permanently.

She arrived, petite and brown as a nut, with a crown of heaped blonde hair, heavy eye make-up, a radiant smile, the most exquisitely elegant feet I'd ever seen, large daisy earrings and a taste for exotic and colourful clothes; a cocky little sparrow dressed as a bird of paradise.

With her came two Great Danes and a small terrier. Her first look at the property didn't impress her greatly, but she was funny and cheerful and we immediately became friends. She had a wacky sense of humour and a very positive outlook on life. Picking her way through the jumble of stuff framed by head-high nettles that had valiantly withstood the summer heat, she rolled her eyes and waved her hands at the panorama of mess.

'Look at it, just look at it!' she exclaimed, running a hand through her hair. 'Have you ever seen anything like it?' I hadn't.

'Never mind,' she smiled, 'give me a couple of days and I'll have it looking nice.' I thought she was being wildly optimistic.

She commanded Bill to unload dozens of pots of plants from the truck she had arrived in, and distributed them around the outside of the building. She didn't know what most of them were called. 'What's this one?' I asked, pointing to a few withered sticks poking out from a clump of baked mud.

'Oh, it's nice, that one. Sort of feathery leaves. It just needs a drop of water. That one over there has big shiny leaves, and this one smells wonderful at night. I'll have to get some petunias.'

I think she liked petunias not only for their long-lasting displays but because they were one of the few plants whose name she knew. She barked a stream of orders at Bill, who dug into the truck and pulled out some garden furniture, two swinging sofas, and a collection of large umbrellas.

'Put it there,' she ordered, pointing vaguely. 'No! Not there, there!'

Bill patiently moved all the bits and pieces around until Gloria was satisfied.

'There you go,' she said cheerfully, surveying her new home.

The two huge dogs staggered around in the waist-high dead grass and weeds, and the terrier chewed frantically on a plastic frog that squeaked loudly until it was fatally punctured. Gloria hadn't yet seen inside the 'house' part, and I decided not to be there when she did.

***

As I hadn't been anywhere other than the vet and the local supermarkets since my arrival, I went to the annual threshing festival at a nearby rural museum dedicated to the farming life of bygone days. There was a procession assembling outside the museum. Men dressed in traditional farming costumes of black smocks and trousers, red neckerchiefs and black hats, were accompanied by their ladies in long black skirts with white aprons, black triangular shawls, and narrow cylindrical lace hats two feet high. How their wearers managed to keep them perched on top of their heads, and why, was a mystery. Behind them came a long cavalcade of mules, ancient ox-wagons laden with children dressed in old-fashioned clothes, babies in antiquated prams, heavy horses and tractors of all sizes and ages wending their way around the village, followed by an aged fire-engine and a band of drums and bagpipes. For half a mile, the crowd followed on foot to a field where the men cut the ripe wheat by hand with ancient implements and tied it neatly in stooks with a length of stalk. Along came a very elderly tractor-driven contraption that threshed the stooks.

We stood round the edges of the field beside the carts and livestock, watching the threshing, and a lady played lively jigs on a fiddle. It was a captivating glimpse of farming life fifty years earlier.

Some months later when I was talking to a local farmer, I said how much more romantic farming had been before mechanisation. He snorted and replied that there was no romance in trudging behind a horse all day. Ploughing and sowing had been exhausting work for both man and horse, walking many miles in all weather, often for very little reward... and when the workhorse could no longer work there was no retirement for it. It was just another mouth to feed and would be slaughtered. He recalled a very hard life as the son of a farming family and was thankful that his own life was far easier physically.

I picked up a handful of the cut wheat and made my way home, passing some French people who were going towards the field. Seeing the wheat in my hand, one of them said: 'Taking the wheat brings bad luck,' or possibly: 'We're too late to see the wheat being cut, what bad luck.' My French wasn't good enough to understand exactly what they were saying, but it stayed in my mind.

Over the next week several things went wrong: Tinkerbelle wouldn't start, Hecate, tore herself badly on barbed wire, I was stung by a *mouche plate* and numerous small things made me think about the 'bad luck' I had heard, so when Terry arrived we took the little bundle of wheat and returned it reverently to where I had found it.

***

When I arrived home from the festival, Gloria trotted over to the car.

'Come around this evening and have a drink with us. An estate agent we're in business with is coming over.'

I asked what sort of business they were involved in, and Bill explained that many English people in Spain were interested in moving to France, so he was going to introduce purchasers to the agent.

'He's a bit mad,' they warned me. 'If you come around, you can help us entertain him.' I was proud and flattered to be invited to help entertain a mad person.

Gaston wore large sunglasses and had a florid face that matched his Hawaiian shirt. Although he spoke fairly fluent English he was quite drunk, so his words were distorted, like a record playing too slowly. As soon as we were introduced, he told me that he was bisexual and that he had learned his English in bed with English girls. 'Piiiloowtook' he called it. Pillow talk.

Bill and Gaston had formed a partnership, but talking to them it was clear that neither trusted the other, nobody knew what anybody else was doing, and it was a relationship doomed to end in failure. Bill had already introduced two potential clients to Gaston, both of whom had agreed to purchase properties. The first had sadly succumbed to a heart attack a few minutes before signing the final contract, and the second had changed his mind at roughly the same time.

Their hopes were resting on the arrival of Bill's third introduction, who was on her way up from Spain in one of his furniture trucks. They were optimistic because she had sold her mobile home in Spain and was coming to France with cash and the intention of buying a property. It

62

seemed certain she would become the partnership's first client. We drank a toast to her swift and safe arrival.

Next day, she clambered down from the furniture truck with the help of three strong men. Mrs Malucha was a gigantic 76-year-old lady of Polish origin, with a pudding bowl haircut and an alarming habit of erupting unexpectedly, and for no apparent reason, into thunderous guffaws of laughter. She settled into a plastic garden chair that immediately began to transmogrify beneath her invincible buttocks.

Entrusting her to my care, and instructing me to keep her comfortable, Bill and Gloria drove away to find her a suitable house. Despite her age and size, Mrs Malucha was rather green around the edges. She had sold her mobile home in Spain at a loss because of 'something to do with currency' and had put herself into Bill's hands in order to move to France, a country she had never visited and knew nothing about.

I asked her what had attracted her here, and she replied that it was the weather. Spain was unbearably hot, and England was far too cold, but she understood from Bill that the climate in France would suit her very well indeed. I didn't want to burst her bubble by telling her that in summer France can be almost as hot as Spain, and winter sometimes even colder than England.

Three hours later, Bill and Gloria returned with the joyful news that they had found a dear little house that would suit Mrs Malucha perfectly. They had made an appointment for her with the *notaire*, when she would sign the preliminary contract and pay a deposit. She could stop and have a look at the property on the way to the *notaire's* office.

Delighted with her good fortune, Mrs Malucha sat squash-buttocked in the shape-shifting garden chair, chain-smoking, bursting into paroxysms of wild laughter, and asking what time we were going to eat. Not only was she a chain-smoker, but she appeared to be a chain-eater, too. Gloria made a large dish of corned beef hash to keep her going until dinner.

She was thrilled that her ideal house had been found so quickly, and looked forward to moving in, despite the fact that she didn't know anything about it or its location and hadn't even seen a photograph. I asked Bill how long he thought it would be before Mrs Malucha could take possession of her new home. 'Monday,' he replied. It was Thursday.

'Are you sure? It usually takes several weeks to complete a purchase.'

'Gaston has taken care of everything. She'll be given the keys when she pays the deposit.'

I was surprised, but very glad for Mrs Malucha's sake, and impressed at the speed with which the sale was happening. Bill mentioned there was no electricity in the house, so he would install a generator, and no bathroom, but he would build one. It would only take a week, he said.

Gaston owned a house in a nearby village which was at the disposal of any potential buyers arriving from Spain. Mrs Malucha could stay there until her house was ready. Bill and Gloria decided to move in there too, with their 10-year-old grandson who'd come out from England for a holiday, plus two of the truck drivers who'd delivered Mrs Malucha from Spain, and Gloria's three dogs. It made sense as Bill had nowhere for them all to stay.

***

Bill introduced me to Carole and Norrie, a British couple who lived about twelve miles away and who would soon become great friends. Carole's French was fluent, and she was accompanying Mrs Malucha to the *notaire* to translate proceedings. They collected Mrs Malucha and stopped for a coffee along the way. Mrs Malucha complained that she was hungry, breakfast being almost an hour behind her. Unlike their English equivalents, French cafés generally only serve coffee and alcohol, but Mrs Malucha was not convinced until she had questioned the contents of every visible container on the shelves and satisfied herself that there was nothing edible within them.

'I'll just have coffee then, if there's no food,' she said sadly.

'Well, I'm having a *pastis*. Anybody else fancy one?' said Norrie.

'Yes,' roared Mrs Malucha, brightening up, 'get me one as well.'

'What, as well as coffee, or instead?' asked Norrie.

'Both. Coffee and *pastis*.'

Norrie returned with a tray and placed a coffee and a glass of *pastis* on the table in front of her.

'What's this?' she asked, pointing at the cloudy yellow drink.

'That's the *pastis* you asked for,' said Norrie.

Mrs Malucha was crestfallen. 'Oh, I thought you were talking about Cornish pasties,' she said.

***

After signing the initial contract Mrs Malucha learnt that her house, which she hadn't seen, was fourteen miles away from our hamlet, and half a mile from the nearest shops. There was no public transport; Mrs Malucha couldn't drive and could hardly walk, but she didn't seem concerned.

'I expect I'll find somebody to run me around,' she said, beaming pointedly in my direction.

In honour of Mrs Malucha's successful purchase, Gloria prepared a celebratory lunch at Gaston's house. It was very pleasant, with everybody in high spirits, sitting in the garden and toasting Mrs Malucha. As we were clearing away the main course in preparation for dessert, Gaston arrived. His car screeched to a halt and he leapt out, scarlet-faced, and screamed abuse, saying that nobody had any right to be there except Mrs Malucha. We had ten minutes to vanish or he would start shooting.

We scraped up bowls of food, dirty dishes, glasses and bottles, piled into an assortment of vehicles and high-tailed it back to Bill's barn, leaving Mrs Malucha to fend for herself.

Back home, we were hardly out of the cars when another bunch of people arrived. Gloria's friend from Spain, Elsa, had come to stay, unannounced, with her teenage daughter and her daughter's nubile friend.

You had to feel sorry for Bill. He had four caravans, two of which were uninhabitable, and a huge open barn with no internal walls and no sanitary or cooking facilities, and he had to provide accommodation for all these people. Hats off to him, he set up a shower and somehow connected it to electricity so there was hot water, but it still left something lacking in the sleeping and toilet arrangements.

Elsa would share one caravan with Gloria. Bill and their grandson would occupy the other caravan, the hired drivers could sleep in the truck, and the two girls bedded down in a tent I lent them. Elsa and Gloria had to take it in turns to stay awake, as the two drivers kept trying to get into the tent with the girls, who made no attempt to discourage them.

My phone rang next morning. It was Gaston, shouting and spluttering.

'You're bloody well going to have to talk to Bill,' he bellowed.

'Talk to him about what?'

'I'm a very important businessman in the community. When we took Mrs Malucha to the *notaire,* Bill turned up in jeans with his arse hanging out of the back, and Gloria was nekkid! Whatever are people going to think of me?'

Curiosity got the better of my impulse to put the phone down.

'How do you mean, Gloria was naked?'

'She was just wearing a thin piece of cotton wrapped round her body. Everybody could see her knickers. She wore nothing underneath. It was disgraceful.'

Gloria did favour exotic costumes that were a little unusual in the villages of rural central France. Relishing the mental image, I said: 'This has absolutely nothing to do with me. If you don't like the way they dress, you'll have to tell them yourself.' I replaced the receiver.

In the afternoon, I crashed out behind closed shutters hoping to catch a few hours' rest. The metallic clang of the gate, some loud whispers, the rattle of the latch and the squeaking of the ancient door on its hinges woke me up. I opened one reluctant eye to see one of the nubile girls glaring at me.

'I want a proper toilet,' she snapped. 'We're meant to use a Porta Potti behind a curtain!'

I could sympathise with her: it was pretty distressing. It wasn't much fun using our own chemical toilet, which rocked playfully from side to side on the uneven cobbles of the goat shed, but it did offer a degree of privacy and a delightful view of the flowering cherry tree through a hole in the wall.

'So do I. But I'm afraid I don't have a proper toilet, either.'

'You **must** have one!' she yelled.

'Yes, I know I must, but in the meantime I'm afraid I don't. I'm sorry.'

She flounced away, banging the old door behind her. A few moments later, a piercing whistle from the grandson roused all the dogs, who had until then been sleeping quietly. They all started milling around and jumping up and down while the boy threw stones and sticks for them, chasing them around while whooping like a Red Indian. I abandoned all thought of a siesta.

Sinbad was still with me and I was getting pretty tired lugging the great cage to and fro each day, but in view of Bill's beleaguered circumstances I didn't like to mention it. I'd only been here a few weeks – the tranquil and gloriously solitary life I had envisaged was already in a state of disarray, but this was only the beginning. It was going to get much, much worse.

Chapter Fourteen

Over the next few days life lapsed into blissful peace. Apart from the grandson and the younger girl wanting to play with the dogs, the comings and goings at Bill's didn't greatly affect me. Yet.

Terry arrived and remarked on the encampment around the corner. I explained the events of the preceding week, and he said: 'Don't get involved with them. Just say no.' Easier said than done.

Gloria's friend Elsa was preparing to return to Spain with the two girls. She was waiting for her brother and his family who were driving from England to spend the night here, and next day they'd all set off together.

Gloria came to say that Elsa had driven to Paris to meet them, but on the return journey they had become separated and by nightfall there was no sign of him.

At just after one o'clock in the morning, our telephone began ringing. To reach it we had to climb down the rickety ladder into the barn, go out of the barn, around the garden and in through the front door to the small room where the telephone lived. By the time we had properly woken up and heard the ringing, and reached the phone, it stopped ringing. We stood around for five minutes to see if it would re-ring, which it didn't until we had retraced our steps to the bedroom. I forget to mention that there was no electricity neither in the barn nor the bedroom, so this was all done by torchlight. Once more we fumbled for the torch, climbed down the ladder, crossed the barn, scrambled round the corner and in through the front door and to the small room. The phone stopped ringing once again. At 3.00am it rang once more, and once again stopped when we reached it.

A few minutes after six o'clock, off went the phone again, and Terry managed to reach it.

'It's me,' said a male voice. 'Can you come and get us?'

'Who are you?' Terry asked.

'Are you Bill?'

'No, I'm not Bill. Who are you?'

'But that's Bill's phone, isn't it? It's the number he gave me.'

'No, it isn't Bill's phone. Who are you, and what do you want?'

'I'm Elsa's brother. We got lost. I'm in the village. We've been sleeping in the car park all night. I kept ringing but you didn't answer. Can you come and get us?'

Terry said: 'I'll go and tell Bill to come down for you.'

Ha, I thought. What happened to 'Don't get involved with them. Just say no.'?

He replaced the receiver, raised his eyebrows and went to tell Bill someone in the village was waiting to be collected.

'How is it,' he asked, 'that person has our phone number? Why didn't he ring Bill?'

'Bill doesn't have a phone.'

'You're joking. Why doesn't he?'

'Well,' I explained, 'apparently somebody ran up a huge bill on his phone, and it was cut off and he can't get it put back on unless he pays the outstanding bill, which he can't.'

'So you mean he uses our phone?'

'Yes, but he's going to pay for any calls he makes. I time them and write them down, and he won't give our number to anybody except for emergencies.'

'I don't think that's a good idea,' Terry said. Well, neither did I, but somehow it had happened.

***

Later that day Gloria came around, her usual cheerful self.

'He's a drug addict,' she chirruped.

'Who is?'

'The brother, that one who ended up in the car park last night. He's with his wife and they've got three little ones with them. They're all very pale.'

'How do you know he's an addict?'

'He told us. He's got needles, and a prescription.'

Terry rolled his eyes at me, and we went out for the day, away from the squealing pubescent girls, the hyperactive little boy, the randy drivers, the drug addict and his pale family, and any other odds or sods who might turn up. We didn't get back until nightfall, by which time Bill and all the guests had left for Spain, leaving just Gloria and the dogs.

The next day, Terry and I started blocking up the hedges to prevent the dogs escaping. Quite soon the novelty of having trees to bark up, mole hills to investigate and dark mysterious corners to explore had worn off, and once they'd tired of their own acre and a half, they set out to explore further afield, terrifying the neighbours. I trotted along behind them as they peeled off in opposing directions, waving my arms wildly and shrieking: 'It's OK! They're very friendly. Biscuits! Dinner! Walkies!'

The first time they failed to return by nightfall, I lay sleeplessly and tearfully wondering what fate had overtaken our beautiful boys. Just after 3.30am all the dogs in the hamlet went off suddenly, barking and yowling. Carrying my trusty torch, and wearing nothing but a quickly snatched-up hand towel and the spiky pink plastic sandals, I sprinted to the end of the lane and found them, coated with mud, skinny as toast-racks, red-eyed and footsore, but evidently extremely satisfied with their expedition. Sometimes they vanished for days on end, but were always found, safe and well, being sheltered and fed on one neighbouring farm or another.

These escapades were becoming ever more frequent, so fence-blocking was a priority. Armed with rolls of wire, hammers, sticks and nails, we had just set off towards the meadow when the phone rang.

I ran back to answer it. It was Elsa, calling from Spain.

'Have you heard from my brother?' she asked.

'No. Should I have?' I replied, trying not to sound exasperated.

'I've lost him at the border. Let Gloria know, and tell her I'll ring back later. If he turns up back there, tell him to stay put until I phone. Cheerio.'

Obediently, I went to let Gloria know that the addict was lost, and that Elsa would phone later.

Terry was furious with these intrusions into what was intended to be our peaceful life, so I'm afraid I took the phone off the hook for the day, and what became of the lost addict and his pale-faced family we never found out.

***

Terry left the following morning, and Gloria arrived to say she was going to visit Mrs Malucha who had been stuck for several days in the middle of nowhere in Gaston's house, with no transport, no telephone and no way of communicating with the outside world.

Gloria wondered whether I'd like to go along to keep her company. Why not?

The great lady herself was sitting at a primitive trestle table, on a wooden chair, which with a single gas ring, a tiny refrigerator and a small bed made up the entire furnishings of the house. Quite understandably, Mrs Malucha was not in good spirits.

Ignoring Gloria, she hollered: 'Sue, phone the American!'

'Susie,' I corrected. 'Who is the American?'

'Phone him and tell him what they've done to me. Look at me, left here like an animal! I've been frozen.' With the temperature up in the high 30s, I suspected she was exaggerating, but I did feel sorry for the poor old soul.

'What do you want us to do?' asked Gloria.

'Get me out of here, Sue,' she said, still ignoring Gloria. She heaved herself up from the chair, which expelled a wooden sigh of relief and, dragging a battered suitcase behind her, made for the door. Gloria shrugged. We trotted behind her, jamming her and her suitcase into the car.

'Where do you want to go?' enquired Gloria.

'I don't care, just get me away from here. Leaving me here like an animal. Wait 'til the American hears about this. You'll phone him, Sue, won't you?'

'Susie,' I corrected.

After a lengthy discussion, we installed Mrs Malucha in a small hotel nearby, to her total satisfaction and my heartfelt relief. I need not now worry about phoning the American, she said kindly, because the hotel was perfectly comfortable and she would be happy there. Her property purchase didn't seem to be making any progress, and it concerned me that she was going to run up hotel bills, but as she didn't seem at all worried as long as the food was good, and the helpings generous, it wasn't my business. Maybe now I could get on with my new life.

Before he left, Bill had pumped up a plastic swimming pool and filled it with water. Gloria was happy to float about in it on an air bed for most of the day, and to potter around watering her plants. I enjoyed a few days of peace until Bill returned from his travels and came to say Gloria wasn't well. She suffered badly with asthma, although she was such a bright and cheerful soul and never mentioned it herself.

'Would you keep an eye on her? I'll not have her getting upset.' With that, he was gone, leaving me responsible for Gloria's emotional and physical wellbeing.

No sooner had he vanished in a cloud of vehicular farts than my phone rang. It was the hotel where Mrs Malucha had been so happily ensconced for the last week. The hotel was very sorry, but Mrs Malucha had to leave and would we please come and collect her straight away. According to the manager, there was some mysterious law that prohibited ladies of Mrs Malucha's age from staying in their hotel for longer than one week. I didn't believe that but said we would come and collect her.

Gloria and I debated what could be done to accommodate Mrs Malucha until the purchase of her house was completed; there was still no indication of how long it might take.

Mrs Malucha was delighted to see us.

'Hello, Sue!' she yelled merrily.

'Susie,' I corrected.

The hotel was wonderful, she said. The rooms were warm, the food was excellent, and the proprietor was in love with her. This was normal: ever since she was a young girl, men had found her irresistible. She batted her enormous lashless eyelids. Gloria and I smiled politely. She was sorry to be leaving, but she understood that rules were rules.

We brought her back to the hamlet, where she wedged herself into a plastic chair while Gloria cooked her a meal and we discussed her options. She couldn't stay at that hotel. She refused to return to Gaston's house and she was not going to stay in one of Gloria's caravans.

'Can't I come and live with you?' she enquired plaintively.

'No,' I said.

'Well, you'll have to drive me back to Spain. I don't think I'm going to like France after all.' The prospect of conveying this yelling, chain-smoking, eternally hungry giantess several hundred miles over the Pyrenees in Tinkerbelle, who had great rust-holes in her lower regions allowing unimpeded views of the passing tarmac, was intoxicating: what a great story it would make. But who would look after Gloria and the dogs? It wasn't going to happen.

There was only one place Mrs Malucha could stay, and while she tucked into another meal Gloria prepared a caravan for her. With very

72

bad grace, she allowed us to heave her up the steps into the mouldy caravan, where she locked the door, drew the curtains and turned on her radio full blast. As I walked back to the house, the phone was ringing. It was the American Mrs Malucha had mentioned, calling from Spain, and wanting to speak to Mrs Malucha right now and he didn't want any excuses or else I was going to be in real trouble. Leaving the receiver dangling in mid-air, I watered the pot plants on the window sill and then strolled back to Mrs Malucha's caravan and tapped on the window. I had to tap several times before she snorted: 'Go away!'

'Mrs Malucha, the American wants to speak to you. He's on the phone. Can you come over?'

The caravan shook and rolled and groaned, and after a couple of minutes the door opened.

'Help me down, Sue,' she said.

'Susie,' I replied mechanically, bracing myself as she extruded herself through the doorway.

'It's no good, Sue, I can't walk to your house. You'll have to bring the phone here.'

'Mrs Malucha, the phone will not reach here. Just hold on to me, take your time and walk very slowly.' Her weight almost dragged me to the ground. We made satisfyingly slow progress back to the phone and the rude American who had spent quite a long time listening to the sound of silence.

Propped in a valiant garden chair, Mrs Malucha bawled down the phone, assuring the American that Sue was the only decent person here. She wanted to go back to Spain immediately, if not sooner than that. She would not travel by train or coach, her leg wouldn't allow it. The American agreed to make the 1,600-mile journey and collect her. In the meantime he urged Mrs Malucha to be of stout heart and keep her spirits up, and make sure that I looked after her.

'Don't worry, Sue's here, she's taking care of me. Nothing's too much trouble for her,' she assured him.

I gave her a long cold drink, answered her request for some cake or biscuits quite truthfully that I didn't have any, and steered her back. What it must have been like in the caravan with all the windows closed, I couldn't imagine. However, Mrs Malucha complained that she was cold. She had a heavy sleeping bag and one woollen blanket but she was cold, very cold, and thought it more than likely she would catch pneumonia, if not something worse. She needed more blankets.

All I had was a large pile of dog blankets in a box, so I washed them and tumbled them dry. Although they looked rather hairy, they were clean and smelt fresh. She accepted them non-committally and locked herself back in.

An hour later she opened the top half of the caravan door to howl that the toilet in the caravan was too low; she couldn't bend sufficiently to use it. Gloria gathered up some concrete blocks and we constructed a kind of throne, hoping that the combined weight of the blocks and Mrs Malucha wouldn't plunge through the floor. Mrs Malucha grunted and asked to be left alone, slamming the door behind her.

Gloria made her some lunch, but when she took it to the caravan Mrs Malucha refused to open the door and told her to go away. Gloria left it on the steps where it lay untouched. She tried trays of salad, cold meats, cheese and bread, cakes and cups of tea, but Mrs Malucha steadfastly refused to communicate. The food lay untouched and desiccating in the sun, like tributes to an Eastern deity. Mrs Malucha on hunger strike was a serious matter. Gloria was distressed and starting to wheeze ominously, worrying that Mrs Malucha would not complete the sale of the property.

I was sitting in the garden wondering whether to get drunk, when Gloria arrived looking exasperated.

'She wants you.'

I trudged around to the caravan.

'Now look here, Sue,' began Mrs Malucha.

'Susie,' I replied uselessly.

'I can't stay here. It's too cold. Freezing. Like an ice-box. I'm not staying in here tonight, and that's it.'

'I'll try to find a hotel room for you.'

'No, that's no good. I don't want to go to a hotel. Why can't I come and live with you?'

I could have given a dozen reasons – there was no proper bedroom even if she could get up the ladder, no bathroom, no running water or satisfactory electricity. The floorboards such as they were would not bear her weight. I didn't want her to stay with me, and certainly couldn't afford to stoke her enormous appetite. She chain-smoked and her clothes smelt horrible, and she was nothing to do with me.

I simply replied: 'Because you can't.'

'Well then, how about your friends? Have you got some friends I can go and stay with?'

'No.'

'Then you're going to have to drive me back to Spain!'

'I've already told you, Mrs Malucha, I can't do that. The best I can do is try to find you a nice hotel room.'

'But I don't want to stay in a hotel!' she wailed.

'Then you'll have to sort yourself out,' I snapped. 'I really can't do any more.' I started to walk away.

'Wait, Sue,' she screamed. 'I'll go to the hotel.'

I phoned a hotel and booked her a room. Gloria and I squished her once again into the car with her bags and bundles. It was a very pretty hotel with a flowery courtyard filled with tubs of geraniums and covered in leafy vines, and Mrs Malucha didn't like it one little bit. She couldn't come up with a particular reason, she just knew it was not a good hotel. Politely ignoring her tantrums, the proprietor led the way to a steep and narrow staircase.

'Aha!' crowed Mrs Malucha triumphantly. 'There you are! I knew it! I can't get up those stairs with my bad leg!'

'Oh yes you can!' Gloria and I cried in harmony, and with the help of the proprietor we heaved her upwards and into a very pleasant room overlooking the pretty courtyard. Mrs Malucha was swift to pick holes in her new accommodation.

'It's going to be too cold here. There aren't enough blankets. The bed is too small. There's no armchair, no telephone, no light switch near the bed. What do you think I'm going to sit on all day?'

I asked the proprietor, who was still smiling politely, whether she could supply an armchair and more blankets.

'Just one blanket?'

'Could you manage four?' She blinked and twitched an elegant eyebrow, but went away and returned with a great pile of blankets, and eyeing Mrs Malucha's bulk rather doubtfully said she would try to find a suitable armchair. There was nothing she could do about the light switch, nor the telephone, for which I was supremely grateful, but she would ask someone to come up regularly to check on Mrs Malucha's needs.

'I won't be able to go down for meals,' threatened Mrs Malucha.

'We can bring your meals up for you,' replied the patient proprietor.

Defeated, Mrs Malucha crashed down onto the bed.

'Well, we'll leave you to settle in,' said Gloria cheerily, and the three of us headed for the door. Mrs Malucha's voice followed us, booming: 'Hey! What about my cigarettes? I've no cigarettes. You'll have to go and get me some.'

When I returned with a hundred cigarettes, she was plugged into her radio and feeling rather sorry for herself.

'I don't know what's going to become of me, Sue. I don't want to stay in France. Did you know the people here don't speak English?'

'Never mind,' I said to cheer her up. 'The American will be here on Tuesday to take you back to Spain.'

'But I don't want to be in Spain. It's too hot.'

'Have you thought of going to England?'

'Oh no, I couldn't live in England. They don't let you sing there,' she added mysteriously. Well, having ruled out Spain, England and France, where she had paid a deposit and signed a binding contract to buy a house, I had run out of suggestions and took my leave, promising to return the next day to see how she was getting on.

Mrs Malucha had now taken up several days of my life, Gloria was going down with flu, and I was contemplating whether I could squeeze in a quick nervous breakdown before something else arrived to occupy my time. The American phoned to find out where Mrs Malucha was, and the hotel rang with a message from Mrs Malucha that I was to go to the caravan and find her brown shoes and kettle and take them to her next day.

Predictably, the American didn't turn up, and neither did Bill. Ensconced in the smoky fug of her hotel room, Mrs Malucha became more manageable, asking for nothing more than a wholesale supply of cigarettes and batteries for her radio, and regular large meals, with wine, to keep her happy.

***

Shortly Bill returned, and Gloria flew south to Spain with the swallows, leaving the dogs and the care of her plants to Bill.

'Try to keep an eye on the plants, will you?' she asked me. 'Just remind him to water them a bit, but not too much.'

I said I would. Each time I went to check the plants, they were drier and browner than the time before, and each time I suggested that if Bill didn't have time to water them I could do it.

'No, no, I'm just about to do it. I've not forgotten.' He even went so far as to find a kettle to put some water in. But still the plants wasted away into withered twigs and wilted stems. Poor things.

Two days before Gloria was due to return, Bill said: 'Do you think the plants are looking OK?'

'No, they're dead,' I replied.

'But if I give them some water now, they'll be fine, won't they?'

'Bill, the plants are dead. Giving them water cannot make them be alive.'

'Oh, that's a shame.' He went back to whatever he was doing.

When Gloria returned, she ranted and raved for a few minutes, then collected all her pots of dead plants, stood them outside and gave them a drop of water.

'What are you doing that for?' I asked. 'They're stone dead. Absolutely, completely dead.'

She laughed. 'No, they'll be all right. They just need a bit of time to recover from him,' she said, glowering in Bill's direction. Astonishingly, most of the plants, after a long rest, did start to sprout new growth. Gloria nursed them to full health, and whenever she went away, Bill murdered them again. It was a continuous cycle of death and rebirth; they must have been very confused.

***

Mrs Malucha was still wedged into the hotel room waiting for somebody to do something with her. I was quite fond of her in an exasperated sort of way. I was concerned that she was running up a large bill in the hotel, where she had been enjoying full board and room service for nearly a month without any mention of the house she was meant to be buying. Alas, there was nothing I could do other than urge Bill to go and see her and sort her out, which he seemed strangely unwilling to do.

Carole and Norrie were very concerned for Mrs Malucha's plight. They took her to a solicitor, and Gaston was subsequently forced to return her deposit and pay compensation to her. On the sale price of the property of 40,000 francs, he had been charging her 60,000 francs in 'fees'. He fell out with Bill and threw a punch at him, and then drove his car at Norrie who had to jump into a bush to avoid being run over.

I lost track of Mrs Malucha over the next few weeks and learned she

77

had checked out of the hotel. I thought it would be the last I would hear of her, but no... From time to time during the next few years, the telephone would ring in the very early hours.

'Hello, Sue, it's Mrs Malucha,' boomed the familiar voice.

'Mrs Malucha, it's four o'clock in the morning.'

'I know, Sue, but I couldn't sleep, so I thought I'd ring and see how you are.'

'Well, that's kind of you, but couldn't you ring during the day instead, when I'm not asleep?'

'Oh no, it's too expensive during the day. By the way, Sue, have you found my brown shoes and my kettle?'

'Mrs Malucha, nobody knows where your brown shoes or your kettle are. I'm really sorry, but there's no point in keeping asking, because I'm never going to find them.'

She told me she had somehow got herself to England and was living in a nice flat in Portsmouth for the time being. However, one of her suitors had asked her to go and live with him in Switzerland. They were buying a house together, and she was very happy.

A long while later, Carole did find the brown shoes. She took them to Portsmouth and found Mrs Malucha living in sad circumstances in a run-down flat in a depressed area. However, she was delighted to see Carole and equally delighted to have her brown shoes back.

She was an unquenchable old thing. I often wondered what happened to her.

***

Despite his little eccentricities, Bill was a helpful and friendly person. Nothing was too much trouble for him. He tried to mend things for me – the lawnmower, the Hoover, the strimmer – anything in fact that was in need of mending. He provided transport and used his digger to excavate the trenches for us to lay the piping for a drainage system. He did nearly knock down the house in the process, but that was an accident. He was almost obsessively clean, forever washing himself, his clothes, his caravans, his pots and pans, and his cooker. Most times when I went looking for him, he would be cleaning something or other. When we planned a trip to town to leave at 11.00 a.m, by the time he had washed his trainers, changed the hose on his washing machine, cleaned the cooker, changed his socks and brushed and washed the doormats of his caravans, it was 2.45pm. Unfortunately, the outside of his property was littered with decaying machinery, abandoned tools, and fly-infested pools of fluid dog shit ('Turd Hall,' he sometimes laughed). Several times I tried diplomatically, and once or twice quite bluntly, to suggest that he needed to tidy the property, whereupon he would reply, gazing into middle distance, that he was going to get it all sorted out.

'It's summer,' pointed out M. Meneteau one day. 'The countryside looks beautiful. The flowers are all out. The sky is blue. But look at this mess!' He waved his arm at Bill's clutter. Three mouldy caravans were gathered around the entrance to the building. There was a wheelbarrow full of rusty metal and water, weeds everywhere, a great roll of water pipe, some blown-over garden chairs.

'Would you ask him if he could put the caravans and all this stuff,' he indicated the piles of junk, 'around the back of his house, where we can't see it, or in his barn? It's such a shame to see our little village in such a mess.'

I told Bill about the neighbours' distress. Again, he adopted that faraway look on his face, saying: 'Yes, I must do something about clearing up.' But he never did.

During the wet weather, he parked his trucks in the quagmire that formed outside his barn, where they bedded down into the mud. After several minutes of wheel-spinning and mud-splattering, he would trot off to ask M. Meneteau, in a loud voice, stressing each syllable carefully: 'Poss-i-ble trac-tor you?' pointing at the embedded vehicle. M. Meneteau would cheerfully bring his tractor around, couple the truck to it with a chain, and drag it from its muddy prison. Then he would indicate, with sign language, that it would make sense to park the vehicle on the hard surface. 'Mercy, mercy,' Bill would mutter, tucking a bottle of whisky into M. Meneteau's pocket. Fairly soon afterwards, the truck would be back stuck in the mud once more.

Chapter Fifteen

With Gloria in Spain and Mrs Malucha out of circulation, my time was my own. Early each morning and again at dusk, an elderly lady fed her chickens in the small field which backed onto ours, so I wandered down to see her.

Madame Grimaud was a widow whose bent back and smiling, lined face were in their mid-seventies, but her sparkling blue eyes were only twenty.

'What do you have there?' I asked, pointing to a small bowl in her hand.

'Chicken soup,' she beamed, putting it down in front of her hens. 'They love it!'

I wondered if they realised where it came from.

'Those chickens there,' I pointed, 'they're the ones called *cul nu*, aren't they?'

She giggled and ducked her head. '*Cou nu*,' she corrected, laughing. Bare necked, not bare arsed as I had said in my muddled-up French. Strange looking birds, they were, tall chickens with no feathers on their long necks. They looked as if they were moulting, or suffering from some unpleasant disease.

Madame Grimaud's beautiful first name was Eglantine, which means wild rose. She'd lived in the hamlet for 50 years and painted a vivid picture of how life had changed over the decades. While we sipped coffee in her tidy little kitchen, she pointed to her smart gas cooker and the neat row of enamelled saucepans hanging from hooks. These were recent acquisitions that had replaced the original cast iron pot suspended over an open fire, which is how the daily soup had been cooked, and the small coal-heated tripod used for making omelettes. At her back door was the wood oven that had once served her end of the hamlet for baking bread. It wasn't baked every day, and when it was they made enough to last for two to three weeks. The loaves were stored on a rack hanging from the ceiling, where it collected dust, got hard and was shared with those rodents ingenious enough to reach it.

There was a small brick-built stove in her garden, which had been used for cooking the pig food, and an old stone container with a drain hole at the bottom that had served as a primitive washing machine. Dirty linen went into the pot and was covered with boiling water and ash from the fire, which was used as a cleanser before the days of washing powder. The wet laundry had to be hauled down to the stream to be rinsed and then spread over the trees and shrubs to dry. The villagers from Saint-Thomas brought their laundry to the stream too, in the days before there was any running water in the village. They didn't do the laundry too often, said Madame Grimaud – the sheets only got washed about once a month and less often in the winter. I'm not surprised.

She was a gentle and merry soul. When she talked she had an appealing way of bending her head and looking at me sideways, smiling and flashing those lively eyes. I could see her as a beautiful and flirtatious young girl. She was always happy to pass the time and describe her life as a young woman – hard work and simple pleasures.

Her days had started at 5.00am milking the goats by hand, and then taking them to the fields to graze. The goats needed milking three times a day. Water had to be carried from the stream, two buckets at a time. When the stream dried up, as it sometimes did for long periods, it meant walking to the well on the other side of the hamlet and laboriously drawing up the water. The villagers produced most of their own food, even their own oil made from poppy seeds and walnuts. There was very little money, and they paid the travelling butcher, fishmonger and grocer partly in eggs for the few things they couldn't produce themselves, like salt, sugar and coffee.

During the war, life had been even harder. There was nothing in the shops, not even soap, so they made their own. Sometimes the Germans came to the hamlet, and she would go with the other women and children to hide fearfully in the woods while the soldiers searched their houses for the hunting guns they had ordered the men to surrender.

The nearest thing they had to a holiday was a day's visit to relatives – not only was there no money, but their animals needed constant attention. Young girls cycled to the local fêtes to dance and meet eligible young men from the neighbouring villages, always with their parents, because unmarried girls were not allowed out without a chaperone. It was at one of these revels that Madame Grimaud had met her future husband.

Her father-in-law, she told me in a lowered voice, had hanged himself. He'd lived with them and been very ill for a long time. One day, he sent her husband to do something with the cattle, and her to do something else, which would keep them out of the way for a while. When one of his nephews came to visit him, he was hanging from a walnut tree in the garden. They'd cut the tree down, afterwards.

One day, she took out from a cupboard a tin box containing printed menus from village festivities decades ago, some old photos and certificates, and a card with a beautiful and poignant French poem printed on it:

It is a hot day in August 1944.
A man is driving his oxen along the road,
urging them to move faster, not to drag their heels,
but to get a move on
as they pull their load of beets and hay through the village,
past the watching German troops.
Come on, he encourages the sweating, straining animals,
let's look bright and lively, not like a funeral cortège.
He smiles, and sings to encourage them.
Once they are out of the village, however, his tone changes.
You'll think me strange, he tells them,
asking them to walk slowly, as he allows himself to weep for his dead son,
whose body lies hidden beneath the straw and hay.
The oxen somehow understand that they are pulling the young man
whose voice they knew and loved,
taking him home to his weeping mother.
'Be careful how you go; mind the holes and bumps in the road,
so you don't bang his head against the cart,' says the father.

The poem was written to commemorate the death of a young man from a hamlet half a mile from where we live. Wounded at the battle of Champagné St Hilaire, he died of his wounds the following day, in the arms of a friend, in the blood-soaked room of the café-restaurant at Joussé.

LES BŒUFS – 14 août 1944

Sur la route blanche et poudreuse
Sous ce chaud soleil de mois d'août
Avancez! mes bœufs, avancez!
La cariole est voyageuse
Lourde à trainer, mais malgré tout
A l'aiguillon, obéissez!
A me suivre, vous êtes braves
Mais bien trop lent à mon désir
Avancez! mes bœufs, avancez!
Nous transportons des betteraves
Du bon foin qu'on hume à plaisir
A l'aiguillon, obéissez!
Passons au travers du village
Devant ces allemands balourds
Gais et fiers, et le pas léger
C'est un innocent attelage
Mais de sa récolte trop lourde
Il me faut vous encourager
Avancez, mes bœufs, avancez!
L'ennemi m'a-t-il vu sourire?
Ne soyez pas si nonchalants!
Pour vous aider, je chanterai!
Ne prolongez pas mon martyre!
Mes bœufs, vous êtes ruisselants
De peine, mais moi je ne pourrai
Plus longtemps donner le change
Vous paraissez trop ténébreux
Mener un train d'enterrement
Avancez! mes bœufs, avancez!
Vous allez me trouver étrange
Ne plus me comprendre, mes bœufs
Allez lentement, doucement!
Vous voici maintenant en plaine
Allez posement, noblement
Laissez mes larmes lentement
Couler. Laisser crever ma peine.

Vous vous traîner péniblement
Ayant compris obscurément
Vous que charmait sa voix si forte
Que sous cette paille et ce foin
Cachant à tous mon desespoir
Doucement, mes bœufs, avancez!
C'est mon fils mort que je rapporte!
Mon fils! Ma raison de demain
Mons fils! Qui fut à son devoir
Mons fils! Lequel aimait tant vivre
Et qui partit pour le maquis
Pour que sa France de nouveau
Soit une France grande et libre!
Mon fils est mort pour son pays
Que pouvais-je donner plus beau?
Il fut blessé dans la bataille
Et ne mourut qu'au demain
C'est pourquoi, dans mon tombereau
Avancez! Mes bœufs, avancez!
J'emporte, caché sous la paille
Un francais, mon fils, au dédain
Des SS, de la Gestapo!
Mais que sa pauvre tête inerte
Ne heurte pas la tombereau
Evitez les trous, les cahoots.
La route est maintenant deserte
Le mère attend votre fardeau
Avec ses pleurs et ses sanglots
Avancez, mes bœufs, avancez!

14 août, 1944. Lendemain de la bataille de Champagne Saint Hilaire. Evocation de la mort du volontaire Robert Armand en les bras de Mitsou dans la chambre ensanglantée des Lhuguenot, Café-restaurant de Joussé (Vienne). Mai 1945 – Jean Coste

In that box of souvenirs, I felt, was the whole story of Madame Grimaud's life.

***

In the nearby town of Gençay, there's a busy market every fortnight. It spreads over the town centre, selling saddlery, tractors, piglets, plants, fresh fruit, vegetables, fish, meat, cheese, bread, flesh-coloured corsetry complete with little rubber suspenders and circular-stitched bras with cone-shaped cups, kitchen equipment, sweet roasted peanuts, fishing tackle, jewellery. A small tent dispenses plastic cups of red wine to huddles of farmers, and eels grill to charred fragrance over a coal brazier.

I went with Bill to buy some chickens. The livestock area was rather harrowing, with rabbits and poultry crammed into tiny cages, or tied to each other by their feet in piles on the ground. I had planned to buy a couple of big, fat motherly hens, but was seduced by a pair of Silkies with their soft fur-like feathers, and two bantam hens, so I acquired twice as many birds as I had intended and none of them either big or fat.

'I wouldn't mind a couple of hens,' Bill murmured, 'but I don't want more than two, because Gloria's allergic to eggs, so it'll just be for me. Do you think I should get the black ones, the white ones, or the brown ones with no feathers on their necks?'

I said I had no preference, so he bought two of each.

'You're going to have a lot of eggs, Bill. What are you going to do with them?'

He muttered something incomprehensible and pointed. 'What are those grey things?'

'They're guinea fowl. Very noisy creatures. For heaven's sake, don't buy one of those!'

Bill didn't buy one. He bought two. Then he bought two white turkeys. There was no stopping him now. He'd developed poultry mania, and quickly built up his flock. We accumulated a large stack of cardboard boxes tied with string, emitting rustles and squawks, and were on our way back to the car when Bill saw the geese.

'Ee, I've got to have one of those. I do like a nice goose egg. But it will have to be a female.' Well, yes. There were three geese in a pen, and I asked their villainous-looking owner whether amongst them was a female. He subjected them each in turn to an intimate and undignified gynaecological examination against which they all fought spiritedly. The first two were rejected as males, but it seemed we'd hit the jackpot with the third. This was a female, he assured us. She was inserted indignantly into a cardboard box to join the stack.

With the boxes and their feathery occupants piled into the back of Bill's car, we headed home. 'I'll be off to Spain next week,' he announced casually.

'But all these birds – who's going to look after them?' I asked stupidly, already knowing the answer.

'I'll only be gone a couple of days,' he said.

***

Once home, my chickens investigated the rustic run and rickety coop I had built for them. The Silkies and one bantam quickly snuggled down. However, as soon as she was out of her box, the other bantam flew up to the barn roof, where she stayed wobbling on the ridge until nightfall. Then she flew into M. Meneteau's plum tree and settled for the night. Nothing I could do would dislodge her from where she perched on a branch ten feet above my head, looking down with a smugly triumphant expression that I suspect poultry seldom have the opportunity to exercise.

The terrestrial bantam, whom I named Lizzie, was a pretty black-feathered creature, with a golden lacy veil over her head and back, black legs and little silver toe-nails. She was the first of the girls to lay an egg and announced the event with the pomp and circumstance befitting a royal birth. She yelled her head off for an hour, describing how she had done it, what it looked like, and where it was, whilst the other birds stood around her in a semi-circle listening raptly.

Sandra, the arboreal bantam, was beige with black speckles, rather like a small pheasant. Although she persisted in roosting in the plum tree, she descended daily to dutifully lay one small egg. With their snowy white plumage, turquoise wattles and brilliant red combs, the Silkies were enchanting. The hen was slow to get going on egg production. For several weeks, she did nothing but wander around scratching in the garden and eating, while the cockerel offered her fragments of leaf or pieces of dried grass, which she took and stamped upon. He did a little war dance on one leg to impress her, without success, and leapt on her when she wasn't expecting it, all to no effect. It was only after he spent a whole day bellowing '*cocorico*' loudly and repeatedly into her ear that she finally started laying.

In turn, the hens became broody and began producing an endless supply of babies. The chicks were adorable, little bigger than bumblebees. Their mother, aunts and father were very attentive to them, making sure the dogs didn't get too close, rooting up insects and teaching them how to scratch and dig. I could watch them for hours. Each night, Sandra flew back to her home in the plum tree, abandoning her young to fend for themselves; they were lucky to have a diligent father who scraped them up under his wing.

Whilst the shed I'd contrived for our poultry was primitive, at least they had somewhere safe to sleep. Bill's didn't have anywhere. He used one section of his open barn for the storage of his clients' furniture, a cornucopia of wardrobes, mattresses, tables, chests, boxes of clothes, pictures, gardening tools, plant pots, leather chairs – you could name just about anything and find it there. He moved his poultry in there, and they took to their new quarters with enthusiasm, perching on top of wardrobes, scraping nests into armchairs with their lethal claws, and shitting all over everything as only poultry can.

We constructed a makeshift pen in one corner, out of people's furniture, and at my insistence installed an overhead light to supply some heat for one of the little white turkeys who was looking very fragile. M. Meneteau wandered over and said he didn't give good odds on the turkeys' survival.

'White turkeys,' he spat. 'They're useless. They all die.' Not if I can help it, I thought.

Forward planning wasn't Bill's strongest point. Although it was obvious that the birds couldn't continue living on his clients' furniture indefinitely, he had made no provision, or provision for making provision, for their accommodation. Time slid by and in another two days, he would fly the coop leaving me with not only Sinbad, who was still in residence, but eleven other assorted birds in various states of health, with nowhere safe to live.

I also had a suspicion that he was going to try to leave the two Great Danes with me. Gentle and affectionate as they were, they were both chronically ill with a disease contracted in Spain, the canine equivalent of AIDS. They also suffered from permanent diarrhoea. With our own five dogs, two parrots, Sinbad, our own poultry plus Bill's birds, and remembering how Bill's 'couple of days' I was to look after Sinbad had turned into 10 weeks, I didn't want any more responsibility or mess to clear up.

'Bill, the birds must have a proper place where they can be locked up, otherwise a fox will get them.'

He promised that before he left, he would build an enclosure for them and asked whether he could use the telephone to call Gloria in Spain. While he did so, I sat in the adjacent room keeping a record of how long the call lasted, because he was a bit of a chatterbox and I was getting quite worried about my phone bill.

The conversation went like this: 'Yes, I'm leaving here on Thursday. Oh, you don't want me to bring the dogs with me? Yes, but I can't leave them here on their own. No, I don't really think so. Not very. No. Well, I'm coming down in the car; I'll have to put them in the back. Do you think they'll be OK in the back, all that way? Will they have enough room? You don't think they'll suffer, the two of them, being so big and having to squash into the back of the car for such a long journey? They're big dogs to have to travel so far in such a small car. Do you think it will harm them? No, of course I won't forget to give them water. Yes, it's a real pity we can't find someone here to keep an eye on them, but I wouldn't dream of asking Susie; she's got more than enough to do with all the... I mean, her own animals.'

Finally, I heard him say: 'OK then, love, I'll see you on Friday. And don't worry, I'm sure the dogs will survive the journey.'

I smiled innocently when he came into the room, saying: 'Right, thanks a lot. By the way, I forgot to say, don't mention anything about the birds to Gloria, will you? She might not understand.'

I was almost certain she wouldn't understand why her husband had bought 11 birds that were of no practical use to him, which he was not going to be here to care for, and which had nowhere yet to live. I didn't understand it.

Anyway, the birds were now a *fait accompli*, and with the help of our obliging friends Carole and Norrie we fashioned an enclosure from pieces of angle iron and chicken wire dragged out from amongst Bill's mess. Norrie built a two-storey roosting area complete with a neat little ladder to give easy access for the birds, who did not seem to appreciate our efforts and scattered in every direction while we tried to round them up and get them into their new home – a project that took the four of us more than two hours.

As Bill was preparing to leave for Spain, I could hear him telling

Norrie how worried he was about having to take the two huge dogs all the way in the back of the little car. Norrie looked politely non-committal, and finally Bill loaded the animals into the vehicle and drove off, with very poor grace and a big black frown on his face.

**

The smaller of the two turkeys didn't look at all well, standing hunched up and trembling, and it was touching to see that the goose, the other turkey and the white chickens tried to mother it. They stood close and fetched it morsels of food which it pecked at despondently. Bill hadn't left any food for his birds, seemingly under the impression that they fended for themselves. His poultry found multiple ways of escaping from their pen, meandering around the hamlet pecking at plants and scratching in flowerbeds. And disappearing. Most evenings, as the sun was going down, M. Meneteau would appear on the lane shepherding a diminishing bunch of poultry in front of him.

'They were over the other side, in the maize field,' he would say, apparently not bothered at finding himself in the role of chicken-herder.

The smaller turkey was blind in one eye, and never seemed to grow.

As Tinkerbelle was temporarily off the road, Bill had kindly left a car which I was welcome to use. Although the brakes, steering and tyres were all defective, it was at least insured, and I wasn't in any position to be choosy. I went one day to buy food for his poultry, and when I returned the birds had staged another mass break-out. After rounding them all up, I couldn't find the small white turkey, until a feeble cheeping attracted me to the 10-foot deep hole intended to accommodate Bill's septic tank. There was a foot of water in the bottom, but the turkey had managed to get itself onto a dry ledge, where it was peeping mournfully and waiting for someone to rescue it. M. Meneteau obliged, leaving his lunch uneaten, fetching a ladder, climbing down into the pit and hauling the bedraggled bird out. Later that afternoon, it went missing again, and after climbing over the old bikes, washing machines, mattresses, rolls of barbed wire and flower pots that decorated Bill's garden, I found it tucked into the rim of an old tractor tyre.

Each night, when I locked the diminished herd into the pen, the goose shepherded them into a corner and wedged herself up against them protectively. The small turkey continued to ail. I took it to the vet in a cardboard box tied up with string; M. Audoux diagnosed a blocked sinus and flushed it out. I was given a supply of needles, syringes and a large bottle of slimy stuff to inject it with twice daily. Madame Meneteau came around cheerfully morning and evening for five days to do the injections, while I held the turkey tightly and looked the other way. I couldn't have known then that the time was coming when daily injections would become part of my life.

***

Bill hardly ever appeared and when he did, seemed to have totally lost interest in Sinbad and the poultry. I was responsible for their nutrition and welfare, including the intensive nursing of the small white turkey, so I moved them all into our garden one afternoon, driving them along the lane with the aid of a small stick. They settled contentedly into the hay barn where the kitchen had once stood, apart from the little turkey which insisted on staying with the bantam hens, one of whom snuggled up to it closely at night to shelter it, undaunted that it was four times her size.

As my three hens were giving me as many eggs as I needed, I gave Bill's two remaining hens to M. Meneteau, mentioning that they had still not begun laying although we had had them for two months. A few days later, he explained why. They were all cockerels, sold for their flesh.

On one of his brief visits, Bill made faint rumblings about a plan to install an old transport vehicle in his field and colonise it with pheasants. He said that he had noticed none of the local restaurants had pheasant on the menu, and he saw an opportunity to set up a business supplying them. He seemed to be under the impression that the birds would fend for themselves as far as feeding, watering, cleaning and security were concerned, so I wouldn't have to worry about that. But I did. I worried day and night about the possibility of finding myself mother to a flock of pheasants. When he started rubbing his hands together and saying he was going to get a piggy, I panicked.

I just adore piggies but I didn't want to have to look after one. I phoned Gloria in Spain to share my fears with her.

'Oh God,' she said, 'if he had a brain, he'd be dangerous. Don't worry, leave it to me.' Bill never mentioned the piggy again.

Chapter Sixteen

Despite all I could do for him, the little turkey didn't make it, but the other one kept growing. It became enormous. I gave the new additions names: Alice the goose, Blue the remaining guinea fowl and Toby the turkey. We called them the Gang of Three. They were always together exploring, and their explorations led them into the house.

We'd started work making a bathroom, laying a concrete base for the floor, and then fitting the bath, bidet, loo and washbasin. The Gang of Three watched intently while we mixed cement, plastered and tiled, as if they were hoping to learn how to do it themselves. Toby and Alice were huge and started challenging the dogs for their food. The dogs ran more in confusion than fear from the two great white birds. A large turkey, fully inflated and a great goose with wings akimbo galloping after five dogs is quite a sight. Outside of mealtimes, they all lived in harmony.

When I sat reading in the garden, the birds lay at my feet with the dogs, although the guinea fowl was a restless creature and could only keep still for a couple of minutes before turning its attention to my shoes and trying to eat them, or wandering around the perimeter of the fence very slowly, with its beak touching the ground, like Sherlock Holmes searching for a clue. Despite its ungainly body it was surprisingly nimble, and would sometimes, without any apparent stimulus, break into a fast run and, leaping into the air, turn a complete somersault. If I hadn't seen this with my own eyes, I would never have believed it. Guinea fowl are not aerodynamically designed, but Blue turned somersaults, and when she landed, she carried right on with whatever she had been doing before this original idea popped into her little mind. Sometimes, for variety, still with her beak to the ground, she would run in circles at top speed for two or three minutes, and then continue her strange slow walk. She took a fancy to our chicks and appointed herself as their nanny. She shepherded them daily around the field, and once they had conquered their initial terror they took to her and accepted the little morsels she offered them.

Things began to turn pear-shaped when Alice started making

persistent amorous advances to Toby, and it became evident that Alice was no more a goose than I was a shooting star. Alice was a gander and the target of his affections was a turkey stag. An angry turkey stag is an awesome sight, and Toby was very angry, and he was very, very big. In the centre of his chest was a single coarse black feather, and above his beak was a red wobbly thing that dangled rather pointlessly. When Toby's dander was aroused, the wobbly thing extended itself several inches, and turned crimson; at the same time he puffed out his feathers to double his size; he roared, and he stamped his feet, and the ground shook.

Alice, rejected, became angry too. The two birds faced each other, Toby stamping and Alice screaming with rage. They launched themselves into battle. Alice shrieked, Toby bellowed, the dogs gathered to watch and barked encouragement. Alice tugged out clumps of feathers from Toby's angry chest, and Toby kicked hard with his sturdy toes. I waded in with Wellington boots and a yard broom to separate them. Toby retracted his crimson wobbler and wandered off to look for food, but Alice was mortally offended, with a dragging wing, and crept into a corner refusing to move or eat for two days. Both birds were heartbreakingly depressed by this change in their friendship, and every so often terrible fights would break out again. It couldn't continue – one of them would have to go.

After numerous phone calls, I found a French gentleman who was starting a small turkey-breeding business and wanted a good healthy turkey stag. I had his solemn oath that Toby would live out his natural life in comfort, and we made a rendezvous for Toby's new owner to come and collect him.

Two gentlemen drove up in a small van. One was short and round, dressed in the typical blue overalls of French country-folk, with a beaming smile stretching across his polished rosy cheeks. His companion was tall with dark, curly hair and a spectacular handlebar moustache. The shorter gentleman clutched a large bottle of clear fluid in his hand, and his companion a small wooden crate, the sort of crate an average-sized chicken could fit into.

'Madame,' beamed the short gentleman, 'have no fear! I promise you, your little turkey is going to a good home, with lots of ladies to enjoy. He will be well cared for. You have my word.'

I thanked him profusely, because believe me, finding a good home for a turkey in an area of France that is almost entirely populated by farmers and carnivores is not at all an easy task. He proffered the bottle, assuring me that it was the best *eau-de-vie* I would ever taste.

Just then Toby stalked up to see what was happening, and the two gentlemen stared at him in astonishment.

'That is your turkey?'

'Yes. Is there a problem?'

'But he's magnificent! What a splendid turkey! We were not expecting such a big, fine bird – what do you feed him on?'

I explained that Toby, by choice, lived mainly on dog food. Shaking their heads in wonder, they proceeded to try to get him into the little crate. It took a lot of folding and holding while Toby put up a heroic fight, but finally he was secured, and extremely angry.

'Don't worry, my son,' the short gentleman told him. 'You'll be home very soon and wait until you see your wives! You are going to be a very happy turkey!'

With many handshakes and promises they drove away, leaving me with a bottle of fire water and a gander called Alice, who started entertaining himself playing with the doormat, or maybe trying to kill it, or mate with it.

Blue, the guinea fowl began roosting on the sofa next to our oldest dog, Natalia.

***

On one of those days when I didn't have any visitors or commitments, I sprawled on the sun lounger. The dogs stretched out on the grass. Despite a drought that had lasted several weeks, a small underground spring kept part of the garden permanently green and moist. Alice settled himself in the shade, while Blue squawked and yelped her way around the perimeter of the garden. The sky was the palest blue; the fruit trees were in blossom, the oak and lindens in full leaf. The wind was warm and gusty, and the horizon that had been brown for several months had suddenly become flushed with green as new crops started to emerge. I watched the big glossy rat who lived in the barn emerge from his den in the stone wall to help himself to the chicken food, looking left, right, and left once more before running out, grabbing a mouthful and flashing back into the wall again. The parrots sang along with the wild birds and the swallows twittered noisily. Alice tilted his elegant head on one side and observed them with a bright blue eye, rather questioningly, as if wondering how they could fly so fast, or why they bothered when they could be sitting comfortably on a cool lawn surrounded by daisies. He had transferred his amorous attentions to me since Toby's departure, and I had to keep a broom at hand to fend him off when he became too passionate. The bruises from his most recent show of tenderness were only just starting to fade.

Suddenly an egg appeared on the middle of the lawn where Blue had been sitting. One minute it wasn't there, then it was, like a rabbit from a magician's hat. It was slightly larger than a hen's egg, and rock-hard. The shell seemed unbreakable: it bounced like a ball when I threw it down the garden. Wizzy retrieved it enthusiastically for several minutes, and when he gave it a hard bite it broke with a loud crack. Having discovered the secret of this novel missile, he waited each day for the egg to appear. At first, Blue laid haphazardly wherever she happened to be at the critical moment, but once she started to get the hang of it, she settled down on a pile of straw in one of the barns. There she sat for about half an hour with a blank stare until the arrival of the egg, which Wizzy immediately collected and took away to eat. Each day, he settled down beside her on the straw and waited. As he became more and more impatient, he poked his snout under the rear end of the vacant-looking bird every few minutes to see whether the egg had arrived. Tipped onto her beak, she remained motionless until he removed his nose and allowed her to settle back, getting on with the business in hand. He tracked her daily as she meandered her noisy way around the garden, waiting for the first sign that the magic egg performance was imminent, wagging his tail ever faster as Blue settled down on her pile of hay.

Alice, whom we renamed Alex, turned his affections to Hecate, our younger bitch. He followed her everywhere, ferociously attacking anybody or any other animal that came near her. She disdainfully ignored his approaches, going about her daily affairs with the gander trotting along beside her. If Hecate sunbathed, Alex sunbathed. When Hecate drank, Alex drank. When Hecate curled up on her cushion and went to sleep, Alex curled up right next to her, keeping one eye open to ensure no harm came to her.

For a while, this was amusing and endearing, but Alex needed a mate of his own kind. Geese are notoriously difficult to sex, which was why

Bill had ended up with a gander in the first place. M. Meneteau said sometimes the females had narrower beaks; somebody else said you could tell them apart by the width between their legs. I found somebody who had what he believed to be a female goose. I met him in a car park. He arrived carrying a very beautiful but enraged bird encased up to her neck in a brown paper bag tied in place with a piece of string.

I drove Lucy-Goose home, took her out of the soggy bag and introduced her to Alex.

For four long days and nights, he harried her. He bit her, chased her, bashed her with his wings, tried to drown her, drove her from her food, hissed and generally terrorised her in every way he could devise.

On the fifth day, I decided to take her back to where she had come from. She was so tired and bedraggled. Then suddenly, Alex's hateful shriek changed to a gentle croaking, and he led her lovingly to the plastic paddling pool that served as their pond. He ushered her in and they became inseparable. Except for Blue, who shuffled along behind them wherever they went, Alex chased away anything that came near Lucy – whether it be dogs, lawnmowers or people. Visitors cringed outside the gates and would only come into the garden if Alex wasn't around – if he appeared they climbed onto the garden table or ran for the house.

M. Meneteau mentioned that Lucy would soon start laying and I should expect Alex to become belligerent. It was impossible to imagine how much more belligerent he could be. I could hardly wait. Where Lucy was concerned he was a model of gallantry, shepherding her around the garden croaking tender goose-talk to her. They shared a happy life for nearly two years, until the morning when we found Alex had lost a battle with something stronger than himself.

Lucy was devastated and went into such a state of depression, I was afraid she would die of grief. I popped her into the car and drove her to *le Marais aux Oiseaux* on the Ile d'Oleron, a hundred miles away. Originally a haven for migratory birds in distress, they also accepted other creatures – unwanted pet rabbits, tortoises, and domestic poultry, all of which live in an expansive area of woods and marshland. There Lucy would have other geese for company.

Chapter Seventeen

We had rodents. A dynasty of rats set up home beneath the chicken house. Glossy, bright-eyed and cunning, I found them interesting and endearing. I watched them help themselves to food and water, always alert for danger, teaching their young to look carefully in both directions before venturing out. The mice thrived too; a battalion of four came up through the floorboards in the evening and shinned up the legs of the parrots' cages, helping themselves to sunflower seeds while I sat reading a few feet away. Three of them concentrated on stocking their larder, while the fourth trundled around collecting fallen feathers and manoeuvring them, with quite some difficulty, back to the nest. Their home must have been something rather special, decorated with bright red, bright green, dark blue and grey feathers.

I found a mouse sitting comfortably on my bed one morning, and they quite often scampered over my head during the night. One regularly sat on the lid of a particular saucepan to perform its ablutions. When I picked up a bunch of grapes from the table, I found a field mouse clinging to them. After staring at me for some time and twitching its whiskers, it ate its way through a whole grape whilst sitting on my hand.

Neither mice nor rats troubled me. Although it wasn't ideal having them living in our house, I wasn't afraid of them. Some people don't understand claustrophobia; I don't understand fear of mice. They are so small and furry. Spiders are different and give me the screaming habdabs. The greater French farmhouse spider is a terrible creature, with a 5-foot wingspan, fierce eyes, and muscles the size of tennis balls on its uncountable legs. They growl like tigers, deep in their throats, trap you with webs stronger and thicker than steel hawsers, and hang you by your ankles while they chew your ears off.

A friend was overrun with cats because one of her neighbours refused to neuter her own, which were constantly propagating. She knew of some young kittens needing homes. I went to see them and said I'd take the one that came to me first. A grey and white one with markings on his face, like the Phantom of the Opera galloped straight into my arms.

I called him Beau and he did a sterling job of rodent control. A while later, my friend phoned to say she had another cat that needed a home as her other cats would not tolerate it. They chased it out of the house, where it sat outside on the window ledge tapping on the glass with one hopeful paw.

'Honestly,' she said, 'it's just heartbreaking to see his poor little face at the window. I've made him a bed in one of the rabbit hutches and put a duck-down duvet in there for him, but he's desperate for affection.' So that's how Louis joined the family.

Beau finished every scrap of whatever he caught, but Louis was an epicure and only ate those parts that particularly appealed to him, so it was common to find a little set of clawed feet, a disembodied head, a backside and tail left behind.

**

We didn't have sufficient land to support our two horses, but neighbours were happy to rent us their grazing, so we arranged to bring Cindy and Leila here.

Terry hired a transporter and drove them here with the help of our daughter Julie. Little Catherine came too. They arrived shortly before midnight on a late autumn evening. As we lowered the tail of the transporter, the mares stepped down the ramp, gazing about them and surveying their new home with the regal air of a pair of duchesses arriving at a state banquet. They stood for a moment in the dark, and then wandered off beneath the stars and started tearing at the lush grass.

A little later, I led them into the small barn I had lovingly spent four days preparing. I'd pulled down the rotting boards of the ceiling, dug out the dried manure and scraped it off the walls, hacked the giant spiders' webs from the beams, disinfected the floor and laid down a thick bed of fresh straw. They went in obediently enough and chewed politely on the hay nets I'd put up for them. In the morning, they kicked down the door and took off to the field. From then on, they steadfastly refused to go into that barn.

As well as the delight of the horses' arrival was the pleasure of having some of our family here for the first time, and we all somehow managed to survive the primitive living conditions and lack of bathroom. My granddaughter Catherine was one of those children who are difficult to feed, the dreaded fussy eater. The only thing she was eating at the time were sweet red peppers, until she discovered the walnuts that had fallen from our tree. With her little 5-year-old hands, she somehow managed to break them open with the nut cracker, and that was all she ate for their entire five-day stay.

At 4.51am in the morning following their departure, the sound of madly barking dogs and whinnying horses woke me. I pulled on a dressing gown and a pair of socks, jammed my feet into Wellington boots and found a torch that produced a faint glimmer of light. I waved it around until it illuminated two large figures. Behind them lay an acre of meadowland and a large weather-proof open barn filled with hay and buckets of water. There had been no need for them to force themselves over two strands of barbed wire and a fallen elder tree, only to land up in a neglected area of about thirty square yards where there was nothing but weeds and rolls of discarded chicken wire in which they were caught up. Having discovered for themselves that theirs was a wasted mission, they were unable to extricate themselves from the entanglement and had panicked.

Cindy's tail was caught in a roll of chicken wire which was holding her back and getting her further tangled up in the undergrowth. Leila had tried to step back over the barbed wire and had both hind legs trapped between two strands that tightened every time she moved. I ran back to find a strong pair of scissors and, jamming the almost extinct torch between my knees, managed to cut away Cindy's tail from the wire, turned her around and led her to freedom. That left Leila trapped in the barbed wire that was attached to a fallen fence post. She was calm and stayed still, as I lifted and twisted the fence post until I could free it from where it was trapped beneath more wire. With the tension released, Leila was freed and wandered off into the darkness. The torchlight died, and I returned to my cold bed.

Next morning when I went to feed them, I found them both trapped in the same area, from where they gazed at me mournfully as if they had been imprisoned there against their will. I released them once again, reflecting that there is no understanding the mind of a horse.

It was the first time in 37 years of owning horses that I had had sole responsibility for them; previously, I'd kept them in livery yards where there was always somebody to ask for advice. I hoped I was going to be able to care properly for them. Being able to see them from the bedroom window standing on our own land was one of my greatest joys.

Madame Grimaud, feeding her chickens, beckoned me down to the fence.

'What a pleasure to see horses here again! There used to be so many, we saw them all the time, working the fields. Then the tractors came.' She wagged her head ruefully. 'Times are changing.'

Confounding the predictions of those who had thought they wouldn't endure the journey, they thrived. Old as they were, their coats shone and they had a youthful bounce in them as they explored their new home. Leila herded Cindy around, deciding where and for how long she could stay in any one place. Cindy, ever placid, co-operated. Despite the frailty of the various lengths of fencing and hedging, they seemed content to stay in their allocated space for the time being.

Between our house and Bill's was a small cottage with a field. It had belonged to an old lady whom we had briefly seen when we first came to view our house. She'd been sitting on a wooden bench outside her front door, soaking up the afternoon sun. Before we completed our purchase and moved to the house, she had died, and the cottage was empty. I contacted her son and agreed to rent the field for grazing. A few weeks later, he called, ostensibly to collect the rent, but more just to chat. He was a sociable and interesting man, and offered to show me inside his mother's cottage. She was 93 when she died, and had left the place immaculate. The oak parquet floors and great flagstones were polished like mirrors. The wallpaper was typically French and floral, covering not only the walls but also the doors and inside the cupboards. The door from her bedroom downstairs led into a pretty little sun-trap garden. There was a large empty loft upstairs with stunning exposed timbers.

During the war, Daniel said, the Germans were barracked in the local village. His parents owned a German shepherd dog that only barked when it heard Germans coming, and it could hear them from half a mile away. His father had a radio to listen to the latest news about the war. The dog's bark was the signal to hide the radio, as it was forbidden to own one.

The German soldiers would come to the house bringing food with them, and ask Daniel's mother, who had a reputation as a great cook, to prepare a meal. When she had cooked the meal and set it before them, they would thank her politely and ask her to just taste a little herself 'to

99

make sure it was good.' Daniel said that the soldiers were always well-mannered and friendly until the day when, having heard on the news that the tide was turning against them, his father had been reckless enough to say: '*Allemagne, kaput!*' which had earned him a severe beating.

When they first arrived, the Germans had been billeted in the village school, leaving the children to take their lessons seated under the trees in the courtyard until the soldiers had built themselves a barracks. After the war, the barracks was dismantled by the villagers and moved a few hundred yards down the road, where it became the present village hall.

Daniel's wife, Marcelle, was a small girl at the end of the war. A group of German soldiers had surrendered to the local French militia and were being marched in convoy through the village where Marcelle lived. As the inhabitants stood watching them passing through, an Allied aircraft appeared and began strafing the village, mistakenly believing the Germans to be an active unit. Bullets flew in all directions as everybody threw themselves to the ground or took shelter. Marcelle said that it took many years for her to recover from the terror and to stop running for cover whenever she heard an aircraft. She still looked up automatically at the sound of an overhead engine.

Chapter Eighteen

By late October, the maize harvest began; looking at the withered brown stalks, it was hard to believe that there was anything to reap. The harvesters worked around the clock, glaring-eyed dragons in the night, rumbling through the fields, reducing the stalks to stubble and filling trailers with golden nuggets of corn.

Autumn settled in, and wedges of geese hauled their way southwards, honking to each other over the susurration of their wings, a sight and sound that reduced me to tears then and still does today.

The gold and yellow leaves dropped from the walnut tree, and I used them to make warm bedding for the poultry because, despite the estate agent's assurance, it seemed to me that the weather was becoming distinctly nippy. As winter advanced, migrating cranes followed in the path of the geese. You could easily miss these wonderful overhead sights unless you heard their croaking calls and looked up to see their formations in the sky. M. Meneteau told me how to distinguish flying geese from cranes: geese fly with their legs tucked up, while cranes let them dangle.

***

We didn't have any heating, having naively swallowed the estate agent's assurance that there was no such thing as cold weather south of the Loire.

As the temperature during November plunged to zero and kept slipping ever lower, I was very seriously discomfited. The animals were fine, the poultry in their leaf and straw-lined coop – except for Sandra the bantam who continued roosting in M Meneteau's plum tree – the horses with their shaggy coats and access to a large barn, the dogs in nests of blankets in the straw, the cats seeking out sheltered corners in the barns, and the two parrots' cages covered with a duvet. On the sofa-bed with its thin mattress through which I could feel the springs, covered by a skinny duvet and one blanket, I was colder than I believed it possible to be and still live. The house was damp. The north-east wind shredded the plastic sheeting we had so optimistically pinned over the gaping doorway in the barn, and in came the rain, hail and snow. It was too cold to cook there, so I put an electric kettle in the living room, which wasn't a great deal warmer, and lived on hot drinks, cider and packets of biscuits. The electricity supply wasn't capable of running even a small fan.

The small room which in summer had been a cool haven became icily cold as the days shortened and the easterly wind started to bite. Despite the paint and polish I had splashed all over, it became mildewy in no time at all, with new colonies of mushrooms popping up on the walls. Most of the floor had collapsed onto the pungent earth below. As I lay in the dark, I was aware of things nibbling and scuttling around me. Once I'd tugged on the string that caused the light bulb to go off I was usually asleep in seconds, waking later to the sounds of scraping, munching and scampering. Occasionally, light, fast bodies with cool feet ran over the bed, chittering as they went. I burrowed further under the covers.

Minimum daywear was at least one set of thermal vest and pants, tights, two pairs of long socks, jeans, T-shirt, jumper, scarf, gloves, woolly hat, sheepskin-lined denim coat. I looked like a cross between a scarecrow and a Michelin man. Instead of my usual Chanel No. 5, I now slept fully dressed. And I was still cold. In the morning, I lay under the covers until the dogs demanded to be fed. I spent the rest of the day wandering around, banging my arms against my sides and stamping my feet, scampering around the field with the animals, or huddled in a chair with a blanket wrapped around myself feeling like a Siberian *babushka*. I ticked away the hours waiting for the first signs of evening, when l could feed all the animals and burrow back into my nest.

Terry brought me a thicker duvet and an electric blanket from England. Night time became less arctic but made getting out of bed in the morning more of an ordeal. We had not been prepared for how cold winter can be in an old French farmhouse.

One morning, I awoke and was sure I could hear a stream burbling close by; by the sound of it, almost in the garden. I clambered out of bed, into my Wellington boots and stuck my head outside the front door. There was a brisk brown brook swishing its way down the lawn towards the field. Two things immediately struck me as odd: first of all, we had not had a brook running through the garden when I last looked, and secondly, there had been no rain during the night. I followed the brook upstream through the plastic sheeting into the barn where the provisional kitchen no longer stood on a dirt floor, but in a spreading, chuckling ocean of mud. The copper pipes to the sink had burst, transforming themselves into ingenious water features gushing thin, high-pressure fountains from eight splits. The mud was ankle-deep and rising.

I sploshed to the phone to call Terry.

'I'm going to have to get a plumber in here quickly.'

'No, don't do that. We can't afford a plumber. You'll have to fix it yourself.'

I snorted. 'Don't be ridiculous! You've absolutely no idea what's happening here. The water's flowing through the barn and right to the end of the garden! It isn't a little trickle, it's gushing all over the place, and there's mud everywhere!'

'OK. Listen. Go and find the toolbox, and the blow-lamp. And turn off the stopcock.'

'Where is the stopcock? What does it look like?'

'It's a red-topped tap, and it's somewhere beneath the basin.'

I found it just above the waterline and stopped the multiple squirts. Over the next two hours, Terry gave an elementary plumbing tutorial via the telephone. I did exactly what he said, cutting through pipes with a hacksaw, joining them up with little brass rings called, for a reason I couldn't understand, olives, and soldering the splits in the pipes, all the time slithering and sliding about in the slimy residue left by the receding stream.

I was colder than ever, soaked and filthy, and we still only had the plastic bucket to wash in. The contents of the refrigerator were frozen: butter, milk, eggs, fruit, cheese and bread were all solid. The washing up liquid had turned to crystals and if shaken made a noise like maracas. The jams and sauces in the jars were frozen solid. All our house plants were dead, turned to a limp green mush. My French dream had turned into a nightmare.

***

A week later, six inches of snow fell overnight. The horses' water buckets were frozen from top to bottom, so I scraped snow into plastic buckets and brought it into the house, but after four and a half hours in the icy living room, they were still buckets of snow. I borrowed a small heater and stood them in front of it. Within ten minutes, it had all melted, including the buckets which were buckled and no longer bucket-shaped.

Madame Meneteau lent me some buckets and filled them for me. I thought how ironic it was that Terry and I had almost certainly earned, over the preceding years, more money than all the inhabitants of the hamlet had jointly earned in their lives, yet while they were all cosily comfortable in their houses, with their wood-burning stoves, I was quite literally freezing.

During that first winter, the weather could be bright and sunny one day, and bitterly cold with thick ice the next. Two days later, it might pour with rain, and a day later out would come the sun again. The horses were particularly perplexed – used to the monotony of cold wet English autumns and winters, they didn't understand why the seasons changed here with such rapidity.

Friends urged me to return to England. It was, of course, never an option even if I had wanted to, not with all the animals dependent upon me.

***

A French friend asked whether I would spend one afternoon a week talking with a group of French ladies who were learning English. It sounded like a good idea and would give me a chance to spend a few hours somewhere warm. The ladies were a jolly crowd. One of them had an enormous bosom – *il y a du monde au balcon,* as the French say – the balcony's crowded. She had stepped out of her car the previous week and broken her leg, yet seemed to find the fact that she was encased in plaster from toe to thigh hilarious. She collected things – beer mats, matchboxes, thimbles, phone cards, wine corks; the list was endless. She had more than 1,800 biscuit tins, although not unfortunately the early Huntley and Palmer tin which she said was worth £4,000. One of the other ladies collected straw hats.

It wasn't long before our conversation turned to food. The straw-hat lady asked whether beef cooked with pineapple, served with cauliflower in cheese sauce, which she had twice been served when dining with English friends, was a typical English dish. I assured her that it wasn't.

No wonder English food has a bad reputation!

Christmas wasn't far away. In France, St Sylvestre, New Year's Eve, is the main event, featuring a huge meal. Christmas Day isn't celebrated very much, and there's no Boxing Day. The ladies wanted to know whether English people had the same sort of special meal as they do in France with plenty of oysters and *foie gras*. I said neither of those featured on a traditional English Christmas meal. What would we typically eat, they asked.

'The first course varies. It could be anything – soup, asparagus, prawn cocktail, but the traditional main course is almost always a roast turkey, with two different kinds of stuffing, one in the neck, another in the body cavity. It's served with roast potatoes and mashed potatoes, roast parsnips, brussels sprouts, fried bacon rolls, chipolata sausages, carrots, peas, bread sauce, cranberry sauce and gravy. Sometimes there is roast beef, too, and Yorkshire pudding.

'*Mon Dieu!*' They looked aghast and asked what bread sauce was. As I explained how it was prepared, their lips turned down unanimously and they made retching noises. I didn't mention that it is delicious, and even cold it makes a great breakfast.

'And you eat all that together?' they asked in disbelief.

'Yes. Then we have Christmas pudding, which is set on fire, and served with brandy butter, cream and custard. Then mince pies.'

I listed the ingredients of the pudding and pies.

'And after that, we sit and watch the Queen on television and eat nuts, fruit and chocolates.'

'And then you don't eat anything for a week!' cried one.

'Oh, yes we do. At tea time, we eat Christmas cake or Yule log, made with similar ingredients to the pudding and pies, coated in almond paste and sugar icing. And later, cold meat and pickles, cheese and salad.'

'Why do you have to eat so much?' asked one lady.

'Well, because it's Christmas. It's a tradition.'

'And you don't eat any oysters?'

'No, I don't think they'd mix very well.'

'But you do have wine, of course?'

'Oh yes, we have lots of wine.'

'Ah well, at least that's something!' laughed the big-bosomed lady.

'Will you have all that here in France on Christmas Day?' asked someone.

'No – we don't eat meat at all and neither of us enjoy big meals. We'll probably have some fish, something quite simple, and some good wine.'

'Bravo!' cried someone else. 'That sounds much nicer.'

***

That first winter in France, Terry and I spent Christmas day rendering the walls of what was going to be our bathroom. We mixed loads of cement and wheelbarrowed it through the mud and rubble, while I nipped backwards and forwards preparing our meal in the makeshift kitchen in the barn, clambering over heaps of rock and debris, through a brisk drizzle, to deliver the food to the living room. Despite the cold, it was quite successful. We'd decided that before the end of the year, we were going to have one really good meal in our new home, and so tucked into a plate of oysters for Terry, cheap caviar with sour cream on blinis, a tiny lobster each, and a bottle of good wine. I'd bought a small wooden table and two chairs from a local junk shop to replace the plastic garden furniture, so we ate in comfort. Unfortunately, in opening the oysters, Terry impaled his hand on the oyster knife, which put a stop to any further rendering that afternoon.

Chapter Nineteen

My French was limited to what I remembered from school and what I'd learned from a few books and tapes. I understood the syntax and could construct a sentence correctly, but my vocabulary of *plumes de ma tante* and *Frères Jacques* was not very helpful for day-to-day conversation. When I couldn't find the word I needed, I created one that sounded as if it might be correct and threw it into the conversation. There was a sticky moment in the early days, following a night of tremendous crashing storms. Madame Meneteau asked whether I'd been frightened.

'Oh no, I love...' whatever was the French word for 'storm'? Probably '*rage*'. I tacked it onto the end of the sentence. She smiled a little nervously and said she had to go and pick some cabbages for her sheep. I looked up storm in the dictionary. *Orage. Rage* means rabies.

As my confidence grew, I took every opportunity to speak to French people, and make little jokes. They always laughed, but whether at the content or at some ghastly mistake I was making, I was never sure.

The insurance agent arrived to check the measurements of the property. Why this was necessary I didn't understand, as he had been insuring the same property for the previous owner for a decade. We chatted away for half an hour; I assured him I was blissfully happy living here in our ramshackle kingdom, and he looked politely disbelieving. The more we chatted and laughed, the less certain I became of what he was saying, and the more I doubted he understood what I was saying. Anyhow, we continued chatting and laughing while he measured each building by striding up and down in his boots. One step equalled one metre.

Talking with M. Meneteau was an education, although because of his strong accent and use of the local patois (where the 'j' was pronounced 'h' so *jardin* became *hardin)* it was sometimes difficult to understand what he was saying. I'd have to ask him to repeat it or explain with different words. We discussed matters medical, horticultural, philosophical and ecclesiastical; the other neighbours; the latest English immigrants and anybody local who had recently died. He was beautifully polite and acted as if I spoke the language perfectly. When I failed, or mispronounced a word, he gently added it into the conversation without any comment. I loved this little man and his wife.

While we were talking over the hedge one morning, he gave a triumphant shout, vanished momentarily and reappeared waving a trap and a very tiny mouse by its dead tail.

'Look at the monster! It's been eating my endives,' he said bitterly, stamping on it.

Of course, you will know that endives are what are known in English as chicory. Chicory is what, in English, we call endives. The French language is a minefield, full of words with double meanings or that sound similar to the untrained ear. *Baiser* is one of those words. If somebody says they want to do this to you, you don't know whether you're meant to proffer a cheek or lie on your back. It is also sometimes confused with *baisser*, meaning to lower, offering opportunity to make a frightful fool of yourself and entertain the natives.

Another verbal trap is the word 'preservative,' which in anglophone countries is something that keeps food from deteriorating. In France, a *preservatif* generally means a condom. There may not be a single market in the whole country where the local people have not been astounded to hear an English person enquire whether the jams or juices contain any condoms.

Introducing somebody as *mon ami* leaves the other party at liberty to decide whether it's a friend or a lover. You think you've learned to form the feminine of words by adding to the masculine the final letter plus an 'e'. So *chat* = cat, *chatte* = female cat; *chien* = dog, *chienne* = female dog; *chiot* = puppy, *chiotte* = lavatory.

I took French lessons so that conversations with French people became less of a hit and miss affair and I was more confident that I could understand and make myself understood. There was so much to learn, not only in terms of vocabulary and grammar, but also about the simple use of words. We learned that *mal au coeur* does not mean a bad heart, or that somebody is suffering cardiac arrest, but that the person feels nauseous. To telephone an ambulance and announce that somebody is suffering from *mal au coeur* will not send them racing to the door. The correct French for a heart attack is *crise cardiaque*. As soon as I learned that, I went to tell some newly-arrived English people who lived close by who knew very little French. They thanked me. When the husband had a heart attack his wife called the emergency number it took them some time to respond, as she told them he had *mal au coeur*.

I bought a small black and white television set to watch French programmes. Reception in the hamlet was very poor and the inbuilt aerial couldn't pick up a signal. I went to buy a more powerful aerial but it cost more than the television, so the man in the shop dug out an old used one that I could just afford. He said it would work perfectly in the loft, as there was no way I'd be able to fix it up on the roof by myself. I suspended it from a piece of string, with other pieces of string and some coat hangers anchoring it to a stepladder to keep it at the correct angle. This took many trips up and down the decaying loft ladder but eventually, I could get a decent picture on four channels.

Several times a week, I sat staring at the screen, watching films and old episodes of *Columbo* in French, trying to understand who was saying what to whom. Once I thought I had understood a film right to the very last seconds, but when the *dénouement* arrived I realised that I hadn't actually understood it all, but gradually it began to sink in and make sense.

A lady from Sri Lanka who spoke fluent English had embarked on a correspondence course in the English language, and she appointed me to help her. Once a week, she arrived with books and course papers to complete. It was the first time I had ever had difficulty understanding my own language: the questions were so obscure that they may as well have been written in Aramaic. I could not convince her that she was wasting her money and our time.

One day, she came with her two handsome and hyperactive little boys who rushed through the house and garden, slamming doors so the fragile glass shook, skidding up and down the wooden floors I had laboriously waxed, trying to catapult each other into the air from an old rocking chair, dragging furniture around and rummaging in drawers and cupboards, tipping the contents all over the place, while their mother apparently didn't notice. I hoped that a drink might pacify them, and poured them what I thought was a non-alcoholic shandy. Far from calming them, it had the opposite effect. Being in the room with them was like being in the eye of a hurricane. After they'd left, I collected up the empty bottles, and found that it wasn't shandy, but very strong cider.

She was a nice lady, eventually deciding to abandon the English course and take up the clarinet instead. She came to thank me for all my help, bringing me half a dozen jars of jam made by her mother-in-law. The jars were thick with cobwebs and the jam had green hair growing all over it, but it was a kind thought and I recycled the jars.

Once my French had improved, I started getting to know my neighbours better, and to learn from them more about the history of our hamlet. Jean-Luc, who had given me a lift when I first arrived, and who spoke English a great deal better than I spoke French, described the life he remembered as a child. Listening to him, I realised with a shock that the peace and quiet and wide open spaces that so many of us love represented, for these small rural communities, the closing of a page in their history, and the loss of a way of life that had lasted for generations.

In the old days, the hamlet had been full of life with four small farms and two large ones. One of them belonged to Jean-Luc's family, and the other to M. Meneteau's. There had been a constant movement of people, tractors and animals, and the sounds of chatter, laughter and machinery. The summer harvest was a time of rejoicing. The farmers helped each other, cutting and stacking the wheat by hand to await the mobile threshing contractors who went from village to village. At midday, everybody ate together outdoors, at long tables laid with salads, bread, *charcuterie*, cheeses, and *mijé*, the local mixture of red wine, sugar, bread and iced water. The farmers delivered their wheat to the bakery in the village, where it was baked into loaves for them.

Each hamlet and village held an annual fête where all the inhabitants from surrounding areas went to dance to live music and socialise. It was a rare opportunity for young people to meet others and, with luck, to find their future spouses. Most people travelled by foot, or the better off by bicycle. Jean-Luc's grandfather sold some of his much-loved cattle to buy a car because he wanted to appear wealthy, but his son was embarrassed to be seen in it and preferred to travel by bicycle.

His son – Jean-Luc's father – wanted to make changes to the farm and keep goats instead of cattle, but he waited until his father died. This region is the largest producer of goat's cheese in France. It isn't a taste that appeals to everyone, but goat's cheese comes in numerous forms from white, mild and fluffy to creamy and crumbly and to withered brown hard pellets. We like most types, apart from the very aged cheeses that reek of ammonia.

Jean-Luc explained about the *communaux*, small parcels of land that every village in France is required to set aside under Napoleonic law, so that the poorest inhabitants have somewhere to graze their livestock or grow food. 'You can use it,' he told me kindly.

Over the centuries, the way property had been divided between surviving children of land owners had created a mosaic of odd-shaped little pockets of land. Jean-Luc showed me an old map and pointed out ragged-edged fields with little bits and pieces bitten out of them. 'This was how it was before.' These awkward parcels were time-consuming and difficult to work.

As a local councillor his father had fought for 20 years to introduce *remembrement* in the commune, consolidating those pieces of land into larger and more regular outlines for the benefit of everybody who owned and worked them. However, people did not want change, and there was so much resistance that he withdrew from local politics in frustration.

After his death, *remembrement* did come into effect, and now all the fields have neat edges, but there are very few small farmers left. Most have retired, or sold their farms to co-operatives.

Above Jean-Luc's bungalow stretched a neat row of three old cottages. The one on the furthest end was seldom occupied, but belonged, according to M. Meneteau, to Jehovah's Witnesses, no better than Satanists and cannibals, his tone implied. Next door lived M. St Martin. With his straight back, stern expression and close-cropped hair, a spiked helmet would have suited him perfectly. He looked like a fierce and unfriendly man, and the nearest he got to a smile was a brusque inclination of his head. Yet when one of our horses let itself out of our field, as they so often did, and he found it ambling by the side of the road, he returned it safely home, only mentioning the matter to me a few days later. I noticed in his neat garden pink roses blooming in December. They were still flourishing in January, and their splendour was undiminished in February. I managed to catch him walking his dog one day and asked how he managed to keep roses in bloom throughout the winter. For a fraction of a moment it looked as if he might smile, but he checked himself just in time.

'*Plastique,*' he replied. '*Pourquoi pas? C'est agréable voir les roses dans l'hiver.*' *Pourquoi pas*, indeed?

Madame Grimaud lived next door to them, and fifty yards uphill from her cottage the track turned at right angles. On the interior of the angle, next to a stone well bedecked with pots of plants, was the home of M. Royer, the rotund bachelor with the enchantingly shy smile whose family originally owned what had become our house, and in whose kitchen we had signed the *compromis*. His house and garden were immaculate – no matter what the season, there were always flowers of some sort blooming around his garden gate. Stacked neatly by the fence was sufficient firewood to last him several lifetimes, and he kept half a dozen bantam chickens and a few sheep. Dolly, his beagle bitch lived on a chain in the garden and barn, and seemed happy with her lot. During the hunting season, M. Royer roamed slowly through the fields in his green jacket, wellies and flat cap, with a shotgun slung over his shoulder and Dolly beside him. For all the many times I passed him, I never saw him with anything he had bagged. Usually he would say he had seen pigeons, but they were too far away. I think he simply enjoyed wandering around with his dog.

French cockerels crow in French. They cry: *Cocorico*. M. Royer had a young cockerel that had only got as far as *Cocori*, at which point it tapered off into a sort of gulp. It practised for hours on end, until I felt like shaking the final syllable out of it.

On the corner opposite M. Royer lived the family we called the Roly-Polys. The exterior of their house was a collection of building materials and car parts, overflowing rubbish bins and bags, and washing in a uniform shade of grey pinned to their gate. Housekeeping plainly wasn't Madame Roly-Poly's forte. I couldn't criticise – it wasn't mine either. The two ladies of the household, Madame Roly-Poly and her daughter were immensely round, and very short, measuring more around than from top to bottom. M. Roly-Poly was thin and wiry, with few teeth. They had numerous cats and dogs, and poultry, and when I first arrived, they had a tame magpie that lived on their roof and talked.

Madame Roly-Poly had a passion for birds. She was always willing and pleased to care for any that were in need. I took her a young blue tit I found bumping around in a deserted barn; she tucked it tenderly into the bottomless cleft of her bosom, crooned to it and fed it with extraordinary gentleness.

On a scorching August day, I drove past a field bleached beige by the sun. A lone crow stood motionless in the path of a tractor harrowing the baked earth into a dusty cloud. I stopped and watched it for a few moments, because it seemed to me it shouldn't be standing there so still, with the tractor not far away. Returning fifteen minutes later, I glanced over and it was still there, directly in the path of the tractor. I braked

Tinkerbelle to a rocking halt and scampered across the flints and dust to where the bird sat like a stuffed toy. It looked up at me with some interest and no apparent fear, allowing me to pick it up, carry it to the car and sit it on my lap, where it remained perfectly relaxed as I drove home. I put it in a cardboard box on a bed of straw, in the cool of the living room, with a small bowl of water. It had no sign of injury, and I thought it may be suffering from heat and dehydration.

Leaving it to recover, I lay down on the bed in the corner and drew a cotton sheet over myself. My eyes closed. In the box, the crow rustled and scrabbled. It rustled and scrabbled increasingly noisily. I opened my eyes and watched as it hauled itself to the top of the box, perching there rockily for a few seconds before hopping onto the floor. Without hesitation, it strutted towards the bed, then using its beak and claws, dragged itself up the sheet and onto my leg, where it sat and studied me. We regarded each other for a moment, and then I pulled the sheet over my face. I felt its clawed feet march up my body until it was on my chest; the sheet twitched and was pulled back. Two obsidian eyes stared into mine, its head cocked to one side. I covered my face again with the sheet; the bird tugged it off. We played this game for ten minutes. It behaved like a tame bird. I left it exploring the living room for a couple of hours, and then as the sun disappeared beyond the horizon, I took it out to the field to see if it would fly. It sat there looking up at me and when I turned to walk away, it bounced along beside me like a small, feathered puppy.

I couldn't keep it, with five gun dogs, so I took it down the lane to Madame Roly-Poly. In her gigantically rotund way, she was charmed. A podgy paw stroked the bird where it sat upon my hand. Yes, she would happily take it because her cousins had always wanted a tame crow like the one she used to have, that had lived on her roof. I handed over my new friend. A week later, I asked how it was faring.

'Ah, the cousins are delighted! It is very happy, living in their garden, coming into the house, and even though it's stripped all the fruit from their cherry tree, they love it.' It stayed with them for several years before flying away one day.

The Roly-Polys were relative newcomers to the hamlet. They were not a farming family and did not mix with the other inhabitants, most of whom had lived here for generations. They had their own social circle, and during the summer months they often ate out of doors with their friends, playing music quietly. I found them friendly, although a little shy, and they always had a kind word for our dogs. The only thing about them that disturbed me was that every so often they killed things in the pathway. Sometimes it was a pig, sometimes a goat, occasionally a goose. If on a Saturday morning a number of cars appeared and parked on the lane, it was a signal to disappear and stay away for a few hours. Later, there would be ominous galvanised buckets outside their house, and magenta rivers running down the lane. Sometimes the dogs appeared with gory stringy lumps in their mouths, and guilty expressions. Other times, there might be a great pile of white feathers, signalling that the Roly-Polys had one goose less. Once they kept two beautiful baby goats, like real live Bambis, who lived in a dark shed where they could just peep over the top of the door. The Roly-Poly grandchildren tied coloured bows around their necks. One day they had gone, and in their place were two snowy white skins and eight tiny hooves hanging from a cord.

As dusk was falling one evening, the phone rang. It was Jean-Luc.

'Susie, do you have your dogs with you?'

'Yes, why?'

'Well, there is a dog like yours injured on the road.'

I ran to count the dogs and found Vulcan was missing.

'Please come to our house.' said Jean-Luc. 'We will help you.'

With a sinking heart, I ran down the lane, hearing anguished yelping and seeing a cluster of cars grouped on the road. Five cars formed a barrier to prevent any traffic going through, and a crowd stood around Vulcan, who lay on the side of the road, crying and lifting his head. M. Roly-Poly was there stroking him, and he reassured me: 'Don't worry, madame, he isn't badly hurt. He'll be OK.'

'Can he walk?' I asked.

'No, he doesn't seem able to, but we're certain he is only shocked.'

I galloped back up the hill to get Tinkerbelle and a blanket, with which we lifted the dog into the back of the car. I thanked the crowd for their help. The driver of the car that had hit Vulcan started talking earnestly. I couldn't understand him.

'What's he saying?' I asked Jean-Luc.

'He says your dog has damaged his car, and he wants you to pay for it.'

I stared at the dilapidated jalopy, which was a mass of dents and bodywork panels in varying colours, and I stared at the driver.

'Where is the damage?' Mr Roly-Poly asked the driver, who pointed to a small dent, one of many, on the leading edge of the bonnet. Mr Roly-Poly lifted the bonnet, gave a push, and let it drop. 'There you are, the damage is repaired,' he told the driver.

'Bravo!' called someone from the crowd. We all shook hands and I drove back home to see how badly Vulcan was hurt. He had a collection of superficial cuts, and was shaken and feeling extremely sorry for himself. I gave him half an aspirin with a bowl of sweetened milk and he settled down on my bed for the night. The following morning, he was his bouncy self once more, and spent the day trying to find a way to get back down to the road.

In contrast with the Roly-Polys, whose garden was decorated with supermarket trolleys, maggoty bones and overflowing dustbins, M. and Madame Meneteau's house and garden were neat and spotless. In every season, Madame Meneteau always had something in bloom; her step was swept, the flower beds weeded, the car polished.

Madame Meneteau was about the same height as her husband, which wasn't very high at all. Her strong, kind face wore a permanent smile; she had a charming way of tilting her head to one side as she talked. Behind their white-painted and blue-shuttered house was a large barn filled with firewood, neatly cut and stacked. Rabbits, hens, ducklings, guinea fowl and pigeons lived in pens, all destined for the table. They kept half a dozen sheep whose lambs delighted us in the spring, when they wobbled around, bouncing into the air on all four legs, climbing woodpiles, chasing each other until they collapsed in tired woolly piles. M. Meneteau grew all their vegetables in neat, hoed rows, and their fruit trees yielded cherries, apples, apricots, pears, quinces and figs. They often passed bowls or bags of fruit and vegetables over the hedge to me.

The first time M. Meneteau asked whether I would like some leeks he had just picked, I said 'Merci' – thank you. He shrugged and walked away with the leeks. I mentioned this to a French-speaking friend, who laughed.

'When you're offered something and you reply 'Merci', it's understood as 'No, thank you.' You have to say, yes please... 'Oui, s'il vous plaît.'

***

Madame Meneteau was born in our living room, growing up there with her siblings and her farming parents. When she talked about her life, it brought home to me just how hard it had been for women in those days. Only a couple of days before her baby was due, she had been in the fields harvesting maize. There were no machines then, and the cobs were chopped from the stalks by hand, the grains then beaten off the cobs with a piece of wood. The women also had to prepare meals for all the workers, and to hand-shear the sheep, to hand wash the greasy fleeces in hot water, and then tease and spin the wool, knitting it into socks and waistcoats. Despite their heavy work burden, those were sociable times, before the advent of television. In the afternoon and evening, the ladies sat together by the pond, knitting and chatting. On Sundays, the men entertained themselves by playing cards in the village cafés.

There were no clothes shops; people bought fabric and had it made up for them by tailors and dressmakers like Madame Grimaud. Healers had their own curious methods for dealing with injuries and disease, and it was more usual for the healer than the doctor to cure burns, which Madame Meneteau said they did simply by touching the patient. Skin complaints like ringworm, eczema and impetigo were rampant, often transmitted by cattle; the healers treated these by cutting a small piece of the patient's hair, dabbing something on it and then applying it to the affected area. M. Meneteau, earthier than his wife, said. 'Piss. We used our own urine to cure skin problems.'

Between their property and Bill's domain was a large barn and a small abandoned house smothered by a vine. The lane continued for another 20 yards before it ran out at our gates.

That was the full extent of the hamlet and its inhabitants. It was generally utterly peaceful, the quiet broken only by the day-long call of the cuckoo in early spring, a sporadic tractor trundling up the track to the fields of sunflowers and maize, the triumphant yells of chickens fresh from laying, and at night, beneath the beauty of the moon and stars, the croaking of frogs and crickets, the nightingales' song, and the hoots and screeches of owls.

Chapter Twenty

That first winter was short, and thank goodness for that. Spring came in with carpets of violets in hues from almost black to almost white, cowslips, buttercups and celandines, daisies and those little blue flowers with the white hearts whose names I can never remember. The transition between seasons took me by surprise, changing overnight like painted scenery on a stage. Cold, wet and dull grey one day, warm and dry with blue skies and blossom the next.

The swallows and the cuckoo arrived together on 21st March, and the hoopoes soon after.

I heard heavy machinery at work in the fields and was sad to see they were gouging up the copses and hedgerows. M. Meneteau was incensed.

'Fools,' he shouted across the hedge, 'they don't know what they're doing. Look at them, tearing everything up. People don't know anything about farming these days. They're spoiling everything. Pouf! Our fathers knew the right time to plant, and so did we. We knew when it was mild enough, wet enough, warm enough. Now they have men with computers who analyse the soil and twiddle knobs on their machines, and that tells them what to plant, and when, and where. They fill the land with chemicals. Bah! We used animal manure. And the food tasted better.' He spat on the ground and stamped away.

When I walked the dogs in the fields in early spring, tractors were fertilising the fields, spraying them with the green-brown sludge scraped out from the sheds where the cattle had over-wintered. The dogs loved to roll in the gorgeous aromatic gloop. Some people complained about the smell; I loved it.

***

Bill hadn't been around for several months, but he had taken Sinbad back to Spain with him, so there was a little more space in our living room. I hadn't seen Gloria since the previous summer, and she hadn't made up her mind whether to stay in Spain or move to France. When

Bill returned in April, he began a new business, selling the piles of second-hand furniture in his barn. He placed advertisements in a local English-language magazine.

The first I knew of this new business venture was when my phone started ringing and people were asking about wardrobes, pianos, bicycles and beds. As Bill did not want to go to the expense of installing a phone, he had decided to use my number.

When people called, I said Bill was absent just at the moment but would call back as soon as he returned. Then I would pass the message to Bill so he could return the calls, which he almost never did. Prospective buyers became angry and indignant when they didn't hear from him, complaining about my inefficiency and asking whether my boss was aware that I wasn't doing my job properly.

A haughty woman rang to enquire about a piano he had advertised. It was rather beautiful, with a marquetry peacock on the front. For several weeks, it had been sitting in his driveway, in all weathers.

The woman wanted to view it immediately. As Bill's barn was jammed with bags of cement, reels of cables, packing boxes and a jumble of assorted old furniture, we humped the piano onto a trolley, dragged it into my living room and gave it a polish.

Bill rang the interested lady, explaining that it had been in the family for years; the children had learned to play on it. Yes, it was rosewood. 'Walnut,' I hissed. 'Walnut.'

The woman asked what make it was, and whether its frame was wood or iron. Bill said he'd just have a quick look. She lost interest, and after a fortnight the piano went back to stand in Bill's driveway when he abandoned his new business. My phone continued to ring for months, at all times of the day and night, as he had not cancelled the advert.

'I'm calling regarding the pine dresser.'

'Do you still have the leather three-piece-suite?'

'I'd like to buy the grandfather clock.'

'Run and get Bill for me, will you, love?'

Strangers phoned asking if I had rooms to let, knew anybody who did, could find them property to buy, or knew where Bill was. I didn't, because he'd vanished again.

When he came back, he brought Gloria and the dogs with him. She had decided to move here permanently – to keep an eye on what he was up to, she confided.

One afternoon, she invited me to go to the village to meet an elderly English couple who had recently moved from Spain. The husband was a gentle, vague soul who volunteered to make tea, and returned with a tray beautifully set with cups, saucers, spoons, small plates, a large plate of very hard sweet biscuits that scratched your teeth, a bowl of sugar, a jug of milk, and a teapot filled with scalding water. Gloria excused herself and disappeared into their kitchen, returning with some teabags that she discreetly dropped into the pot.

They didn't own a motor car, said the wife 'because it would cause pollution', although her husband subsequently mentioned that it was because he had been unable to learn how to drive.

With town and the nearest shops six miles away, they were dependent upon taxis and friends. The wife hinted at a disability sustained during the war whilst carrying out top secret work for the British government; she was prevented by the Official Secrets Act from giving any details. It meant that she could not do any kind of physical work, although she spent most of her time gardening and appeared quite able-bodied. Her husband did the housework, the laundry and the cooking. She nagged him mercilessly – his defence was to remove his hearing aid, tapping and reinserting it several times before giving an apologetic little smile, shaking his head sadly and saying the device would have to go back to be repaired. It seemed to often be away being repaired.

I wondered why Gloria had introduced me to people with whom I had nothing in common, and the reason became clear later that evening. Bill came to say the old woman had medical appointments in town and would need transport for several days running. As he was leaving for Spain early next morning and Gloria was busy gardening, he had said I would take her there and back. She would pay for fuel.

I didn't mind helping, but recently Tinkerbelle had started making sinister clanging and thumping noises interrupted by screeches and I wasn't sure that she would be a reliable taxi, but Bill brushed aside my concerns.

'Oh, you don't need to worry. Those old puddle-jumpers all make noises like that,' he explained. 'It's perfectly normal. Don't worry.'

On the first day, I took the old woman to town and mooched around for a couple of hours waiting for her, then stowed her back into the car.

We'd driven about a mile, when Tinkerbelle made a terrible grinding noise and belched a cloud of pungent black smoke from beneath her bonnet. As my passenger said she couldn't walk, I decided to try to drive to the nearest telephone box a mile further on, and call for help.

Miraculously Tinkerbelle summoned up her reserves and surged forward, roaring throatily back to life almost as if she was making a heroic effort to reach the call box. We almost made it when she suddenly became unnaturally still and silent. Further clouds of smoke billowed from her engine. Tinkerbelle wouldn't move another inch.

Fortunately, Gloria had a mobile phone and I was able to contact her. Leaving her gardening, she came and collected us. My passenger paid me fifty francs for fuel, and I was left with a car which was immobilised six miles from home and no longer usable.

Still, said Gloria, Bill and his friend would return in a few days, and as they both knew all there was to know about 2CVs, they would get her going in no time at all. I wasn't to worry.

In those days, l was still sufficiently naïve to believe Tinkerbelle would soon be back on the road. When Bill returned, he diagnosed a terminal disorder of the gearbox and promised to pick up a cheap second-hand one in Spain on his next trip.

Tinkerbelle sat despondently for many long weeks waiting in vain, until Terry was able to find a replacement gearbox and bring it out from England.

***

The old couple from the village went to Spain for a holiday and I was surprised when the husband rang one day. Without any preamble, he said: 'Would you mind switching on your fax machine? We're selling the house and want to send you the inventory. You'll have to collect the keys from the *notaire* so you can show people round.'

I replied truthfully that I didn't have a fax machine and hung up. I'd only met them twice.

They returned some months later, having decided, after all, not to sell their house, and I was soon running a regular taxi service taking them shopping, and their cats to the vet. They always paid for the fuel, and entertained me to tea, plying me with the frightful little teeth-scratching biscuits. When they learned I didn't have hot water and was still washing in a bucket, they insisted I must use their shower. It was very small and the water wasn't terribly warm, but the old lady kept phoning to say they had put out clean towels, were waiting for me and how they so enjoyed my visits. I didn't want to appear ungrateful. I used the shower twice. The second time, as I came out, I overheard her telling one of her visitors that I was 'an absolute pauper,' and 'always asking to use their shower.' I declined any further invitations and went back to my bucket.

Chapter Twenty-one

Before I met Bill, I had expected to be the only English person in the area, but through him I discovered a large and diverse British community.

This is not Paris, the Riviera, the Atlantic coast, or a major town. It is a rural, agricultural area with a sparse population, where property prices are low. As older people retired and died, the younger generation moved away from the rigours of farming to work in towns. They left behind an abundance of old French farmhouses in states of disrepair but still attracting hefty tax bills. Their owners were only too pleased to get rid of them and their liabilities.

Low prices made large properties with land affordable in an area enjoying almost as much sunshine as the south of France. A British couple who moved here saw and seized the opportunity to link up with a local French estate agent. They advertised widely in the French life magazines, and it was through them that we had found our property. Soon many more British estate agents would spring up in the area, but they were the forerunners.

With all the alarming stories about the complications of buying property in France, particularly for people who didn't understand the language, being able to deal with an English agent put people's minds at rest. Everybody was happy. The French were selling property they didn't want – at prices beyond their dreams, the British were buying the property they did want at prices they could not have believed possible, and the agents were thriving, not only earning generous commission on sales but also through introduction fees to insurance companies, builders, banks, hotels, restaurants and furniture dealers.

France offered the perfect opportunity to start a new life. The digital age was still a fledgling, and people who wanted to disappear or reinvent themselves could quite easily do so. Addresses of isolated properties were vague and the internet would be virtually inaccessible in *la France profonde* for another five years, so if somebody chose to call themselves Colonel This or Doctor That, or hinted that they were a war hero or a commando, they could do so. Mostly these claims were publicly accepted and privately disbelieved.

It was a diverse and transient community. There were people escaping from broken marriages or running from the tax man. Others were seeking a way out of the rat race to bring up their families and become self-sufficient. Some were retired people on small pensions and there were others like us who had been affected by the recession and were trying to recover.

While our conditions were primitive, there were many in far worse circumstances. I did have a roof, sound walls and a door in the living room, but through that first winter there was a family with three small children who were living in a tent inside an open barn without electricity or running water, and a couple, their two teenagers and a mother-in-law in a small caravan also with no running water.

We became friends with a couple in their seventies who had bought a 'house' for £1,000 which had only three walls, a tree growing through the middle of it and no roof. They were sleeping beneath a black plastic sheet tied to some branches, while he tried to build up the walls and make the place habitable. Like many others they found themselves in these dire circumstances through no fault of their own. They had owned a thriving greengrocery until a major supermarket was built less than a mile away. They lost their home and all their money, and were just surviving on what she could earn teaching English. Later, once he had managed to create a couple of primitive rooms, he collected empty plastic bottles to act as wall and ceiling insulation.

Other friends collected fallen branches to burn. They were stopped one day by a *gendarme* who told them that taking wood without permission of the owner of the land is a criminal offence carrying a prison sentence and heavy fine. The law dated back to times when there was no other form of heating or cooking, and firewood was precious. Without it people had no means of keeping warm or preparing food.

Some people were only just managing to eat.

People appeared out of nowhere and quickly disappeared. Many only stayed briefly, drifting down to Spain in search of warmer weather and cheaper living, or returning to England because they missed their family and friends. There were the P&O or Brittany Ferry 'builders', men with little or no knowledge of building but ready to have a go if anybody was prepared to pay them. They were often here one day and gone the next, leaving unfinished work and angry, poorer people.

Relationships sometimes broke down and spouses or partners disappeared leaving their other halves in desperate situations. As it was a small community, everybody seemed to know everybody else's business, and what they didn't know they made up. I knew intimate details of the financial situations, the background, habits and sexual behaviour of all the friends of a neighbour who happily divulged everything she had been told in confidence to anybody who would listen. Friends and I had fun amongst ourselves starting outrageous rumours and seeing how quickly they came back to us and how much they had been embellished on the circuit.

There were a few British residents who had lived here for decades and were more French than the French, speaking the language more 'Frenchly', and keeping themselves at a distance from the newcomers.

One of my French friends enquired if all British people were heavy drinkers, because she lived near a bottle bank where British-registered cars frequently came and deposited dozens of empty wine bottles.

'They are not local,' she said. 'They don't live in the commune.'

Sometimes people confessed they felt guilty at the number of empty bottles they accumulated over a week, so took them far away, or by night, so their neighbours didn't see. They used to say that you could tell a Briton from a local in the supermarket, because a French person would have a basket containing a packet of ham, a tin of green beans, a baguette, some fresh meat, fish and cheese, and the British would have a trolley piled with beer and burgers.

Friends in England asked how we found the French, and to me they seemed the same as English people, except they spoke a different language. Some were smiley, some were dour, some were instantly friendly, some weren't. Some were tolerant of our foibles, others were shocked by our bad manners. It wasn't the snapping fingers and yelling 'Garçon' ill manners – I think we had moved beyond that, but the fact that we walked into small shops, restaurants, post offices or waiting rooms without saying hello to everybody. 'Messieurs/dames' was sufficient, with a brief smile and nod of the head. It is what people do here, but unfortunately it was not something taught in French lessons in British schools, so to many people we had a reputation for being rude when we were merely ignorant.

I hope I haven't given the impression that everybody I met was a drunk or a scoundrel. Most of the people I knew and who became friends were ordinary, hard-working people who had either had some bad luck, or simply wanted to follow their dream of living and bringing up their families in France.

Although times were hard and uncomfortable for many of us, there was a strong community spirit and people helped each other in all kinds of ways. It was a hotchpotch of different social backgrounds, accents, age groups, attitudes, creeds, united and supportive of each other, lending help and equipment, sharing information and advice. I look back on it as a time when strong and lasting friendships were built. Despite the financial problems, life was simple and sweet when the sun was shining and the sunflowers were in bloom, when we shared meals and cheap wine. Gardening was limited to pots of geraniums, nobody was interested in what car you drove or whether you had satellite television. Nobody had a swimming pool, decking, patio furniture or a lawnmower; when we wanted to swim, we went to the river at the campsite in town, or to one of the many local lakes. Those were happy and relaxed times, some of the most enjoyable years of my life in France.

***

It astonished me when friends didn't fall head over heels in love with our new home. They stared in blank-faced disbelief at the bare stone and dirt walls and floors, the holes where the doors should be, and the dozen or so electrical extension leads which served the house from the sole socket in the living room.

They were shocked that we lived six miles from town, by the frightful mess of Bill's place, by the absence of a lock on the only working door, and the lack of glass in some of the windows.

'My God, you can't live here! It's falling down! What on earth do you do for heating? You'll never get it finished – it'll cost a fortune.'

'Susie, you can't stay living like this. Can't you move to somewhere normal, or back to England?' asked one very dear friend.

'Seriously, you've got to get away from here,' another advised. Irrespective of weather, financial dilemmas and problems with the animals, I'd never wanted to live anywhere other than that house since the moment I saw it. Not for one moment had I ever felt unsafe leaving our doors and windows open and unlocked by day or by night.

Where else would we find neighbours who were always kind, always considerate, always ready to help? Where else could we have toads coming into the house on warm summer evenings and spending the night sitting fatly in flowerpots, or see the twinkling green lights of glow worms blinking in the grass? Who would have rescued the plump hedgehog trundling around the patio with its body wedged into an ancient horseshoe from which it couldn't free itself, whose irritable whiffling combined with a metallic scraping, clunking sound woke me up? Where else could we lie in bed and hear a symphony of owls performing throughout the night, or the nightingales who sang to each other from spring to summer, and watch the sun float up over the hill opposite the tiny bedroom window in the morning?

A friend visited during October, and we went out for a meal in the evening. Most restaurants were closed. In the rural areas, they generally only opened at lunchtime outside of the holiday season, and we had to drive a long way to find somewhere to eat.

'Susie, you can't possibly stay here,' he said earnestly. 'You'll be bored out of your brains. Look at it.' He pointed to the quiet square in town, deserted at 10.30pm. 'There's nothing happening.'

I tried to explain that it was the nothingness I loved: the being able to park my car easily, and without having to feed money into a machine; the polite, gentle people; driving home at 2.00am through deserted country lanes and not being afraid. Lying in the dark listening to the night noises, or standing outside, sometimes when the stars came down so low that they grazed the rooftops, and the moon lit up the countryside. I described how one night, coming home very late, I had seen the house shining in the dark, lit by the Milky Way hanging so low over the roof it felt as if I could touch it.

These were the things I saw, while others saw only cracked walls and a sagging roof.

As a matter of fact, there wasn't nearly as much nothingness as I would have liked. Forgetting for the moment the perpetual round of trying to mend things that were falling to pieces, like gates and fences, the pitiful efforts at home improvement and the garden I was trying to develop, I had numerous creatures in my care, all of which needed regular feeding, continual medical attention, clearing up after, and frequent hunting down and retrieving from far-flung places. If I didn't shop and cook, I didn't eat. I washed dishes and clothes, occasionally swept the house, translated, took phone messages, and baby-sat animals for other people.

And there was Bill next door.

When I pointed this out to a friend, he replied: 'It's funny, somehow I imagined that living in France all you would have to do was sit in the sun reading, picking flowers and drinking too much wine.'

Funnily enough, I once had a similar vision.

Living in France is not synonymous with being on holiday. It's like living in England, except it's foreign and much more fun. The weather is generally better, and the wine is cheaper.

***

Bill introduced me to a lady running a business transporting mobile homes from England to the south of France. Carole B (not Carole M who had become a friend during the Mrs Malucha episode) could not have looked less like a heavy goods vehicle driver. Tall, slim, elegant, with perfect ivory skin, large grey eyes and copper hair, she would have looked at home on the catwalk. To watch her climb into the cab, then nonchalantly steer a 120-foot rig through the twisty country roads and reverse it into a parking area was a sight to behold and stop the traffic.

She was a gentle and tolerant mother to two of the most diabolical little boys I had ever known. The elder one, Christopher, had a passion for snails; he collected them and let them crawl all over his face and body, watching their slimy progress with wonderment. Sometimes he kissed them, pressing them fervently to his lips. His younger brother, Joseph, found them fascinating too; if when we were out walking he found a snail, or a slug, he'd crouch down beside it saying: 'Look, it's boodiful.' We'd all agree that it was 'boodiful', and Joseph would stay behind despite all our urging him to catch up with us. After spending a long time crooning to the 'boodiful' creature, he would grind it into the ground with his little boot, then stand looking at the sticky patch with a huge grin of satisfaction on his face.

They sprinkled their freshly-varnished staircase with handfuls of dust and grit, and decorated the newly-painted blue wall with black paint. Their new cream leather suite formed the background for abstract art created with a selection of colourful and indelible felt-tip pens. You parked your car at your own risk and had to watch the boys constantly to prevent them reorganising the bodywork with one of their father's hammers. Honestly, who would have thought that these two little horrors would grow up to be respectable hard-working men? Nobody who knew them at the time.

Despite the dreadful kids, we quickly became firm friends. On the first day we met, I asked her if she knew where I could buy feed for the horses.

'Come on,' she said, 'I'll take you there.'

She hoisted the 50 lb sack and dumped it in the car, drove me home and unloaded it. I showed her around, and she remarked that there was a lot of work to do to make the house habitable. I laughed and said that it was fine during the summer. I looked forward to one day being able to soak in a full bathtub of water, as the plastic bucket in the garden did have its limitations.

Before she left, she invited me for a meal that evening. When I arrived, I found a deep bath awaiting, with piles of warm fluffy towels heaped on a chair. I spent a blissful hour submerged in bubbles, and then sat down to a perfectly cooked hot meal, served at a table standing on a proper floor. It seemed a long time since I'd done anything similar.

I now had two close friends. Both called Carole.

Chapter Twenty-two

With their amorous reputation, people imagined that as a woman living alone I would be a constant target for the attentions of every neighbourhood Frenchman. As humiliating as it was, after a year I hadn't needed to administer even one rebuff, although M. Meneteau had once told me shyly that he loved me, but I think he was having a little joke.

It wasn't that I wanted to attract advances, but the fact that I hadn't had any was a little demoralising.

I'd almost given up hope, when it happened. We'd found an Englishman to do a few jobs, putting up fences and laying a concrete floor. For the first couple of days, he was respectful and polite, then he started calling me 'love' and 'darling' and telling slightly risqué jokes. It is customary in France for people to kiss or shake hands each time they meet, and when they part: in an office, everybody kisses or shakes hands with their colleagues until everyone has been kissed or had their hand shaken by everyone else, which is why it quite often takes a long time for the telephone to be answered early in the morning. M. Meneteau said that when he was a child, this kissing was limited to relatives, and one peck per relative; then the custom was extended to two pecks, and to friends; now, he said, everybody kissed everybody, and the two pecks had become four, and heaven knew where it would all lead.

The builder, who was spending ever longer intervals sipping tea and recounting the tragic breakdown of his marriage, had always followed the handshaking custom until one morning he unexpectedly lurched at my cheek. As I was brought up to be polite, I accepted the peck without flinching, which was a mistake, because next morning I got pecked twice. The peck as a polite greeting should be delivered without any other form of body contact, but his pecks were starting to be accompanied by a hand that tried to slip around my back. I evaded this with a nimble little manoeuvre that a sensitive person would have recognised as rejection, but my man persisted, until the morning he tried a full frontal assault, asking me what I would do if he kissed me properly. I looked into his eyes and said sweetly, with a friendly smile: 'Kick your balls out through the back of your neck.' Our relationship deteriorated rapidly after that, so soon I found myself looking for another builder.

He must have released the blockage, because soon I had suitors queueing up. A local Frenchman, with sharp blue eyes and a ferocious wife who cleaned her fingernails and picked her teeth with a Bowie knife, had been helpful in finding hay for our horses, and subsequently turned up with some seed potatoes. He began dropping in frequently to ask if there was anything I needed. It only took one brief look to know this chap would not be satisfied with a chaste peck. I could field his ribald suggestions by feigning a failure to understand what he was saying. By some cruel coincidence, it seemed that whenever he showed up, one of the cats would be sitting on my lap, a fact that gave him endless opportunity for insinuation. I found his visits unnerving, so I kept a handbag beside the front door. Every time I saw his car approaching, I grabbed the bag and trotted towards my car, waving calling merrily: 'Ah! How are you? What a shame, I've got an appointment at the doctor/dentist/vet/ironmongers/whatever: I have to dash.' He seemed to get the message eventually and stopped his uninvited visits.

Not long afterwards, a Frenchman to whom I'd been introduced at a friend's house turned up at the gate. He was a notorious womaniser – I was surprised to see him as we'd only exchanged half a dozen words, he lived 15 miles away and I hadn't told him where I lived. Some friends had dropped in for coffee but he was not deterred by their presence, making the reason for his visit clear through innuendos and sultry looks. He left an hour later, unfulfilled, subsequently reporting back to our mutual friends, who relayed the message to me, that I was a *chaud-lapin*. A hot rabbit. A sex maniac.

The ancient cow-dung that held together the walls of our house was falling out in lumps and chunks. Terry did as much as he could, but some jobs were too time-consuming and we were introduced to an elderly French builder. Although in retirement, he was happy to undertake a few jobs now and again. After satisfying himself that we were decent folk, he agreed to come and repair our walls, at a price we could afford.

François arrived punctually each morning, on his scooter, with a degenerate little home-made cigarette clamped between his lips, which were often blue with cold. After shaking hands politely, he worked quickly and skilfully until exactly 12.30pm when he presented himself, hands and face washed, for his lunch, which I provided. Ignoring the knife I laid on the table, he used his own Opinel to slice the bread and cut his food. When he had finished the main course, he would enquire whether there was any cheese, which of course there was, because what meal in France is complete without cheese? He washed it all down with a beer, followed by a small cup of strong black coffee. At precisely 2.00pm he was back at work, continuing until 5.00pm, when he swaddled himself in jacket and helmet, then inserted another odious little cigarette into his mouth. Having worked his hands into the furry gauntlets that were an extension to the handlebars of his scooter, he kicked the latter into spluttering life and set off for home, with one hand raised in salute.

The first week went smoothly. On Friday, we bid each other *'bon weekend'* and 'see you on Monday.' On the Saturday afternoon, he arrived unexpectedly, to enquire whether his work was satisfactory, and to deliver a brown paper bag full of gladioli corms. I assured him that it was, thanking him graciously, although gladioli are not my favourite flowers and smashing holes to plant them in the rock-hard surface of the garden was something I could have done without. I offered him a beer, and after he had drunk it, he rose from the table. Instead of shaking hands, he planted a beery kiss on my cheek. Skilled, reliable and affordable builders were as rare as hens' teeth, so I accepted politely.

Monday morning, promptly at 7.55am, he arrived and held out his wiry little hand. As I took it, I found myself in a vice-like grip, being pulled into his chest and kissed vigorously, the icy tip of his nose stabbing my cheeks. Tuesday morning, I thrust a steaming cup of coffee into his hands to distract him from the kissing ceremony, but no... He placed it on the table and launched himself at me. I wondered how long it was going to take him to finish the work. I couldn't afford to lose him.

I felt sorry for him. He was sad because his wife had left him, as he told me repeatedly. His poor little face was a network of broken red and purple veins, extending into the whites of his eyes. He lived a lonely life between his neat bungalow with its beautifully tended garden, and the local bar. He began inviting me to dances and dinners, all of which I gently declined, pleading imaginary prior commitments. These invitations were always delivered by telephone at around 10.30pm and accompanied by little hiccups, or maybe sobs. They were never mentioned the following morning.

Our relationship continued on an even keel, with the facial rituals each morning and evening being, I felt, a reasonable bonus for his excellent work, until he overstepped the line. As we shook hands preparatory to the kiss/nose thing, he jerked my hand in a quick downward movement into his expectant crotch. He was extremely strong for such a little man. I resisted an almost overpowering urge to punch him in the head, and instead pretended to trip, lurching forward into him and knocking him off balance. I retrieved my hand and handed him a cup of coffee with a big smile.

Thereafter I started getting up earlier, leaving the coffee to waft invitingly on the table whilst I busied myself shovelling manure in the barn or clearing up the dogs' mess to coincide with his arrival, calling out a cheery greeting whilst flourishing the shovel. This was an effective repellent and must have made some impression on him, because we reverted to a brief polite handshake and peck morning and evening.

I felt unkind until M. Meneteau mentioned obliquely one day that I should be careful, because 'la petite misére', as he was rather unkindly known, was not to be trusted and had a bad reputation as far as women were concerned. Shortly afterwards, another Frenchman I knew came around to the house and saw François working there. He stared at the little fellow, who turned his back and continued working. It was unusual behaviour, because no matter who turns up where, people normally greet each other with a handshake and a few words. The visitor warned that I should be careful of François and confirmed M. Meneteau's warning. Once I realised I was not the sole object of his affections, I no longer worried about rebuffing his advances.

When Terry arrived, he was amused when I told him about my unwelcome suitor. 'It sounds as if he's lonely. Let's take him out for the afternoon,' he suggested.

We invited François to come with us to visit the newly-opened Monkey Valley just four miles away. It is a magical place where 25 species of monkeys live freely in the trees and bushes. There are no bars, and no cages; they are free to roam where they want, will feed from your hand and sit on your shoulders. It's a conservation project and an opportunity to see these creatures living as normal and enjoyable existence as possible outside of their natural habitat.

François was delighted, stylishly dressed in pressed trousers, polished shoes and a smart jacket, emanating a pervading aroma of beer. He conversed energetically with Terry, a one-sided exchange as Terry's French was minimal and François' English non-existent, but he was happy to chatter on.

The first monkeys we saw were the tiny, squirrel monkeys with their shrill, bird-like calls. It is a rule at Monkey Valley that while the monkeys may touch humans, we must not touch them as they can interpret that as a sign of aggression. That didn't stop François. He was entranced by the little creatures, and he was also, we realised with dismay, horribly drunk. He started making loud, monkey-like noises, chittering and chattering and lunging at the monkeys running around our feet. People were staring.

Terry shepherded him firmly on to the next colony, the Barbary apes, then on to the lemurs, who enjoy sitting on visitors while eating their snacks. One perched on Francois' shoulder. He told it emotionally and loudly that he loved it, and that he had once had a cat that looked very similar.

We moved on to the central island where the gorillas live, a stern silverback male and his wives and children. As we watched them being fed, the crowds stared disapprovingly at our guest's loud shouts and uncertain steps.

Next to the gorillas were the pygmy marmosets – the smallest monkeys in the world. They are barely larger than sparrows, with the tiniest faces, and they move slowly, like chameleons. During our visit, they were very publicly and enthusiastically mating, a fact that even in his inebriated and wobbly state François noticed and commented on, turning to call the passing crowds to watch, encouraging the little creatures excitedly, and jabbing me rhythmically in the ribs with his drunken elbow. He laughed and clapped and stamped his feet, turning ever redder in the face. I willed the ground to part and allow me to slip beneath it. We dragged him onwards, past groups of astonished monkeys who broke off what they were doing to watch him perform a variety of drunken imitations, scratching his armpits and rear end, rolling his eyes and swinging his arms wildly around while making clicking, growling and whooping sounds. It was a memorable afternoon.

Chapter Twenty-three

During our second summer in France, I dug a small pond that attracted scores of amphibians, butterflies and birds; clouds of goldfinches came there to drink, fluorescent dragonflies zinged above the surface, and swallowtail butterflies danced in the lavender round the edges. Newts, frogs and toads found their way to the pond within a few days. I wondered why, as they could only have come from the stream a couple of hundred yards down the hill, an arduous journey for their small legs through long grass, bushes and fields of stubble. I watched a large frog ambushing the butterflies, cramming them into its mouth with podgy fingers. Fish appeared too, their eggs translocated from other water on the legs of birds.

In the warm evenings, large winged creatures, striped yellow and brown, began coming into the living room through the crack under the door, and then blundering noisily around the electric light bulb, from where they fell to the ground and whirled about on their backs trying to regain their feet. I scooped them up on a piece of card and tipped them out through the door; it was a time-consuming procedure because they kept crawling back in again.

One morning M. Meneteau came around to warn me about the *frelons,* of which there were a great number and which he said were very dangerous. 'Be careful. Their sting can kill a child, or a sick person, or a dog. Certainly, it could make you very ill.'

I hadn't any idea what a *frelon* was, so I asked him to describe it. 'A large winged creature, striped yellow and brown.' They sounded familiar. I looked up *frelon* in the dictionary. 'Hornet', it said.

Taking his advice, I blocked up the bottom of the door to stop them getting in. They flapped angrily at the windows and buzzed menacingly.

We had bought and fitted a staircase in the barn to replace the wormy ladder leading to the bedroom, and run an extension lead for a light so that I could sleep up there. To see my way upstairs, I had to first switch on a bulb hanging from a piece of string in the barn. When I did that, in came the hornets through the sheet of plastic where we still didn't have a door. They flapped around, banging into the bulb and dropping to the ground. Once I had got upstairs and switched on the bedside light, I had to come back down and switch off the light in the barn. While I did so I had to leave the bedroom door open so that I could see my way. As soon as the bulb downstairs was switched off, the hornets made a dash for the upstairs one, so by the time I'd got back to the bedroom, they were swarming around. I tried to knock them out of the door with a magazine, but they came in squadrons of about twenty, so by the time I'd knocked the third one out the first two were back in action. The only solution if I didn't want to risk being stung, was a merciful swift whack with the fly swatter.

Every night, there were more. Going to bed was exhausting – it took ages to clear them out. When I discovered that they were living in the chimney, I lit a roaring fire. This filled the living room with smoke and extremely angry hornets. I barricaded myself and the parrots, dogs and cats in the little room next door until they'd calmed down. Three hours later, the hornets had all disappeared, so the next evening I repeated the fire trick. They never came back, but one of our neighbours had a thriving colony living in his roof the following summer.

On summer nights, I fell asleep to the sound of the birds singing and frogs croaking to each other; and when I woke, they were still going. In the fields, flamboyant sunflowers were at their radiant and frivolous best, little knowing how fleeting was their life. In just a few weeks, they would be hanging their black and withered heads in shame, dying beneath the wheels of the combine harvesters.

***

Terry arrived in the early hours one morning, walking softly. When he opened his fleece, two enquiring little black faces peered out from where they were snuggled between his neck and shoulder. The first young housemartin stepped without hesitation onto my outstretched hand, while the second decided to fly around the room and attach itself to a beam, from where we caught it without difficulty and slipped it into a box with its companion. They settled quickly. Terry described how at mid-point across the cold, windy Channel he was watching a flock of birds swooping round the deck of the ferry as daylight faded. As he leant on the rails, one of the birds landed on his wrist, and a few moments later, a second bird joined it. They huddled together, and he put a hand over them to shelter them from the drizzle. For the rest of the journey, he stood on the deck keeping the little birds as warm as he could. When the ferry docked, they refused to fly away but climbed a little further up his arm into the comfort of the sleeve of his fleece. He tried to release them once he reached woodlands, but his little passengers would not disembark, clinging like feathery limpets to his clothing. He drove 250 miles with the birds cosily nestling on his shoulder.

In the morning, they were composed inside their box, and looking at us with perky interest. I phoned the *Ligue pour la Protection des Oiseaux* in Poitiers to ask for advice. The lady there didn't seem surprised to learn our visitors had travelled so far sitting on my husband.

'You can just let them go,' she said. 'They'll sort themselves out straight away and join up with others.'

As we opened the box, they flew like arrows from a bow, soaring up and out of sight in seconds.

I knew about the *Ligue pour la Protection des Oiseaux* because a short time before, an owl had caught the tip of its wing in a knot of wire 15 feet from the floor in Bill's barn. The poor thing was swinging helplessly upside down and we couldn't reach it, so I went to see if M. Meneteau had a sufficiently long ladder. He didn't, but he came to see what was happening. As we looked up, the owl spun frantically by its wing tip until it broke free, crashed to the ground and scuttled awkwardly behind a pile of timber. I dug it out and put it in a box of straw, under an infra-red lamp. Phone calls to vets and a wildlife park referred me to the *LPO*, the League for the Protection of Birds, who rescue and rehabilitate wild birds.

'Leave it until dark, then see if it can walk. If so, take it outside and see if it flies. If not, bring it to us tomorrow.'

I was going to feed it some cat food, but most serendipitously one of the cats had left an intact dead mouse on the doormat that morning. I removed it from the waste bin, brushed off the dust, and put it in the box with the bird.

An hour later, I found the neatly processed remains of the rodent. The owl gazed at me hopefully, so I gave it some raw liver which it snatched. When I took it out of the box, although it could walk, both wings were dragging, so next morning I drove it to Poitiers. A young woman wearing thick leather gauntlets examined it.

'Ah yes, a female barn owl. Very strong beak and claws. You must wear gloves when you handle them, they can hurt you badly.' I can't say I'd noticed.

The owl was entered into a log, and I was invited to telephone in a few months to find out how she was doing. When I did, they said she had two broken wings, which had been mended at the veterinary centre. She would remain in captivity while she healed and grew new feathers, then they would release her back into the wild.

***

We needed to take the water supply down to the tap that watered the horses, so I began hacking at the ground with a crowbar to dig a trench for the pipe. Beneath the grass, the soil was tightly packed with rocks and stones. You couldn't have put a needle between them.

Madame Meneteau watched me digging. She pointed to the great pile of stones that bore no relation to the relatively small hole I had dug.

'There are a lot of stones in your garden!'

'Yes. It's absolutely full of them. I don't understand where they all come from. There isn't a square centimetre where there isn't rock.'

'We did it when we were children!'

'Why?'

'Because when it was a working farm, the carts used to sink into the mud when it rained. Our parents sent us into the fields with baskets. We had to collect the stones and pack them into the mud. We collected so many stones!'

'Yes, I believe you! How would you like to come and take them all out?'

She laughed and handed a bowl of strawberries over the hedge.

I jabbed the crowbar into the ground once more and revealed a large grey rock that looked like a baby hippo. I tickled it with the crowbar but it did not move, so I tickled it a bit harder, and harder still. I wiggled the crowbar down its side and started heaving until it moved. It was one of many, a whole cluster of them in precisely the spot where the trench had to go. I used the tip of the crowbar to find their sensitive spots, and, with a wiggle here and there, eventually I moved them until I had a great pile, 160 in all, lying on the grass waiting to be rehomed.

My triumph was short-lived. The heavy black and blue flexible pipe that was to go in the trench refused to uncoil. Like a great snake, it writhed and twisted. Every time I straightened it and pushed it into the trench, it jumped out and tried to rewind itself. Both my energy and my patience were now very thin, and I banged the snake with some of the hippos to make it stay flat. Because the trench had been previously occupied by more hippos than earth, and because it was far too shallow, there was insufficient soil to bury the snake. I would have to find earth from somewhere else, but some other time. It had taken seven hours under a sizzling sun to get this far. There was little to show for my labour apart from the upheaved hippos and half-submerged snake.

Before he'd left the previous day, Terry had installed the bathroom fittings and a water heater. The bathroom had no ceiling and no door because there was no wall to set the door into. The sheet of polythene draped over the beams afforded little privacy if anybody wandered into the barn. For many months, I had dreamed of lying in a deep bath of hot water in our own home, so after today's efforts with the hippos, I decided to take an inaugural bath to soothe my tired muscles. I collected a book, a glass of wine, some clean clothes, a pile of fluffy towels and some fragrant bath oil, humming a contented little tune whilst turning on the taps. Sadly, they were locked solid. Even with a plumber's wrench, I couldn't budge them a fraction or squeeze a single drop of water from them. Such is life, sometimes.

I staggered to the bed and lay comatose until darkness fell and I had to feed and water the animals, after which I sat weakly with a glass of vodka and composed 'Ode to a Crowbar':

Crowbar, crowbar, I love you.
When nowt else works, you always do
When the pickaxe won't pick
And the shovel won't shove
You keep on crowbing,
Crowbar, my love.

I wondered if I might be going slightly barmy.

Chapter Twenty-four

We managed to find somebody to knock a doorway between the 'living' part of the house and the barn where the kitchen and staircase to the bedroom were. It wasn't something we could do ourselves, because the three-foot-thick wall was built from compacted flints, rocks and dust tenuously held together with dried dung. Watching him smash a hole through the wall was one of the most nerve-wracking experiences of my life. He left for the weekend, leaving a thin segment of wall intact and a stick jammed into the gaping hole to hold up the remaining part. I quite expected the whole house to fall down as during the night I could hear small stones dislodging themselves and trickling onto the floor.

Once the opening was made, I could walk to the barn without having to go outside and around the house, but it left approximately four cubic yards of rubble to dispose of. I spent many months filling holes in the field and sifting out larger stones to use as borders for flower beds.

I don't feel I was cut out for hard work. I've never been very strong, can't stand heat, don't do well in the cold and am physically quite weak. However, things needed doing, and I had to get on and do them when there was nobody else around.

One cold rainy night, I was woken by a distant horrible crash. A really loud crash, then silence. My initial reaction was to stay where I was and hope the crash belonged to somebody else, but the more I hoped, the more I thought about it, and the more I thought about it the less enthusiastic I was about getting up – the more I knew that unless I found out the cause of the crash, I was not going to get back to sleep that night. Out of bed, on with boots, hat and gloves. I sploshed down the garden, flashing a torch around until it picked out two horses' bottoms sticking through a great hole in the wooden wall of the barn. This led into M. Meneteau's vegetable garden, where they were chewing his cabbages.

I found a hammer and some nails. The torchlight was fading. I elbowed the horses back away from the cabbages. I tried unsuccessfully to hold the torch in my mouth, and then clutched it between my knees, recovered several planks of wood from the other side of the hole, and started nailing them neatly back into place. I wondered whether the neighbours were lying in their warm beds, speculating what *l'anglaise* was doing hammering wood at midnight. The horses were now eating the piles of hay left in the barn for them. Proud of my handiwork, I retired to bed. In the morning, I examined my midnight carpentry project. It had looked fine in the dim light of the torch, but cruel daylight revealed the truth. I was crushed to see that it was higgledy-piggledy, with gaps where there shouldn't be and the planks all over the place. I went and found my trusty crowbar, undid the previous night's effort and re-nailed the planks. The nails didn't seem quite long enough, or sharp enough, and the planks were a bit splitty, but it was the best I could do. I was never going to be a carpenter.

Although I no longer rode the horses, they still found ways to entertain and exercise me. During the summer, they stayed out in the field at night until the sun came up and the flies came out, when they took themselves into the shade of their barn. Even there the flies pestered them, and I could hear them stamping and snorting irritably throughout the day. I made them some cotton fringes for their eyes, out of thick white woolly mops and stitched a couple of old flowery-patterned duvet covers into lightweight fly-sheets. They looked a little strange, like small medieval destriers, but it kept the flies off.

About twice a month, they breached the electric fencing and went walkabout. Leila, the more dominant of the two, herded and pushed Cindy into the wire, where she would receive a shock; with the jolt ahead of her and her bullying companion shoving her from behind, Cindy would lunge at the wire and drag it down. Leila could then step over comfortably and they were free to wander where they pleased.

A French lady arrived at the gate one afternoon and asked whether I'd lost two horses.

'No,' I replied. 'I don't think so. Our horses are in that barn.'

I pointed to the barn where they had been when I went to check their water an hour previously.

'Well, the people in the village were certain they belonged to you.'

'Where were these horses when you saw them?' I asked.

'Trotting around in Saint-Thomas.' She looked at me a little curiously. 'They were wearing fancy dress.'

'Oh, *merde*,' I cursed. 'Thank you so much, madame. They do sound like my horses. I'll go and catch them.'

I found a couple of ropes and set off in pursuit. I met my little warhorses on their way back home, clacking down the road at a spanking trot, heads and tails high, ears pricked, and duvet covers billowing around them like giant wings.

Quite often they took themselves off to another nearby field and grazed quietly, but every once in a while they vanished into the hundreds of acres of sunflowers and maize that surrounded us, when all I could do was wait for them to return, either under their own steam, or attached to kindly strangers who had been directed to me. Most people within a radius of several miles knew about the English woman with all the renegade animals.

On a blistering summer day, I started tiling the floor of the small room next to the living room. We had laid a concrete base and I was mixing tile cement, spreading it on the floor and positioning the tiles. It was tricky, because no walls were parallel, no corners formed right angles and I had to decide which layout would look the least odd. After I had shuffled the tiles around for a while, sweat was running down my face and neck, so I took a few minutes to lie in the cool of the shuttered living room. The phone rang. It was Jean-Luc's girlfriend.

'Susie, your horses are on the road.'

Why did they have to be on the road? What were they hoping to find? They'd been dozing in the barn last time I saw them. Because of the dirty task I was doing, I was wearing a very old pair of leggings full of holes and ladders, and in which the elastic waist had gone, and a baggy T-shirt smeared with blobs of paint and encrusted with dried cement. My footwear was the pair of plastic sandals. I grabbed some ropes and sped off down the lane in time to see two fat rumps jogging up the hill on the other side of the road. Jean-Luc's girlfriend came by in her car and I jumped in. We followed the horses for half a mile as they charged across a dusty ploughed field, then they veered away from the road and I had to abandon the car to keep them in sight.

Young vines were somehow maintaining their green crispness in the stifling heat and every so often the horses stopped to nibble at them. I could get within a few feet of them before they tossed their heads and trotted off again. The discomfort of chasing horses over a roughly ploughed field in flimsy sandals cannot adequately be described: you have to experience it yourself, as pieces of grit work themselves inside your sandals, under the straps, under your soles, between your toes, and between your heels and the backs of the sandals. It was agony, compounded by impossible heat, rising panic, increasing exhaustion and the necessity of holding up the ragged leggings in order to prevent them from slithering down my hips. Reaching a fence, the runaways changed direction, found a gap and shot through it.

I hobbled along behind, desperate to keep them in sight, finding myself scampering between orderly rows of tomatoes. A man and child were hoeing around the vegetables. '*Bonjour, madame,*' they called politely, as if dishevelled women and fat horses habitually ran through their garden. Very soon I was going to have to give up the chase; my heart was pounding, I was soaked through with perspiration and starting to see double. The horses were showing signs of flagging too, tired by negotiating the deeply rutted fields. They stopped to nibble at a hedge, so with a lunge I managed to grab a handful of mane and get a rope onto a halter. With one secured, the other was content to follow behind as we trudged around trying to find a pathway, and then to discover where we were because I had no idea.

A bent old gentleman was leaning over his garden gate. He raised his cap as I hobbled past. '*Bonjour, madame.* Isn't it rather hot to be taking your horses for a walk?' The subjects in question were lathered into a soapy foam of sweat and their heads were hanging almost to the ground.

'Please, can you tell me where we are?'

He mentioned a name I'd never heard of.

'I'm trying to get back to Painville.'

'Oh, that's simple. It's just over there,' he pointed, 'no more than two miles.'

Really no distance at all. It only took an hour for the three of us to stagger back. In the meantime, the tile cement had set hard in the bucket and had to be thrown away, but that suited me just fine because the last thing I wanted to do, apart from scuttling about in a ploughed field again, was lay any more tiles.

***

I wanted to plant shrubs against the walls of the house where the rocks flourished. Sometimes it could take several days to extract a particularly huge specimen. Many of them went right up to and in some cases slightly beneath the walls of the house. As I tugged out the umpteenth boulder,

I had a vision of that corner of the house gently subsiding into the void left behind, followed by the rest of the building caving in behind it.

The wisteria cutting given to us by the people who had sold us Tinkerbelle had survived being eaten to the ground by sheep, chewed to the ground by dogs, masticated to a pulp by the geese on its third try, and once again chewed down by dogs. With very little hope after the fourth assault, I put a protective net around it. Lo and behold, off it went again. Within a year, it was over six feet tall. Some survivor. You had to be resilient to last around here.

As a spasmodically enthusiastic gardener, I thought I had acquired green fingers or, as the French say, a green thumb, because whatever seeds I planted, whatever twigs I stuck in the ground, they all grew. I congratulated myself on my new-found talent. After a relatively short time, I discovered that everything flourished in the fertile soil despite the stony substratum, and the neat garden I had created transformed itself rapidly into an impenetrable wilderness, with twigs exploding into towering bushes so that smaller plants gave up the hopeless struggle for light, surrendering themselves to the brambles and nettles. In almost no time at all, we were living in a jungle. The more I chopped and hacked at the rampant greenery, the faster it grew.

Apart from drought and flood, moles, slugs, snails, greenfly, blackfly, red spider mite, leather jackets and dozens of other pests and diseases, the great enemies of the French gardener are the *Saints de Glace* – the Ice Saints. Every day of the year is dedicated to a particular saint (some have to share a day because there are so many of them). The saints Mamert, Pancrace and Servais belong to 11, 12 and 13 May, dates which, in 1897, suffered serious overnight freezing. St Urbain, on 25 May, is regarded as the last Ice Saint, after which the night-time temperature is unlikely to drop below freezing. Jean-Luc told me that in 1966, it snowed on 15 July. If you joined in a gardening discussion and said you'd planted a particular plant, or taken some geraniums outside, it was an invitation to the warning: 'Ah! Beware! Don't forget the *Saints de Glace!*'

From the hedges and fields, I harvested walnuts, blackberries, blackcurrants, nasty little worm-ridden apples, rock-hard pears, sweet chestnuts, and mushrooms. Although we had several books to help distinguish edible fungi from toxic ones, when you held a specimen in your hand and tried to identify it among a whole load that looked similar, when a shade of pink or a length of stalk could make all the difference, eating it was like playing gastronomic Russian roulette. Madame Meneteau mostly knew which mushrooms were safe to eat and I would take them to her for advice. One day, I found a large patch of voluptuous fluted yellow fungi that I hoped might be *chanterelles*. Were they edible? I asked hopefully.

'They might be,' she said, 'but I'm not sure. Why don't you try just eating a little bit?'

'Because I don't want to die in agony,' I laughed.

She recommended taking them to the local pharmacy, as French pharmacists are trained to distinguish those mushrooms that could kill you from those that will not. Our mushrooms sadly fell into the former category.

That summer the weather was particularly humid, so the living room floor I had painstakingly sanded back to clean wood, and oiled, was covered in green mildew, as were my leather shoes and a handbag. I dragged the furniture out into the garden so I could scrub the mould from the floorboards. The neighbours said their wooden floors were also covered in mildew, something they had never known before. It was attributed to unusually high humidity.

Since we'd arrived we'd experienced the coldest winter for twenty-five years, the highest winds, the driest spring and then the most humid summer. I wondered what extreme to expect next.

Chapter Twenty-five

One Sunday morning, I drove to town to buy a *baguette* from the new bakery, taking one of the dogs with me for company.

I queued with half a dozen cheerful and friendly people buying *fougasse, pain, croissants, couronnes, tartes à l'abricot, éclairs* and *brioche,* and bought a small *baguette.* On the way back through town, I noticed a young pigeon strutting backwards and forwards distractedly, watching its reflection in a shop window. I could see there was something not quite right about it, so I got out of the car and picked it up. It pecked me hard. In the few seconds this had taken, a line of traffic had built up and people were hooting impatiently. I got into the car with the pigeon, which the dog wanted to sniff. The pigeon didn't want to be sniffed and struggled. More cars hooted. With my left elbow holding the dog back, and the bird in my left fist, it took several backward and forward shunts to get the car around the corner one-handed without damaging it, whilst the hooting grew more impatient and arms started waving out of car windows. After two or three embarrassing minutes and much manoeuvring, I rounded the bend. In the rear-view mirror, I saw drivers pointing at me and gesticulating. Never mind, the road ahead was clear and there was a small copse behind the treasury offices, so I stopped the car there, pushed the dog off the pigeon and put it on the grass, where it wandered around rather forlornly, attempting to fly without success. Something had pulled out all its tail feathers, so now it was quite helpless. It was very young, with straggly wisps of cotton wool-like hair poking out between its few feathers.

Driving home holding the dog off the bird was going to be dangerous, so I stuffed the pigeon up inside my T-shirt and set off again. It didn't nestle quietly, but used its scythe-like claws to haul itself up until it could get its head out through the neck of the T-shirt. The dog clawed at my shoulder in excitement. This wasn't going to work. My skin was lacerated, bleeding into the T-shirt and I couldn't take any more pain. I put the pigeon into a convenient cardboard box in the boot and set off yet again. Although now relieved of the agony of the raking claws, it felt as if something was still scratching me. I was certain I could feel my skin moving. I scratched at an arm, leaving tiny spots of blood. My neck itched, so I scratched that and more tiny ruby pinpricks appeared. My hair was itching, both arms, my stomach, my nose. I looked in the mirror and saw dozens of tiny, blood-coloured dots waltzing around on my face.

Back home, I handed my find to Madame Roly-Poly, warning her that it had things on it.

'Oh yes, that's normal – bird fleas. Poor little thing, it's just a baby. You're hungry, aren't you?' she crooned at the bird as it pecked at her thumb.

I stripped off, showered in scalding water for a long time (yes, we had a working shower at last!), put all my clothes in the washing machine, soaked my trainers, burned the cardboard box, fumigated and hoovered the car. The *baguette*, which was the cause of the entire episode, ended up in the bin.

Blue the guineafowl taught herself to sing – an appalling racket, being a combination of shriek, groan, screech and honk, uttered rhythmically from first light until total darkness had fallen. It sounded like somebody sawing sheets of metal with a blunt saw. While the volume she attained was impressive, her melody did not improve, and her grating racket outweighed the benefit of the daily egg. The noise reverberated around the whole hamlet, endlessly, every day. She had also developed a strange habit: suddenly and unexpectedly running full tilt at unsuspecting people then pecking them hard on the shins. She would have to go.

Very fortunately for Blue, the first person I approached said she would be glad to take the bird, but she would have to get her brother to kill her, as although she could kill rabbits and chickens quite easily, guinea fowl were notoriously difficult to despatch. Much as I wanted to be rid of Blue, I could not condemn her to a painful death.

I called the sanctuary where we had taken Lucy, and they said they would be happy to welcome Blue, so Terry and I packed her into a cardboard box and drove her there, still bawling. There she was instantly accepted into the bosom of a flock of similarly noisy birds. Without pausing for breath, she melded into the crowd and became indistinguishable from the rest.

Chapter Twenty-six

I had not unpacked the suitcases full of smart suits, neat skirts and high-heeled shoes from my previous life and for which I no longer had any desire nor opportunity to wear. Everything that was of practical use was stained or torn. Carole B arrived one day to say we were going clothes shopping. Clothes shopping is my very worst chore, but I was happy to have a break from digging rocks and dealing with mildew.

The clothes shop was unusual, located behind the cement factory. There was no sign on the door, and unless somebody told you about it you'd never find the place. The clothes lay in piles several feet high all over the floor, arranged into sections. Men's shirts; denims; sportswear; dresses; coats; nightwear; children's clothes; underwear; men's jackets; jumpers; shoes; and several miscellaneous heaps. It was not for the faint-hearted. You had to climb onto the piles and delve into them, and a faintly unpleasant smell lingered from the product that was used to fumigate the garments.

The stock came from donations from all over France. Suitable items went straight away to needy areas worldwide, and what remained was sold by weight, for a modest 25 francs per kilo. It was a gigantic collection of rags and riches. Unworn designer clothes and shoes; stained night-dresses and clothes with cigarette burns, zips removed, or gaping holes. For the discriminating shopper willing to invest time and effort there were some wonderful bargains, and there was no excuse for anybody not to have a comprehensive wardrobe for every season.

The clientele included the really poor, travelling folk, market traders and wealthy professionals. My bank manager always looked as if she had stepped off the pages of *Vogue*, and almost all her clothes came from there. There were no social barriers as everybody united in a common quest and helped each other. When somebody wanted to pull out something from beneath a huge heap, other people would dig in and help them burrow through the pile. Shoes were piled up haphazardly, but seldom was a pair found together. Somebody found a shoe they liked, waved it aloft, and all the other hunters dug through the pile to find its partner. Someone discovered a gigantic pair of bloomers waved them in the air laughing; fat ladies, encouraged by their friends, tried determinedly to squeeze into thin dresses; the two resident dogs bounded around asking people to throw rubber toys for them; children climbed up the clothing piles and tumbled down; somebody took off their jacket to try another, and in no time another customer had picked up the discarded garment.

'Ah! No!' cried the owner, snatching it back.

There didn't appear to be a name for the place, so the English called it the Rag and Louse, and the French, a little more delicately *Chez Dior*. It quickly became a regular haunt where I went with friends to spend a couple of hours laughing and replenishing our wardrobes. I came home with plastic sacks full of clothes that went into the washing machine. For the first time in my life, I enjoyed clothes shopping.

Our next trip was to the local rubbish dump, which at the time was just a large area of land where people tipped stuff they no longer wanted. There were old beds, piles of magazines, doors and windows, glass jars, chairs with broken legs, plastic containers, broken flower pots, ornaments, fridges, washing machines, melamine kitchen units and anything else that people wanted to be rid of.

'Shopping' at a rubbish dump wasn't something I had ever done, so I was initially hesitant, but when I found a dozen other well-dressed people rummaging around and dragging things triumphantly to their cars, I was happy to have a go too. Once you began exploring, it was astonishing to see what people threw away. Over a couple of months, I acquired a large collection of perfect cast iron saucepans and frying pans. And it was all free! All they needed was a thorough wash and seasoning. I also came home with a pristine cane rocking chair, ten yards of brand new hosepipe, and numerous other treasures. I laughed to myself thinking how much I had enjoyed these 'shopping trips'. Up to three years previously, I regularly shopped at Harrods and found it a dreadful ordeal. I wondered what friends and family would say if they could see me now, digging around in piles of junk like an urchin in a Dickens novel.

In a rural and, at that time, depressed area, there was almost no hope of finding employment. The few jobs that were available inevitably went to French people. I had registered as looking for work. After a long wait, I was sent for an interview with a local college, to work as a typist for the principal, having filled in a form saying that I was a fast and accurate touch typist, which I was on a standard qwerty keyboard. However, French keyboards are not qwerty; they are azerty, with many letters in different places, as well as a host of other characters with accents on them that are not found on qwerty keyboards. It doesn't need saying that the typing test was a complete disaster and I was not sent to any further interviews.

I worked as a cleaner for a few months, but the husband kept touching my backside and telling me I had nice thighs. His wife insisted that the very high beams must be hoovered weekly, which involved perching on a stepladder and holding a heavy vacuum cleaner in one hand while hoovering with the free hand, and it was only going to be a matter of time before I broke my neck, broke the vacuum cleaner or broke the husband's nose. You can tolerate quite a lot when you are in need of money, but there are limits.

***

Carole B asked if I would like to work as her secretary as she had taken advice and formed a French company. I would become part of the French system, paying tax and qualifying for health care. Carole M, our mutual friend, who had helped build Bill's poultry palace and translated for Mrs Malucha, also worked for Carole B. She worked five mornings a week, and I worked the afternoons. One aspect of the job was applying for and chasing up the necessary permits to allow the extra-wide loads transit through France. Each load required a separate permit from each of the *départements* it traversed, which could be as many as six or seven. The application forms were unfathomable, peppered with incomprehensible acronyms. In more than one *département,* the issuing authorities showed a definite antagonism, whether towards foreign transporters, transporters in general, or Carole in particular, I didn't know, but they made the whole process incredibly difficult and protracted. Having to telephone these people and try to get them to return the permits in time was a daunting experience. If the vehicles were moved without the permit, the transporter faced heavy fines, so it was essential that we had them.

During the low season, which was most of the summer when the mobile homes had been delivered to site, we tried to keep Carole's fleet of trucks moving by sub-contracting from other hauliers. My job was to telephone French haulage firms and persuade them to give us some work. Liaising by telephone in a language with which you are not really competent, and talking about a subject with which you are not familiar is an ideal way to learn the language. As you can't see the person you're talking to, can't gesticulate or draw a sketch and you have to listen very carefully to understand what they are saying, using whatever vocabulary you have to explain yourself. Before making a call, I searched the dictionary for the necessary words, then wrote them into what I hoped were intelligible sentences. It was the perfect way to improve my French.

The money was useful too. The first thing I bought was a wood burning stove. Although it was high summer, the memories of that first bitter winter remained.

***

My perfect mother-in-law Sophie came to stay. In her mid-eighties, she was still fit and full of fun. Before her arrival, her first visit to France, she hadn't any idea what to expect of the country. 'Do they have fridges?' she enquired.

Once she was here, the lovely summer weather, the peacefulness of the life and the tidiness of the countryside seduced her. She took in her stride the lack of flooring, doors and walls all over the house, the bumping around in Tinkerbelle, and was happy sleeping on the divan in the living room. She sat in the garden watching the chickens and playing with the cats, or watching the geese in the pond.

'Yes, it's lovely here,' she reported on the phone, 'the weather's wonderful, and they've got swans on their lake.'

***

Autumn started settling in; the roar of the chainsaw replaced the grumble of the cement mixer; the fields were bathed in morning mist and smoke curled from chimneys. Chestnuts fell and lay on the roadsides like families of little green hedgehogs and the hunting season went into full swing. Some evenings they started hunting towards nightfall, with the sound of yelping dogs, shouting men, and gunfire in every direction lasting until midnight, panicking the horses into galloping crazily around

150

in the dark, leaving them sweating profusely and blowing hard. The hullabaloo had to be heard to be believed. The French hunting horn sounds like one of those children's party squeakers with a feather on the end. When some of the dogs got lost or stuck down holes, instead of seeking them out their owners just squeaked on the horns. The horses didn't like that, either.

Carole B found a stray dog, a sad-eyed, beagle-type bitch limping along a road many miles from the nearest village. She wasn't much of a dog to look at: long-bodied, long-tailed, long-eared, short-legged, with a black and tan coat that looked wiry but felt soft. Her white muzzle indicated advanced age. Her left eyelid turned almost inside out.

I had never seen a dog who knew such fear. Any noise or sudden movement caused her to cringe to the floor, but Carole's ghastly children could do what they wanted with her, and her tail, which was almost as long as her body, would wave behind her. She adored them.

I'd tried unsuccessfully to find her owner. If there was anything we didn't need it was another dog to feed, but each time I saw Amy, as Carole's boys had christened her, my heart ached. She wasn't suited to living in a busy house/office with constant noise and movement.

One afternoon, I put her in the car and brought her home, bringing our canine headcount to six. Despite living now in an environment where she was loved and secure, she still clamped her tail to her belly and flattened herself to the ground if I picked up a magazine, or if somebody walked past her carrying something. Her fear was too deep-rooted to be overcome. We had her neutered and tattooed, and her damaged eyelid repaired.

***

During the summer, I'd bought a pile of old firewood from a neighbour which was stored in a barn next to Bill's establishment. The only way I could get to it was via Bill's drive, which was a public right of way. During one of his long absences, something belonging to Bill had disappeared, and he had aroused the indignation of the neighbours by asking me to go and see whether they knew anything about it.

'We are not thieves!' yelled M. Meneteau, stamping his foot and spitting.

Bill installed a motion detector lamp on the wall, and M. Meneteau came to ask what it was, wondering if it was a spy camera.

I explained that it was a light that would come on at night if anybody walked past it.

M. Meneteau considered that for a few seconds, and then he asked: 'But if Bill isn't here, and the light goes on, what is the point?'

A little while afterwards, Bill and I unfortunately fell out. What had begun as a simple misunderstanding developed into a minor war and we stopped speaking to each other. In protest against what he believed was the theft of his property, before returning to Spain, he erected an edifice of scaffolding poles, rolls of barbed wire and heavy wooden planks across the entrance to his land, blocking the path to my firewood. The only way I could access it was by lying on my stomach and writhing beneath the barricade. The neighbours watched anxiously and said that I should report the situation to the local mayor or to the police, as it was an offence to prevent somebody from getting their firewood. Instead, I spent the next few weeks becoming increasingly agile and progressively shredding my clothes until I'd collected all the wood.

I ordered a further supply from a wood merchant. Three cords – ten cubic yards – should be sufficient, friends told me, to see us through the winter. When the wood merchant phoned to say he was on his way to deliver the logs I waited excitedly, looking forward to having a neatly stacked woodpile like my French neighbours. By 2.30pm, it was cold, and drizzling, so I went into the house to have a cup of coffee. Ten minutes later, there was a knock on the door, and there was the beaming wood merchant to say he had delivered the logs.

I was astonished to think that he could have off-loaded and stacked them in such a short time. I thanked him profusely, gave him a cheque and went to accompany him to the gate.

That is when I learned that it was not he who stacked them into the neat piles, but me. He had tumbled the logs onto the drive behind my car. Until they were moved, I would not be able to go anywhere. Numb with disbelief, I watched him trundle away with a cheery wave, then I stood and stared tearfully at the logs and my immobilised car. The forecast was for the current drizzle to turn to heavy rain, and if the wood got drenched it would be useless. I started stacking it in the storage area 60 feet from where it lay. It took me five hours, until long after dark. When I had put the last log on top of the wobbly heap, the result in no way resembled the neat piles my neighbours had, but at least I could get to the car, and cover the pile with a tarpaulin. Offhand, I couldn't remember ever being quite so physically exhausted as I was then. I was soaked in perspiration and the last thing I wanted to do was sit by a fire.

The forecast rain arrived in torrents, and twenty-four dogs' paws transformed the living room into a sea of mud. Then the electricity failed in the kitchen, leaving us in the dark with no means of cooking or heating water. In the garage, there was a small two-ring cooker weighing about sixty pounds. I floundered with it through the mud to the living room where the power was still on, but by then I was too tired to eat. I curled up on the settee and went to sleep, thoroughly disgruntled with this exasperating day. None of the books I had read about a new life in France had mentioned anything about power cuts, torrential rain and mountains of damp logs.

Chapter Twenty-seven

A friend from England phoned one day to ask if Terry seemed all right, because she had seen him and thought he wasn't looking at all well. His face was grey, she said, and his hands were shaking badly. When I called him, he said he was just fine. I mentioned that somebody had remarked on his hands shaking, and he thought he was probably drinking too much coffee.

Over the following weeks, he began phoning every evening, complaining of severe headaches. I told him to see a doctor. When he first said that his headaches had been diagnosed as a blocked sinus, I remember thinking: 'That's what the little white turkey had.'

Weeks passed and he didn't get any better. The painkillers weren't working and during his visits, I was shocked to see he was stumbling, talking incoherently and unable to do simple tasks. It seemed strange that a blocked sinus should have such a drastic effect, but his frequent visits to the doctor always produced the same diagnosis: it was nothing more than a blocked sinus that would sort itself out in time.

For our second Christmas in France, he came to stay for three weeks. When he arrived after his 14-hour journey, he staggered from the car, holding his head and had to go straight to bed dosed with painkillers. Next morning his headache was gone, but he seemed vague and uncoordinated.

The more I thought about it, the more I was unconvinced about the blocked sinus. I asked myself whether his condition could be psychosomatic, a reaction to the demands of this farmhouse that required never-ending supplies of money to hold it up, the animals who seemed to be constantly in need of veterinary treatment, the car and household equipment that was falling to pieces, and of course, my day-to-day living expenses. Tinkerbelle had needed a complete set of new tyres and brakes as well as a host of smaller components, and in the past year, my computer had gone through two modems, one hard disk, a motherboard and a monitor that had gone up in flames after one of the cats piddled on it.

He'd been ill now for several months, but somehow he kept producing the income we couldn't survive without. I had my job with Carole B, but a month's pay would possibly sustain the animals and myself for ten days. Her business was in trouble. Following some very poor advice and turning her successful one-woman business into a French company with all the financial obligations that entailed, in no time at all, it was sinking under the insatiable demands of the French exchequer. The bailiff was a regular visitor to her office, and a strange car pulling up outside was the signal for Carole B to disappear through the back door, leaving Carole M to use her charm and streetwise talents to keep the unwelcome visitors at bay.

With the distress of Carole B's situation and increasing concern over Terry's condition, my stomach was in a permanent state of liquidity and I shook constantly. His behaviour became ever more peculiar, and as he kept making the long, tiring journey here he became progressively more frail. I knew he had to be suffering from something far more serious than a blocked sinus, and that either he wasn't telling me, or his doctor wasn't telling him. I feared he was in the early stages of Alzheimer's disease, or had a brain tumour, and this was the only thought in my mind during every waking hour. I needed to be looking after him, and he had to be in England where he could receive medical treatment.

We could not afford to pay anybody to care for our multitude of animals indefinitely. The only solution I could see was to have the dogs put to sleep, and in one of Terry's more lucid moments I told him I was going to do that and come back to England with him. He wouldn't hear of it, insisting that he was feeling a great deal better and that if I did put the dogs to sleep, he would never forgive me. Before he left, he made me swear not to do so.

In his befuddled state, he continued to drive, not noticing that the car was overheating until the engine blew up 200 miles from here. He managed to walk to a garage, from where a lady phoned to tell me he was stranded at the side of the road, with no money nor transport, and the only food he had was a carton of walnuts collected from our garden to take back with him. I had no money, Tinkerbelle was again out of action, and there was no way I could get to him. The garage people were kindly keeping him supplied with coffee and letting him use their phone to keep me up to date.

Each time he phoned, he insisted that he was feeling fine and making arrangements to get back to England. He managed to find somebody to give him a lift to Portsmouth, another kind person took him to London, and an off-duty taxi driver drove him all the way to his flat, free of charge. There is something about the way that strangers rally around to help a soul in need that restores my faith in human nature.

Terry managed to find and buy a replacement engine for the car, and get it back to France to fit, and then continue on his journey home. How he did it, in his condition, remains a mystery.

It was eight months since he had first started complaining of the headaches and having treatment for a blocked sinus when my phone rang one Sunday. His neighbours were calling to say he had collapsed and they were very worried. They had called in somebody they knew to lay her healing hands on him.

I exploded. 'For God's sake, call the doctor. He doesn't need hands laid on him, he needs medical help.'

'But it's Sunday afternoon, we can't call the doctor out on Sunday.'

'Bugger that. Ring the doctor now.'

I called Terry's sister who lived 100 miles away. She took control – an hour later he had been seen by a new doctor, and our daughter Julie was with him. She phoned to say that she was staying with him, as he was not allowed to drive and had to be at the local hospital the following morning.

'Don't worry Mum, he's in good hands.'

'What do they think is the matter?'

'The doctor wouldn't say. We'll know tomorrow. I'll phone you as soon as there is any news.'

I put the phone down, feeling ill, the most frightened I had ever been; terribly frightened for my husband, terribly frightened for the future. I lay awake all night, shivering and trembling, my mind racing until dawn when I could busy myself feeding the animals.

Julie rang.

'It's OK, Mum. He's had a brain scan and he's being sent to a neurological hospital. I still don't know what it is, but Dad's cheerful and there doesn't seem to be any panic. He'll be transferred by ambulance this afternoon. I'll stay with him and keep you up to date.'

There was no panic. He wasn't being transferred until the afternoon. He was cheerful. That must mean it isn't *really* bad news, I thought, but I still quivered through the interminable morning and afternoon, waiting for news.

Late afternoon, I heard from Julie.

'It's serious, but not too serious. You don't have to be worried. He has a large quantity of blood inside his skull – it's called a subdural haematoma – and they're going to operate tomorrow to drain it. Are you going to come over?'

Of course, I would go over. I had to. Half a dozen phone calls enlisted a brigade of helpers who would hold the fort and mind the animals while I was away. There were no local flights between the region and England, and no ferry crossings for the next three days. The only way to get there was by *Le Shuttle* under the Channel, a claustrophobic's worst nightmare. I'd have to leave early next morning to catch the train. As I scribbled lists of feeding and medication requirements for the animals and threw an armful of clothes into a small suitcase, the phone rang.

Michelle, who had wanted me to help her to steal somebody's dog, was calling in her strange croaky voice. She needed blankets to wrap her mother's furniture in, and could I let her have some.

'Not now,' I said. 'My husband is terribly ill in hospital and I'm leaving for England tomorrow morning.' It was 10.30pm.

'But can't you just bring me some blankets for my mother's furniture before you go?'

'No,' I said, 'I'm packing to leave and trying to organise care for my animals. I've had no sleep for two days, will have none tonight, and I can't worry about your mother's furniture now. When I come back, I'll see what I can find. I'm sorry I can't help you now.' I put the phone down.

Half an hour later she arrived at the door. 'Can I take some blankets now?' she asked.

It was quicker and simpler to hand her a pile of dog blankets than to argue with her. She still has them.

Carole B was in England. She phoned at 11.30pm, and I told her what was happening.

'Have you got any money? she asked.

'No.'

'Go to the office and take two hundred pounds,' she said. She couldn't afford it, but insisted I must have it. 'You're going to need it when you get there.'

The office was twelve miles away, and the key twelve miles in the opposite direction. I collected the key just before midnight and picked up the money on my way to the railway station the following morning. I didn't even want to think about the journey on the train through the Chunnel.

By the time I arrived at Frenchay hospital, Terry had been successfully operated on and was fully recovered. The doctor explained how blood had seeped from a small vessel into his skull, forming a mass pushing one half of his brain to one side, putting it under tremendous pressure. Immediately that pressure was released, he was back to normal again.

Four days later, we came back to France for him to convalesce.

It was late spring, and while Terry stretched out in the garden soaking up the early sunshine, we breathed a sigh of relief.

The next afternoon he had a slight headache, said he was hungry and would like to go a local restaurant. We'd ordered our meal and had just taken a bite, when he began clutching at his head and looking very grey. Two minutes later, he was on the floor, slumped against a radiator with his jacket over his head.

The local doctor arrived within minutes, looking like a funeral director, all in black, thin and mournful. I explained Terry's recent medical history, and he flicked a light into his eyes, then pulled his jacket back over his head.

'Madame, your husband is dangerously ill. He must be taken to hospital immediately. I am going to phone an ambulance.'

The paramedics came and wheeled Terry from the restaurant, to the obvious interest of the other diners and relief of the manager.

When the doctor summoned the local ambulance, he had also alerted the hospital in Poitiers. An emergency medical team was already whizzing down the motorway towards us as I followed the ambulance. Keeping in radio contact, the two ambulances met at a junction and transferred Terry to the care of the three specialist doctors in the emergency ambulance. They took blood samples and blood pressure and radioed the results to the hospital.

Being in the ambulance with three of the most wickedly handsome men I had ever seen should have been a pleasure, but I was shaking with fear, my teeth chattering and I was frozen despite the warm evening sun. The doctors were relaxed and cheerful as they flourished needles, connected drips and machines, twiddled knobs.

'Has he eaten this evening?'

'Just one prawn and a little…' I didn't know the French word for piece. 'A little part of a slice of bread.'

'Ah! *Un petit morceau! C'est 'un morceau', le mot que vous cherchez!'* he smiled.

Whenever I hear the word *'morceau'* now, it still takes me back to that moment in the ambulance beside the motorway.

'OK! *On y va!*' cried one of the handsome ones, slapping merrily on the window behind the driver. 'You follow, madame, and don't be afraid, French doctors are very good!'

The ambulance sped away, with Tinkerbelle stuck like glue to its bumper as I had no idea where the hospital was.

As soon as we arrived, Terry was whisked away while I was led to a comfortable waiting room and told not to worry.

I was actually very worried not only about Terry, but also because all the way there the petrol gauge on the car had been indicating that it was virtually empty. I hadn't any idea where or if I would find an open fuel station, while back at home the animals were many hours past their evening feeding time.

A large kindly surgeon in a powder blue gown appeared, smiling as he shook hands, and speaking perfect English.

'Your husband has another haematoma, but there is nothing to worry about. I'll operate in the morning, and he will be fine. You can go and see him, and then you must go home and sleep. First of all, I'll show you the X-rays. Come.'

The X-rays of Terry's brain were pinned up to back-lights.

'Here, you see, the two halves of the brain, and down the middle, the line between them. It should be a straight line, but because of this,' he pointed to a large dark mass to one side, 'which is the blood, his brain is pushed to one side.'

Instead of a neatly bisected oval, Terry's brain looked more like the yin-yang symbol.

He was tucked up in bed in a quiet room, almost asleep. I squeezed his hand, telling him that the doctor said he would be fine and we had nothing to worry about. He nodded wearily and closed his eyes.

I reached home just after 2.00am. The animals had put themselves to bed and stayed curled up asleep. I climbed gratefully into bed and dozed spasmodically through what was left of the night.

Terry was operated on the following morning, strapped to the operating table under local anaesthetic. Two holes were drilled through his skull and a litre of blood was drained out. The surgeon visited him daily while he convalesced in hospital, sitting on his bed and chatting about aeroplanes, boats and other little boy matters.

Subdural haemotomas are the result of a head injury. It had been eight months since Terry first began suffering the headaches, and when we talked later, we recalled it had also been eight months since we stood one night watching the Hale-Bopp comet passing over the house. He had tripped and fallen, banging his head on the concrete.

Despite the words of comfort before his two operations, there is a high mortality rate from subdural haematomas, and a strong probability of permanent brain damage for those who survive. Somehow, Terry had survived two.

We may have been broke, but like our wisteria, we were survivors.

Chapter Twenty-eight

Having a cockerel had been a mistake. My enchanting vision of hosts of chickens happily scratching and pecking their way around our land fell apart as our hens went broody and produced clutches of fluffy chicks. I hadn't taken into account that amongst them, inevitably, would be a certain number of cockerels. The majority of all the chicks grew into little boys and as they grew, they fought. At one count, there were twenty-two cockerels fighting energetically throughout the daylight hours and seven hens watching with mild interest. It was a disastrous situation that could only get worse, so I had to make gifts of the little cockerels to our neighbours. As a non-meat eater, my heart was heavy delivering them to their fate.

If you ever decide to keep chickens and don't know much about them, here's a tip: catching them is quite a lot more difficult than you might suppose. They are fleet of foot and you can look extremely foolish lunging around after them. Wait until dark, when they become tractable; I don't know whether they're worn out, night blind, or whatever, but you can pick them up without resistance, provided they are not roosting up in a tree like Sandra. They appear to be in a state of trance, so if you lift them up, they stay in a sitting position without moving a muscle.

Our new dog, Amy, settled in quickly and demonstrated her gratitude by killing as many of our poultry as she could catch, solving our surplus chicken dilemma. Within a month of her arrival, there were none left.

***

'I need your help, but only if you're not afraid of snakes.'

I knew instantly who had left the message on the answering machine. Gentle, beautiful and charismatic Agnes, whom I'd met recently and instantly loved. She and her husband, a successful author, had been immensely kind and supportive to me in my fledgling writing career.

I called her back.

'There's a grass snake trapped in the raspberry netting. I can't think of anybody mad enough to help me, except you.'

The snake was thoroughly enmeshed in a tangle of plastic netting threaded with long grass and pinned to the ground by raspberry canes. A few feet away lay the decomposed body of another snake that had met a similar fate.

At first it looked as if our mission had come too late. The beautiful black and green reptile lay motionless under a broiling sun, but when I touched its tail it moved slightly.

Agnes could only find a gigantic pair of dress-making shears. We considered our strategy. The snake had gone in head first through one of the small loops of the netting, and then through another, and another, and another in its efforts to get free. About two dozen green plastic circles were digging into its body, giving it the appearance of a loaf in the process of being sliced. Where the netting had cut most deeply, layers of skin were peeling away. The diameter of the netting was at most two inches, whereas in places the snake's body must have been at least four inches thick. Starting at the tail end, crouching in the grass and raspberry canes, we began cutting it free, one holding it while the other manoeuvred the scissor blade between the netting and the skin. It was a laborious and lengthy task, our backs and legs aching as we worked, but greatly encouraged by the increasing movement of our patient we progressed up the body, snipping and pulling away the nylon from where it was embedded in the snake's silky skin. It was by now alert enough to be taking an interest, its head turned to watch us, the forked tongue flickering, but its attitude was relaxed as if understanding that we were trying to help.

As we got closer to the head end and the snake became livelier, Agnes said: 'You know what? It's beginning to look like an adder to me.'

'No, it's just a grass snake.'

'I hope you're right, because I don't want to have to phone your husband and tell him you've been bitten by an adder.'

'Trust me, this isn't an adder.'

The final circle of netting was tight just behind the snake's head, and meant getting very close to the open mouth, but with Agnes holding the several feet of freed body I was able to snip the last of the nylon and pull it away. As if it had never been there, the reptile vanished. It moved so fast we didn't see it go, and had it not been for the aches and pains in our muscles, and the overpowering stench of the decomposing body, we might have thought we'd imagined the whole thing.

My first encounter with one of these snakes was when I had to move the electric fencing to a new area in Jean-Luc's field where the horses grazed. In the long dried grass, I saw what looked like a coiled hosepipe and went to take hold of it. In a blur, the coil transformed into a straight line measuring at least six feet and took off at high speed, whipping the long grass into waves as it went.

I wondered if I was hallucinating in the heat of a French summer, but after consulting *Reptiles and Amphibians of Europe* I learned that Western whip snakes are common throughout much of France, grow up to seven feet in length, and are non-venomous but if disturbed can be aggressive and will bite. It is best not to touch them unless you would like to be bitten. We have since seen many in our garden, but they are shy and generally rush away if you try to get close.

***

Tinkerbelle, bless her, was having trouble keeping up and it was time to bid her *adieu*. Dearly as I loved her, for all her crankiness, there were limits. Every so often, she'd give a rattling shudder and a tinkling sound as something fell out of her. Her ignition key had jammed in the lock and had to be drilled out, then replaced with a switch fitted to the steering column with some insulating tape. Only her left indicator worked, and the windscreen wipers didn't unless the indicator was on at the same time. Having to wear plastic bags to protect my feet from the rain that came in from the corroded bottom of the windscreen was not a sufficient reason to pension her off, even coupled with all the little unscheduled stops we made in strange and inconvenient places, or the loud and embarrassing grinding noise she emitted from time to time. The floor tile that covered the gaping hole in her chassis in front of the pedals could be slippery, but I had grown used to that. Her habit of spewing out her spark plugs periodically and unpredictably, sending them rocketing into the underside of bonnet, for which nobody could find the cause, was particularly alarming. The garage had warned that there was a likelihood of them ploughing through the bonnet, the windscreen and my head. There were the ominous little gurgles, squeals and small jets of steam escaping from under the bonnet, whereupon I would stroke the steering wheel and encourage her gently: 'Just a couple more miles, Tinkerbelle. We are almost home. Please don't collapse here, in this deserted lane, in the middle of nowhere, in rural France, at midnight.'

Our outings were becoming increasingly fraught. She had served well for nearly four years, like some bent and creaky-boned crone still faithfully caring for her employer, but she had earned her retirement as soon as we could scrape up sufficient funds to replace her.

When Terry rang to say he had found a car and it would be arriving within a couple of weeks, I passed the news to Tinkerbelle. She seemed to take on a new lease of life, behaving faultlessly, rolling smoothly and quietly, starting when asked and not making horrid smells with her brakes. It seemed that she was making one last appeal to keep her job, but she had a final trick up her sleeve.

In our local town there were traffic lights at the top of a steep hill, and we arrived as they turned red. This was always a blow as Tinkerbelle's handbrake had stopped working some while back, so she had to be held on the hill with one foot revving the accelerator to stop her stalling, and the other foot on the brake but ready at a moment's notice to switch to the clutch. It was at this awkward moment that her seat collapsed.

The seat of the 2CV is a primitive thing, a metal frame covered with a thick plastic material. Beneath the thick plastic material are some criss-crossed webbing straps attached to the frame by little clips. It is this webbing which provides the support for the driver's weight. When it ceases to do so, the driver finds themselves sitting in a hole on a piece of sagging plastic, with the top of their head level with the centre of the steering wheel.

This is not a satisfactory driving position. You cannot see out of the windscreen for a start, which is generally a bad sign. As there is nothing to support your weight, you have to do so yourself with your legs, while simultaneously operating the pedals, so you are squatting like a horseless jockey, and juggling three pedals with two feet.

In what I regard as possibly my greatest achievement in a motor vehicle, I managed to pull away from the lights and into a slip road. I found a length of rope in the boot and wove it around the metal seat frame, then padded it with a couple of dog blankets from the back seat, driving home in more comfort than style, and parking Tinkerbelle to one side for the last time.

I advertised her for sale, and a Frenchman phoned to say he was interested.

'She's very old. Both her bodywork and her engine need a lot of work,' I told him. 'I don't want you to come all this way and be disappointed.'

He insisted he quite understood. He was a 2CV enthusiast and Tinkerbelle's condition was immaterial. He loved her even without seeing her. It was a brief love affair, because as soon as he arrived, he made most offensive remarks about her, kicked her tyres, mocked her red roof, rocked her from side to side and spat next to her. He offered me half of the pittance I was asking and stomped away with a muttered '*sale anglaise*' when I turned him down. Tinkerbelle remained on her tired axles until Carole B came to visit one day and offered to buy her for the boys to learn to drive. 'They'll love her,' she said, and I thought they probably would.

As I watched Carole winching her aboard the transporter, I felt rather weepy, having an urge to touch her and tell her that I still loved her. She had a lot of character, that little car, and we had shared some memorable adventures.

Shortly afterwards, Carole's business collapsed beneath the weight of French bureaucracy and taxes, and the bank took her house. She and her family moved away, so I lost a good friend, and my job.

Chapter Twenty-nine

We'd had Amy for a couple of years when, during her evening walk, she abruptly sat down and wouldn't go another step. Terry had to carry her, heavy lump that she was. Back home, she flopped into her bed and wouldn't move.

The following day she was still drained of energy, so I took her to the vet. He examined her with increasing furrows on his brow and said: 'She's diabetic.'

The insulin was expensive, and she would need a strict diet of freshly cooked meat and green beans. More expense!

She quickly recovered her bounciness, until a few months later, I found her crouched behind a pile of timber, in a pool of mud, cringing and shaking. I carried her to the house, where she started spinning around and around in circles, alternately yelping and barking.

I phoned the vet who was at lunch.

'Give her sugar, as much as you can get her to eat — it's a diabetic crisis — and bring her to the surgery at two o'clock.'

The sugar mixed with the strings of saliva pouring from her mouth, and her whole body became rigid. She insisted on sitting on my lap with her head hooked around my neck for the 15-mile journey to the vet. Her fat body made it all but impossible for me to operate the steering wheel or see where I was going. She barked and yelled increasingly loudly. By the time we reached the vet, I was soaked in copious floods of Amy's urine.

She was quickly hooked up to a transfusion while the vet examined her.

'In fact, this isn't a sugar problem. She's having a stroke. We'll keep her here tonight, and we will ring you tomorrow morning.'

Off she disappeared into a back room, and I thought we probably wouldn't see her again.

The vet rang the next morning. 'Your dog is fine: you may come and collect her when you like.'

She was proving to be a great survivor, although not quite the low-cost, minimum maintenance pet we had hoped for. With fresh meat, insulin, vet's fees, she was costing more than all the other animals put together.

About a year later, she started bumping into furniture, then running into walls. Her brown, limpid eyes were clouded over. She was blind. She had never conquered her fear, so even after three years of love and kindness, she was still terrified of any fast movement. Once she lost her sight, she lost this fear as she no longer saw anything to frighten her. She became more confident and could soon find her way around the house and garden. Her tail no longer stayed between her legs. She had found peace and started to enjoy long walks across the fields, galloping blindly along with the others and returning frequently to our sides to reassure herself that she wasn't lost. Her beautiful gentle blind eyes saw nothing, but with her ears listening for our voices, her nose following familiar scents, her feet kept to the paths she knew with her extraordinarily long tail wagging high behind her. Despite her massacre of the chickens, and the unwelcome expense of daily medication, she was a joy and an inspiration. As we followed her along the lanes and paths, she stopped from time to time to dig holes, pounce on mice or stand with her head tilted to one side to listen to things she could hear but couldn't see.

***

We had acquired a feral tabby cat that skulked around in the hedges and fields. Whenever we met, it crouched with back arched, ears flattened, green eyes glaring and lips drawn back to show its fangs. Its dislike of us did not discourage it from coming into the house at night and raiding the kitchen, spilling dishes and tearing open any packages it could reach. Our other cats loathed it so terrible fights broke out, accompanied by wailing and the sound of furniture being overturned.

Gradually, it insinuated itself into our life and became Tigger. He monopolised my lap and chased the dogs. The two other cats still hated him, but Tigger didn't care. His arrival made life difficult for Amy, who had adjusted to her sightless world, making her way confidently around the house and garden, wagging her tail a little ruefully when she bumped into a piece of furniture or a plant that had been moved from its usual position.

Tigger had quickly made friends with the dogs, planting himself in front of them to attract their attention. When he stood in front of Amy, she blundered straight into him and he responded by boxing her ears. As such, Amy lived in a state of puzzlement, wondering what it was that kept attacking her, and why. The cat soon seemed to understand that the collisions were caused by circumstances beyond Amy's control, and either got out of her way or simply accepted their intermittent impacts.

Tigger went off to the vet to be neutered, and when I went to collect him the receptionist was looking rather pale.

'Would you mind coming to help me take him, please? He is very vicious.'

When she had gone to remove him from the cage, he had attacked her so ferociously that she had to run out of the room and slam the door.

We went together to the room at the end of the corridor and looked through the window to where Tigger was sitting in the middle of the floor.

'Be careful,' said the receptionist.

I went into the room and Tigger ran to me, purring and wrapping his front legs around my neck.

'Ah, he is a one-woman cat,' she said.

He accepted Terry after a while, but never took to other people.

***

A few months after Terry's operations, my daughter Julie and granddaughter Catherine came to stay for a week, and we were having a barbecue lunch. I'd put bunches of rosemary and thyme over the coals where we were cooking fish. It didn't seem to be burning well, so I asked Terry to relight it. He sprinkled some barbecue lighter fluid onto the coals. There was a very loud bang; the plastic bottle exploded in his hands and erupted into a ball of fire. He was engulfed in flames from his head to his shoes, reeling around and burning.

He fell to the gravel and rolled around, but still he was on fire. Little Catherine was transfixed with horror. I turned the hosepipe on him and drenched him until the flames were out, then filled the bath with cold water. His shorts had melted to his legs, his shirt was burned away, his hair was burned and he had awful wounds on his shins. In the icy bath, the heat from the burns warmed the water, and we had to keep the cold tap running.

Somebody had told me that in France you cannot summon an ambulance, but must first call a doctor who will call the service if necessary. I calculated the time it would take to contact the doctor and for him to get to the house, so decided it would be quicker to drive directly to the hospital in Poitiers. I drove like the wind, screeching around corners, and rushed him into the emergency unit at the hospital. A nurse poured some colourless gel onto his shins, which gave instant relief. She admonished me for not calling an ambulance.

'They would have been able to help your husband far sooner. In future, whenever there is an accident, call them straight away.'

(To call an ambulance in France, the phone number is 15.)

Terry was admitted to the burns unit. The hospital staff, remembering him from his previous stay, welcomed him back cheerily. The surgeon who had operated on him came to visit and to check that he hadn't sustained any damage to his head when he fell. He spent two days in the hospital, undergoing an immensely painful treatment that involved having the burned flesh vigorously scrubbed with a hard linen cloth. This promotes clean and quick healing, which resulted in his wounds leaving almost no scarring at all. He and Julie had to return to England two days later, so the hospital discharged him with sufficient medication to cope with a national emergency, including lotions, creams, bandages, tablets and *tulle grasse*, a large gauze pad smothered with a thick layer of some kind of grease like petroleum jelly. It can be applied directly to wounds to protect them without sticking.

It was not long afterwards that M. Meneteau arrived at the gate one day, limping badly. I asked him what had happened, and he replied that when he was washing out the wooden barrels in which he made his wine, he had accidentally tipped a bucket of scalding water and caustic soda into his boot. He raised his trouser leg to reveal the most terrible burns and sores all down his shin and ankle. What did I think he ought to do?

I had some of the dressings that Terry hadn't used, so I gave them to him and suggested he took them home, asking his wife to disinfect the wounds and cover them with the *tulle grasse*, then go to see the doctor as soon as possible. Later that afternoon, I went to ask how he was.

'Oh, he's fine.' Mme Meneteau smiled. 'The doctor said that the *tulle grasse* was exactly the right thing to do.'

It's a very useful thing to keep in the house. You never know when you might need some.

The hospital seemed to exert a magnetic force over Terry, because it wasn't long before he fell off a ladder while doing some repairs to a wall, cracked his ribs on a beam and was admitted to hospital with a suspected ruptured spleen. Fortunately, that was a false alarm and he was discharged the next day, remarking that he would have been happy to stay for dinner that night, as the menu included a choice of either red or white wine.

***

Having checked out the hospitals and vets, I moved on to the doctors. In French farces, the doctor is usually either mad or incompetent and always prescribes suppositories no matter what the ailment. As such, I'd been worried about finding a doctor, and in particular one who wouldn't prescribe suppositories for everything from tuberculosis to a hangnail.

Carole B recommended a surgery five miles away, where there were two doctors to choose from and a little timetable to learn. Each doctor was available by appointment only on certain days, alternating mornings and afternoons, and not at all on Thursdays. The rest of the time they saw patients on a first-come, first-served basis.

Our doctor spoke perfect English, which was a great benefit for those British who could not speak French, so he was extremely popular. A big man, with thinning sandy hair, blue eyes and a manner that was mostly avuncular with a hint of rakishness, he dressed casually and smoked heavily, although not in front of his patients. On the day I went into his office and noticed the absence of the familiar smell, I asked, 'Have you given up smoking at last?'

'Yes,' he sighed. 'I've given up. If I didn't, I would die. Like a rat.'

He always came personally into the waiting room to usher in his next patient, shaking hands and enquiring after family and neighbours. Despite his heavy work load – his day didn't end until he had finished his house visits late into the evening – he always had time to discuss politics, the weather, his holidays, food and wine, mutual friends. An appointment with him was always a sociable and enjoyable event. He was also an extremely good doctor who looked after us for many years.

With the hospital, doctors and vet all proving themselves, there was only one thing left to check out: the dentist. Each morning, I wake up terrified that I might have a cavity, or a broken tooth. Sure enough, one morning as I brushed my teeth, a large filling fell out. A French friend recommended a dental surgery in a small village nearby.

'He is very kind, and efficient,' they said. Yes, but would he have the necessary temperament and skills to deal with an Englishwoman who was frightened out of her wits?

I set off in tears, and twenty minutes later, lay on a leather couch watching downhill ski racing on a television mounted in the ceiling. Hardly aware of the fingers and hardware filling my mouth, I was still awaiting the moment of agony when something would hit a nerve. The dentist was young, startlingly handsome – and clucked disapprovingly: 'English dentists. I can always tell. Not good at all.'

As I looked into his large brown eyes, his gentle, seductive voice said I needed two fillings, and could he do them straight away? I nodded feebly and braced myself for the worst.

He sprayed something on my gums, waited a minute, injected a local anaesthetic. So far, I had felt nothing at all. Was I comfortable, he asked? I nodded, waiting for the pain that I knew would come. He reached for the drill 'just to clean out the cavity' he explained, and I clutched at the arms of the couch, sweat pouring down my hands and running to my elbows. There was a distant purring noise, while I focused on those gorgeous brown eyes, like pools of dark chocolate ganache. Every two or three minutes, my man asked whether I was comfortable, whether he could carry on, and I gazed back adoringly as he pouted a small sad smile.

'*Et voila, c'est fait.*' he murmured.

And so it was. Really, I hadn't felt a thing. He liked a little joke sometimes. Knowing that each visit was still an ordeal for me, he might show me Polaroid photographs of the bloody gums of a previous patient who had just had all her teeth extracted, and wait to see if I'd fall to the floor. At least I could drive to appointments without crying any more.

Chapter Thirty

During the summer, the parrots stayed in the garden during the day, sheltering from the sun beneath the vines. I often found Rafiki, our African grey parrot exploring the garden, having managed to open her cage. She was always happy to climb upon my hand and return to her cage, until the day when she panicked as a door slammed, and flapped her way into the hedge. From there, she hopped into a plum tree and began scrambling further away, examining the tree bark and leaves whilst whistling and chattering to herself. I scrambled after her over hedges and wire fences, but she kept on going until I lost sight of her as she found her wings and flew away.

For three days I hunted, called, shook tins of food. I put the other parrot cage in the garden and played the radio. Several times, Bill said he had seen her, that she was in a tree or on a roof, but every time it turned out to be a pigeon.

I was devastated and resigned to having lost her for good.

On the fourth day, the phone rang. It was dear old Madame Grimaud.

'Madame, your parrot is in my garden!'

'Are you *sure* it's my parrot, madame?' I didn't want to raise my hopes and be disappointed again.

'Yes. Absolutely. I heard it talking a little while ago. It's speaking English!'

Rafiki was sitting in a walnut tree, surrounded by amused French people, waiting for somebody to bring her something to eat and drink. Bred and raised in captivity, she had no idea how to fend for herself.

'Hello!' she chirped when she saw Terry, sidling down the branch and onto his arm.

She was none the worse for wear, but hungry and slightly dehydrated. With foxes, martens and buzzards in the area, she was lucky to have survived in the wild for so long.

Her companion Cervantes, an orange-winged Amazon parrot, was usually no trouble, being content to sit in or on his cage watching the world go by or playing with his toys. Unlike Rafiki, he was a bird who'd been captured in the wild and had never forgotten or forgiven man's hatefulness. We bought him as a companion for Rafiki, but unfortunately she despised him; he was very sociable with other birds, but if he tried to befriend Rafiki, she attacked him.

At night, the parrots came out of their cages inside the house. After a long period of insomnia, I took two strong sleeping tablets. I'd been unable to get Cervantes back into his cage before I went to bed, then around midnight, I was dragged from my slumbers by mad squawking and the sound of things crashing about. For some reason, he was flying around in the dark, had managed to knock over all sorts of ornaments and ended up on top of the computer with one claw trapped in the casing. It took fifteen minutes to release him, holding his beak at bay with a wooden spoon with one hand and working his claw free with the other. He flew away growling, and I went back to bed. At 5.30am there were more crashings and bangings, squawkings and yelpings. He was sitting on the head of one of the dogs, both of them looking equally startled. It took a broom, a towel and an hour-long struggle to get him back into his cage.

Cervantes craved companionship, and he was never going to find it with Rafiki, so I found a parrot sanctuary near Paris who agreed to take him.

We drove up there with him in a cat basket. The sanctuary occupied the ground floor of a large house. It was filled with parrots, both in and out of immaculately clean, very large cages. They were singing, whistling, chattering, clambering on cage tops and swinging on toys. What was so noticeable about the noise was that it was happy. When parrots are stressed they growl and squawk, but these birds were behaving as if they were having a party. I asked how many parrots were there.

'At the moment, we have one hundred. We work with the police, customs and veterinary services. Some of the birds have been confiscated from people importing them illegally, others removed from their owners because of ill-treatment, and some are found in the wild, lost, with no identification. They will all stay with us permanently. We do not breed, nor do we rehome. At the moment, we are extending the premises because there are always more parrots in need.'

Every bird was let out daily, was fed its own specific diet from the best fruit and vegetables, and was entertained to ensure that its life in captivity was the very best that it could be.

Above the noise was one distinctive repeated cry. From the cat box, Cervantes replied.

The lady who ran the sanctuary led us to a large cage, and inside it was a female orange-winged Amazon. We moved Cervantes into his new cage and set it down next to the female. It was love at first sight, the two birds chattering and posturing to each other.

'This is perfect,' said the lady. 'The only two of this species here, and they have bonded immediately. I shall keep their cages next to each other for a couple of weeks so that they get to know each other, and then I'll start letting them out. The female always shares my breakfast with me here,' she pointed to a small table nearby.

I phoned a month later and learned that Cervantes had found true love at last, and the two birds were sharing a cage. Isn't that a happy story?

***

When we bought the house, the garden and field were kept in pristine condition by M. Royer's five sheep. If I had known then what I know now, I would have asked to buy them together with the house. Those sheep spent their time methodically chewing and munching everything in their path, like living lawnmowers.

For somebody who is neither a gifted nor particularly enthusiastic gardener, it was a mistake to begin digging flowerbeds and planning a vegetable garden. I had no idea at the time how quickly things grew in this fertile soil, nor how sizzlingly hot it could be in summer. Having bought the regulation red geraniums – everybody has red geraniums – I would spend the following weeks watering them twice a day to stop them shrivelling up as the temperature climbed into the mid-40s.

I admired Madame Grimaud's forsythia. The next day, she gave me some cuttings and some small rhus trees. Gloria gave me seeds of something she didn't know the name of, but which smelled nice and could have taught William the Conqueror about invasion. M. Royer gave me some artichoke plants, and an English woman gave me 60 hibiscus seedlings.

Each gift entailed hacking out a hole for it, in the rock-ridden, sun-baked soil. These plants all needed watering, pruning and transplanting, spraying against pests and diseases, protecting from the sun, frost and the creatures that dug them up or ate them. It was a full-time job for somebody who already had a full-time job dealing with the animals and the needs of her English neighbours. The old English woman who had invited me to use her shower and then complained when I did, phoned to say she had several hundred mixed bulbs for me so that I could build a flowery bank in the garden.

After a heavy rainfall, at night, battalions of snails decimated just about everything I tried to grow. Madame Grimaud hunted them, popping them into a flowerpot, showing me which were worth harvesting, and which were too small. I helped her, feeling guilty each time I plucked another podgy snail from where it was cowering beneath a leaf, and apologising as I popped them into the flowerpot. They do have quite cute little faces, but there were so many!

After a night of hunting them by torchlight, I delivered bags to Madame Meneteau and Madame Grimaud. Don't tell anybody, they warned – it's against the law to hunt them at night, and out of season. Who knew!

As a non-meat eater, I don't eat snails, but I'm very happy dipping chunks of baguette into a pool of butter, garlic and parsley.

Sometimes when I was walking the dogs, we met Madame Meneteau collecting dandelions for her rabbits, or fallen beads of maize left after harvesting for her poultry. Nothing went to waste. When I grumbled about stinging nettles to a farmer, he said: 'Nettles are useful. When you plant your tomatoes, dig a trench and fill it with nettles. They provide fertiliser and prevent disease. Plant the tomato seedlings very deep, right up to their necks, so that the stalks produce plenty of roots to keep the plants stable.'

Maybe our French neighbours thought us strange: we kept horses we didn't ride, gun dogs though we didn't hunt, and I only used my gun for target shooting. Sometimes they had a laugh at my expense. In the days when I had thought it was possible to have a vegetable garden and five dogs, I bought a box of seed potatoes. I hoed a bed for them and planted them in rows. My gardening reference was a small book that had cost 45 pence in the early 1970s, entitled Adam the Gardener. The potato-growing instructions were straightforward: you stuck them in the ground, waiting for the green bits to grow and produce flowers. Once the flowers had withered and died, you dug up your potatoes. Simple.

The green bits on our potatoes flourished, but they didn't produce any flowers, even after the things had been in the ground for several months. One day, I asked M Meneteau if he could come to hold one of the horses while I injected it. Afterwards he pointed to our potato patch, asking when I was going to dig them up. I explained that the flowers hadn't arrived yet, and he looked at me a little strangely. 'What flowers?' he asked. I told him about the little book and how Adam said you had to wait for the flowers to bloom and die. His shoulders shook a little, and his eyes filled with tears as he started to laugh.

'They don't all produce flowers!' he spluttered. 'If you don't dig them up soon, they'll be as big as footballs. I dug mine up six weeks ago!'

How stupid of Adam not to have explained properly. I got the fork out, poked around in the ground, and was rewarded with a large crop of very fine potatoes. They tasted delicious and were so big that one was sufficient for two people.

M. Royer kept his sheep – the ones that had previously maintained our land so well – in the field next to ours, which they shared with Mme Grimaud's hens. One evening, I noticed one of the sheep lying in the wet grass, moaning, with the others standing at a distance watching it. It seemed distressed, so I thought I should tell M. Royer. I knew the neighbours thought I was soft in the head where animals were concerned, but anyway, I banged on his front door and interrupted his supper, saying one of his sheep didn't look at all well. He took off his slippers and pulled on his boots, then we walked down to the field. By the time we arrived, the animal was standing up, munching grass and looking perfectly normal. I apologised for having disturbed his meal, and was feeling rather stupid when he smiled (he was a very shy man but when he smiled, it was like watching the sun come out) and pointed: 'Look!'

In the grass, a newborn lamb was struggling to its feet.

'It's a good thing you came for me – it's too cold for it to be out tonight. I'll get them into the barn. I didn't know she was having a lamb. Thank you for telling me.'

I blessed the sheep for giving me an opportunity to make a neighbourly gesture, and for enabling me to enjoy the longest conversation I'd so far had with M. Royer.

When Jean-Luc came and said he was going away for a long weekend, and asked whether I could feed his dog, I was so pleased to be asked I almost burst into tears. Whilst out shopping, I recognised more and more local people who waved and chatted. I started to feel we were beginning to belong, although the sheep whose domain our garden had previously been still glared through the fence with undisguised indignation as we walked where they once had, bleating: *Go home, get off our land, stupid English people and their dogs!*

Chapter Thirty-one

Gloria decided to move with her dogs from Spain to live here permanently. Their property was still uninhabitable. Bags of cement, ladders, timbers, plaster-boards and sanitary fittings formed an obstacle course stretching as far as the eye could see. Electric wires poked out and dangled at face-height, so she and Bill were still living in one of the caravans at the back of the barn, and the dogs lived in another.

The two Great Danes were ageing, and their health deteriorating. One of the symptoms of their illness – Leishmaniasis, or sand fly disease – was terrible nosebleeds. The vet had given Gloria some powder to staunch these haemorrhages before she went on a visit to England, leaving Bill in charge.

The phone rang one night just after midnight, as it so often did. It was Bill who had finally succumbed to installing his own telephone.

'Lolly's having a nosebleed. Can you come?'

The room looked like the aftermath of the *Texas Chainsaw Massacre*, the blood was still pumping fast and Bill couldn't remember where Gloria had left the powder.

We searched in vain, and still the blood poured. I couldn't find any cotton wool, so as a last resort, I took a broom handle. I collected up the cobwebs, until I had a small wad, which we pressed to the nose until the flow finally stopped.

***

A few nights later, the phone rang again just after midnight, but had stopped by the time I reached it. I waited for ten minutes in case it rang again, and then went back to bed.

Next morning, Bill said: 'I rang you last night, before I realised how late it was.'

I asked why he had called.

'Well, I'd papered the hallway, and it looked right nice at first, then all these little bumps and bubbles started coming up. I was going to ask you if you thought they'd go down if I stuck pins in them, but as it was so late I peeled the paper off and saved it. Now I'm going to put lining paper on first, and stick it all back on again.' And he did.

I've never met anybody who was so meticulous and patient. If something of mine broke down, he would willingly drop whatever else he was doing and spend hours dismantling it and trying to get it to work. Mostly it didn't, but it wasn't because Bill didn't try hard enough. If only he would have devoted the same effort to tidying up the bags, sacks, boxes, cartons, vehicles, rolls of pipe, weeds, stone fountains, garden furniture and caravans covered in green algae.

Despite the mess all round her, Gloria was a cheerful soul, happiest when she was floating on an inflatable bed in her plastic swimming pool, in the sun, with a book, a cigarette and her dogs lying nearby. Her other pleasure was her garden – with her green fingers she could make anything grow, even if she didn't know what it was, and of course, she could bring back to life the plants that Bill killed. When she mowed the lawn, she did it in the altogether, and in times of crisis she changed her hair colour or style.

She was like a champagne bottle shaken before opening, and bubbling over with fun. I think the reason we got on so well is that we both had an odd sense of humour, and we laughed nearly all the time we were together.

One day Fred arrived, brandishing something small in his hand.

'It's me toenail – it's come off!' he exclaimed. We both stared in dismay at the thing in his hand.

'Will you stick it back on for me?' he said in my direction.

I have a very weak disposition and faint at the mere sight of wobbly teeth: detached toenails are right out of my league. Quick as a wink and disregarding her glare, I replied: 'Gloria's the one for that. She's more of a nurse than I am.'

From long experience of Fred, I knew there was no point telling him that once toenails have fallen off they can't be stuck back on. As he turned towards her with his offering, I beat a hasty retreat. She called out: 'I'll see you later,' in a tone that was half laugh, half threat. I sprinted home laughing. Later, I asked her how she had managed.

'I got a big wad of cotton wool and shoved it on while he put the toenail in place. Then I quickly wrapped some plaster round it. I don't even know if the toenail was still there or not. It might have fallen off into the grass.'

***

As the opening hours of the post office in Saint-Thomas-le-Petit were erratic, I began going to La Petite-Eglise which was only a couple of miles in the opposite direction, where I could open a new bank account after falling out with my previous bank. The post mistress was slim and very attractive, with dark, wavy, shoulder-length hair and a splatter of freckles. She had two young sons of eight and ten, she collected teapots, snowmen and Father Christmases, and she was a gifted artist producing beautiful animal portraits and scenery. She was also an Anglophile who spoke almost perfect English, always asking whether anybody coming from England would bring her crumpets, custard powder and jelly.

The first time I met her, I was swaddled in thick clothes, because winter had arrived and we still had no adequate heating. We had the wood burner in the living room, but the rest of the house was bitterly cold. I looked like the Michelin tyre man. It took less than ten minutes to open an account, then we chatted. She asked where I lived, how long I'd been here and how I was finding life in France. I said jokingly that it was much colder than I had anticipated, having been told that the climate was always mild south of Loire.

'Come and eat with us tonight,' she said. 'Our house is nice and warm.'

Her name was Agnès, and we became instant friends. I now had two close friends called Carole, and two more called Agnès. How weird was that?

From Agnès, I learned some quaint French. Somebody who isn't quite all there has 'a spider on the ceiling', or 'a little bicycle going around in his head'.

Shortly after I met her, she invited us to an 'evening of friendship' at her home, from 7.30pm onwards. Unfortunately, Terry could not be here, and on that particular evening I wasn't feeling very well. I would have liked to go to bed with a hot water bottle, but as she had been kind enough to invite us to her friendship evening I felt I should make an effort. I calculated that if I arrived at 8.30pm by 10.00pm I could politely take my leave. Setting off with only a sketchy idea of where to go, I spent forty minutes driving around spidery lanes in the approaching dark,

180

tempted to go back home. I stopped to ask for directions at a small bar where the customers were in various stages of intoxication, so I had difficulty trying to explain myself, as they shouted and laughed and beckoned me to join them. When I had made them understand I was trying to find the hamlet where Agnès lived, three of them staggered up and pointed in three entirely different directions, bellowing and emitting alcoholic fumes. I focused on the one who was staggering the least, repeating the name of the place I was looking for. He pointed twice in the same direction, so taking that as confirmation I set off and duly arrived just before 9.00pm.

I was aghast to find a crowd of forty people in the courtyard, all French, none of whom I knew, and Agnès waving me into their bosom, saying gaily: 'Good! Now Susie has arrived, so we will eat.'

This was not the casual gathering I'd imagined, but a formal sit-down dinner, a banquet held in a rustic barn decorated with flowers and paintings. Over the next three hours, we ate through plate after plate of fragrant melon, stuffed eggs, marinated vegetables, followed by a main dish of succulent chicken which I declined, but which came with assorted vegetables and a green salad. Next came creamy cheeses and crumbly cheeses, cheeses that smelt of hay and cheeses that smelt of old socks, blue cheeses, white cheeses, golden cheeses, and baskets of crusty bread.

Friends from the Gironde had brought the melons. 'They're the best melons.' The cheeses had come from friends in Normandy. 'The best cheeses!' Most of the vegetables Agnès had grown in her garden, the bread had come from the bakery that baked the best bread and the wine came from the vineyard of a close relative next door to Saint-Emilion.

All the other guests were family and old friends and I was flattered to be there with them. Although the wine flowed, people drank moderately, the barn was loud with animated talk and laughter, everybody was well-behaved. One old boy stood up and sang, slightly off-key, to kindly applause. The children entertained themselves.

By midnight, we had moved on to dessert – chocolate profiteroles, plum tart, apricot tart, strawberry tart when Agnès's two young sons clapped their hands loudly, shouting: 'Silence. The firework show is about to begin. Everybody outside.'

We trooped out into the courtyard where a group of small children were crouching around a heap of sand studded with fireworks.

'Everybody behind the stones. Nobody must step forward. This is dangerous.'

The elder boy indicated two rocks connecting an invisible line over which we must not step, and we obediently assembled behind it. A child struck a match, and nothing happened. The children examined the firework that hadn't gone off and applied another match to it. It went off this time, starting a colourful and noisy display that had been well put together. For the grand finale, they set off one of those powerful rockets that divides itself into several dozen howling, shrieking things that whirl in every direction. Either it had not been securely placed in the sand and it had moved, or else the young organisers wanted to have a laugh because when it was lit, it shot directly towards the spectators – still standing behind the invisible safety line – at knee-height at about a hundred and fifty miles an hour. Despite our heavy payload of food and drink, we all managed to leap to safety, albeit with little dignity as we clung to and collided with each other.

Back at the table, it was time for coffee, with chocolates, followed by the *pousse-café* – the 'coffee pusher', a small cognac or Calvados, which was naturally the best cognac and the best Calvados. When I made my way home at half past midnight, everybody else was revving up to dance till dawn.

Chapter Thirty-two

The British colony grew. As members of the European Union, we had the automatic right to move and live here. The region was still inexpensive compared to the better-known and more popular parts of *la belle France*. Many visiting friends and family succumbed to the peacefulness and simple charm of the area: the gentle rolling hills, wooded valleys, abundance of ancient buildings, and the feeling that the march of time had bypassed the place fifty years previously. As more English estate agents set up shop, property prices exploded and old houses became scarce. Unlike those of us who had come here with nothing, newcomers were able to take advantage of soaring house prices in Britain and a great exchange rate to sell up, arriving with thick wallets, thus enabling them to employ artisans to renovate property to a high standard as if money was no object. There were ever more British-registered luxury cars on the roads and more English-speaking voices in the shops and restaurants. Local businesses thrived. Builders' merchants and supermarkets expanded, British foods began to appear on restaurant menus – *le fish and chips* and *le crumble* were particularly popular. British products took up increasing space on supermarket shelves.

The Anglophone community created their own social clubs, amateur dramatics groups, Scrabble tournaments, pubs and restaurants. People asked if I thought the French resented the British who were, as one French gentleman said, invading the area. If they did, they were too courteous to show it openly, although occasionally I heard local people lamenting that there were more foreigners in their village than French, and young French couples found themselves priced out of the market.

Many said they were pleased to see the local economy booming and old houses being renovated that would have otherwise become ruins, and hamlets that would have become deserted being restored to life. French people had little use for collapsing old farmhouses. They were bemused and puzzled why the English were prepared to spend huge amounts of money buying them, further fortunes on making them habitable, when for a great deal less, they could have bought a nice, comfortable modern house.

A jovial Frenchman I was talking to one day confided that he much preferred English neighbours to Parisians, who seemed to be universally disliked.

Not everybody who moved here settled happily ever after. Once the initial euphoria faded some found the endless peace and quiet they had thought they wanted was too endlessly peaceful and quiet, so after a few months they were bored. Others had over-optimistic expectations of the weather, or under-estimated the cost of living or ease of integrating into a foreign country. There were people who found that country life didn't suit them. They didn't like the gorgeous agricultural pongs that reeked off the fields, or the clods of tractor-borne dirt shed outside their houses. They didn't like the lowing of the cattle, or the bleating of the sheep, or the crowing of the cockerels, or the fact that their neighbours were all farmers and only talked about farming. Some missed their families and friends in England. Others missed being close to theatres and museums. The odd person here and there even found that they didn't like the French, the 'smell of garlic everywhere' (yes, really!) or couldn't cope with French bureaucracy. A few didn't like the fact that there was a British community already here (yes, really!) They hadn't come to live in France to find themselves living next door to their compatriots. Most people made some effort to learn the language, but there were some who had no intention of doing so, on the basis that they 'couldn't get their tongues round it', or were 'too old to learn new tricks', although all of them peppered their conversations with '*boulangerie*', '*gendarme*' and '*baguette*'. Everybody could manage those three words. I felt that if they made a point of learning one simple word each week, by the end of the year they'd know fifty-five words instead of only three.

Those who made France their permanent home integrated to different degrees: some surrounded themselves exclusively with other English; some like us were equally at home with French or English, and others immersed themselves totally in French life, joining all the local activities and becoming involved in all aspects of their communities, even if they couldn't speak the language. They followed the fortunes of the local football team, played mysterious card games they didn't understand, and bought tickets to the village entertainments; there were people who steadfastly refused to have any contact at all with other British.

Not all those who emigrated to France did so for love of the country. Some admitted they were only there because they couldn't stand living in England any more, chiefly because there were too many immigrants there who couldn't speak English. They were the ones who were critical of the French, and demanded that their local mayors should learn to speak English. This attitude sent shivers up the spines of those of us who loved the country and its people just as they were. We feared that if it continued, the French may start to lose their tolerance towards us. When we met our English friends, we lamented the fact that more English were moving into the area. Often the new arrivals became new friends, and soon they too would be sighing and saying: 'The house next to ours has just been sold to Brits,' and we'd all commiserate.

Chapter Thirty-three

Gloria's heart was in England; life here was too quiet for her bubbly nature, and she missed her children and grandchildren.

'Once the boys have gone,' she said, referring to the dogs, 'I'll go back.'

Because of the dogs, she and Bill always took it in turns to go to England. However, this time they were going together. Fred Bear and his little wife were coming to look after the dogs for five days until Bill returned. Gloria was staying on for a holiday in England.

They were ready to leave, but had to wait for somebody who was going to hire one of their vehicles to come and collect it. When he turned up, Gloria came around and beckoned me.

'Come and have a look at this! Quite a tasty number, the chap who's hired our truck,' she said.

He was a little too tanned, a little too white-toothed, a little too smooth and a little bit too pleased with himself for my taste. He wore tight jeans and a shirt open to his navel, showing a bronzed chest and a thick gold chain. As soon as he had driven away, Bill and Gloria left, she snapping and snarling at him in her normal half-serious, half-joking way, he murmuring under his breath and rolling his eyes.

I decided to have a laugh at Fred's expense. When he wasn't obsessing about money, he had a certain charm and sense of humour that I enjoyed, and he had a kind heart. Somehow our relationship had survived him insisting on lending me money and then panicking that I wouldn't repay it; asking me to keep a sum of money safe for him while he was away, and phoning up to say he was sure I'd stolen it. I'd eaten some splendid meals at their house, and been told that they were down-payments against future favours he would ask of me. He had removed the light from the interior of their refrigerator, and one evening when several of us were eating there, he retired early to bed having removed all but one of the overhead light bulbs.

In the evening after Bill and Gloria had left, I went around to the mouldy caravan where he and his wife were sleeping and knocked on the door. When Fred opened it, I said: 'Bill has just phoned to say the horse is arriving tomorrow, and you need to get a stable ready for it.'

Bill had several times in the past mentioned that he was thinking of having a horse.

Fred's eyes bulged as he said: 'What bloody horse? He didn't say anything about a horse.'

'He said you knew. He told you it may be arriving before he was back, and you would know what to do.'

'I don't know anything about horses!'

'Well, you need to clear out one of the barns, and put in some buckets of water and a bowl for its food. I can let you have some bales of straw and hay to keep you going.'

'I'm not looking after a horse.'

'It's only for a few days. You'll have to. It can't just stand in the drive until he comes back. Plus, you'll need to make some kind of a fence so that it can go out during the day.'

He was crimson in the face and speechless with rage, his hands formed into fists that he was shaking around his ears.

I said: 'You've got plenty of time. It won't arrive until late tomorrow afternoon. The transport company are going to ring when they're almost here, and I'll come to give you a hand unloading it and getting it into the stable. Come over in the morning and pick up the straw and hay. I'll bring you a couple of buckets of feed to keep it going until you can buy some.'

He said that I'd have to take the horse, as I had the place for it, but I replied that you can't introduce a strange horse to others who might injure it, as it was apparently a valuable racehorse. It couldn't come to me.

Leaving him jumping up and down and swearing, I trotted home laughing.

Next morning, he was banging at my door just after sunrise.

'I've been awake all night. We can't look after a horse. I said we'd keep an eye on the dogs, and that's all. Ring Bill and tell him to stop the horse coming.'

'I can't phone Bill, I don't know how to contact him in England, and the horse is already on the way. It will be here in a few hours. Don't worry, I'll help you with it. You just get the stable ready, and get some fencing put up in the field.'

187

He stamped away cursing Bill. I called after him to remind him to help himself to hay and straw, then I sat down and laughed until it hurt.

Throughout the morning and early afternoon, I kept going around and updating him on the impending arrival, advising him how to convert a barn full of junk into a stable, using bits of furniture and old bed frames to make fencing. He became more and more agitated and angry.

By mid-afternoon, he was talking of going back to his own house and leaving the dogs to look after themselves.

I said: 'You'll probably find that you really like looking after horses once you've been doing it for a couple of days. Bill says that Hercules is very gentle even though he's so big. You don't need to be afraid of him.'

I let him shout and stamp his feet and hurl furniture around for ten minutes before I tapped him on the shoulder.

'Fred,' I said. 'Have you ever been had?'

He spluttered, coughed, glared at me, then sat on the ground and roared with laughter.

'You wicked bitch!' he said.

***

Next day, Terry and I set off on a sunny afternoon to go to town to do what the French call 'window licking' – window shopping. There was a car parked at the end of our lane where it joined the road. As we approached, out stepped two men wearing armbands, raising their hands in the air, signalling us to stop.

'Uh oh! Cycle race going through,' I said. During the summer when cycle races were a daily event, it was normal for traffic to be held up or rerouted while the cyclists passed. The armbands walked towards the car, one on each side, and one leaned in on my side.

'*Bonjour*,' I said politely.

'Your papers, please, madame.'

I'd never known cycle marshals asking for motorists' papers.

'Is this normal?' I asked.

'Perfectly normal, madame. It's part of our job. Please step out of the car.'

'What's happening?' asked Terry.

'They want our papers, and we've got to get out of the car.'

We climbed out and handed over the car documents. From our

house, our dogs could hear our voices and were barking madly.

'I'm going to put our dogs away before the noise disturbs our neighbours,' I told one of the armbands.

'Do not move. Stay where you are. Your passports, please.'

Terry handed over his, but mine was in the house.

'Where do you live?'

'Just there.' I pointed to our house. They flicked through Terry's passport.

'You are not Mr Smith then?'

'No,' replied Terry.

I noticed then that the armbands had '*Douane*' printed on them. They were Customs officers.

'Oh God, this has to be something to do with Bill,' I muttered to Terry.

One of the armbands took out a mobile phone and made a call.

'You are to come with us. Please follow in your car.'

'Where are we going?'

'Just to the village. Please follow.'

We set off behind them. After a couple of hundred yards, they pulled over to the side of the road as a police car coming in the opposite direction flashed its lights at them and came to a halt. We all turned around and followed the second car a mile in the opposite direction, until they pulled into a field. The second car disgorged three policemen with guns on their hips and handcuffs hanging from their belts. Two more cars arrived, with more policemen spilling out into the field. I started to feel frightened. Another car arrived and its passenger walked over to us, holding out his hand.

'Good afternoon. I'm sorry you are being bothered. I am a judicial policeman and I'm here to ensure that the police and customs officers carry out their duties in the correct manner.'

'Could you please tell us exactly what this is all about?'

'No, I'm sorry, but we are going to search Mr Smith's house. Is there anybody there?'

'Yes, some English people are looking after the house.'

'Do they speak French?'

'No.'

'Then in that case, madame, I have to ask you to act as interpreter. The law requires that these people can understand what we are saying.

Please will you follow us.'

Back we went, now a convoy of six cars, sweeping into the hamlet and stopping outside Bill's barn, to the great interest of the other inhabitants. Fred and his wife were standing in the space where there would have been a front door if Bill had ever got around to putting one in.

'What the hell's going on?' asked Fred.

'They're cops and customs officers, and they're going to search the house.'

Fred was simultaneously furious, excited, and certain that Bill had done something wrong.

'He's been up to something. I know he has.'

'We don't know that yet,' I said.

A seventh car arrived bearing two more policemen and a German shepherd dog. They set about exploring the barns and the skeleton of the house, pointing at the bare dangling wires, the dusty furniture, a pile of ancient records. The dog showed no interest in any of it.

'How long has the septic tank been here?' asked one of the officers, pointing to the open channel that carried effluent to said tank.

'About two months,' I replied. *Oh no, please don't say they're going to open it up.*

The officers conferred for a few minutes and said: 'OK. We've finished here. Do you please have a table where we can fill out our report?'

While they had been searching, they had also been checking our passports on their computer. Terry had been heroically making tea and coffee for our fourteen new friends. It was quite a task as we only had six mugs, and the instant coffee offerings didn't seem to go down very well.

Eight of them filed into our living room, installed themselves at a table and started putting together their report. We weren't meant to know what was going on, but it was impossible not to pick up the frequent use of the words '*drogues*', 'cannabis', 'Dieppe' and 'Smith'. While several of them made verbal contributions, one of them tapped away at his computer, and two others wandered casually around the downstairs of the house, glancing about. It took them over two hours to complete the report to their satisfaction, then it had to be read aloud to ourselves and to Fred and his wife, while I translated. When we got to the nitty-gritty, we learned that the truck Bill had rented out had been searched at Dieppe. There was half a ton of cannabis aboard.

Fred seemed undecided as to whether to be angry or pleased at this revelation. I said: 'Let's wait and see what happens. Gloria and Bill weren't even in the vehicle.'

As far as Fred was concerned, that was proof in itself. The eleven officials in our living room with their handcuffs and guns watched this exchange with polite interest, then took their leave with much hand-shaking.

Terry and I resumed our trip to town, while the news snaked through the local English community. It was the hot topic until the next morning when we all awoke to the news that Princess Diana had been killed, which overshadowed all other events for the following week.

When Gloria phoned to say that Bill's solicitor had advised him not to return to France, Fred worked himself into a fit of rage.

'If they think we're staying in this hovel looking after their bloody dogs, they've got another think coming!' He was afraid that he'd have to buy the dog food when it ran out. 'I'm not bloody buying it. When it runs out, that's it. They can bloody starve. They said they'd be gone for five days, and we're not staying a minute longer.'

Gloria returned the following weekend, looking worn and bewildered. She took the dogs and went back to Spain.

Although everybody forecast that as soon as he returned to France, Bill would be arrested, much to my surprise he arrived a couple of months later. He said he had been cleared of any involvement with the drugs and was just getting on with life as before. He started coming and going freely, and nobody arrested him. Gloria returned and things became as normal as they ever did in their household. Bill worked on the house; he'd put a staircase in by now and was laying some floorboards when he dropped a hammer on Gloria's head. They settled back into their own tumultuous concept of married life.

Chapter Thirty-four

An English couple moved into a hamlet a mile away. Bill had encouraged them to move here from Spain and brought all their belongings. They weren't very happy with him, because he'd come by a steam cleaner and decided to steam clean all their belongings, including oriental rugs, a three-piece suite and an antique grandfather clock that had stopped working since its treatment.

The poor man fell ill and died very soon after their arrival, leaving a petite fluttery widow known as Princess Tippy Toes, who was always perfectly made up and carefully dressed, quite out of place here in the backwoods.

A week or so after the funeral, quite late one night – *why did calls always come late at night?* – the dead man's son phoned to say his mother was distraught. She had climbed out of the bathroom window and disappeared into the night, dressed in lightweight clothing with no coat. The neighbours had been searching all the local barns, stables and frosty fields, but there was no sign. He was worried out of his mind, and could I suggest anything. I couldn't, apart from summoning the police which somebody had already done, so I went back to bed. The countryside is a whole lot of space dotted with little copses, hamlets and farmyards: impossible to even know where to begin to look for a missing person. I didn't feel I could be of any use, but as it turned out, it seemed I could.

I don't know how much later it was when I heard male voices calling my name and banging on the patio doors that we had fitted to the barn to replace the ineffective plastic sheeting. It was late November, so I was dressed in standard winter nightwear: an odd assortment of long johns, mountaineering socks, a little woolly hat and several jumpers. I descended the stairs and found, standing at the door, our youngest and most attractive neighbour Jean-Luc with his dazzlingly handsome friend, supporting between them a sobbing little bundle that they had found staggering down the road, asking for me. The panic was over, but I didn't feel I'd been seen at my best.

Princess Tippy Toes was very cold, and she was very, very drunk. She alternated between crying, clinging to me and shouting about her son. They had had a terrible row and she was never going to speak to him again. She became hysterical when I phoned to let him know she was safe, and he said he would come to collect her. She screamed and yelled, so I said she had better stay the night and I would take her home in the morning.

I made her a cup of cocoa, wrapped the cleanest of the dog blankets around her, and tucked her up on the settee.

For someone who had lived her married life wrapped in conjugal cotton wool, as she had, the change in her circumstances came very hard. Living in the French countryside can be bliss, but it can be hell too: on icy winter days, logs need cutting and splitting, lugging into the house, and jamming into the fire. Every crack and crevice of old buildings sucks out whatever warmth you are able to generate, replacing it with icy draughts. Chimneys get blocked and instead of filling the house with warmth, fill it with smoke and dust, with layers of ash covering every surface. Torrential rain can turn gardens into an expanse of mud that gets trailed into the house. Marauding cats and dogs knock over dustbins, scattering their contents over the driveway. When you most need it, the car won't start, or breaks down on a bend on a narrow lane, or the boiler fails and there's no hot water. At times like those, you feel you would be happier in a sheltered housing unit. In the summer, there were snakes in her garden and biting insects that brought her out in huge welts... and as a woman alone, she attracted unwelcome attention from local gentlemen.

She did try, and continued to present herself as if she was going for an important job interview, beautifully dressed, with her nails varnished and not a hair out of place. Her very kind French neighbours tried to take care of her, arriving at her front door with little gifts: a bunch of radishes, a small bouquet, a magazine. While they tapped at the door, Joan crouched behind a cupboard in the kitchen until they went away. One day, they persuaded her have dinner with them, and invited me too. I explained that I was a vegetarian and didn't want to be a nuisance – that was no problem, cried Mireille. She loved cooking for vegetarians. She produced a superb meal, which was wasted on Princess Tippy Toes who sat tearfully looking at her watch the whole evening. I felt it my duty to scintillate and spent three agonising hours trying to converse in French, while at the same time politely disregarding the huge lump of boiled bacon that had arrived in my bowl of *soupe au pistou*, that quintessentially Provençal dish. I dreaded to think what vegetarian ingredients the main course might include, but Mireille produced a *pissaladiére* so perfect that it was almost criminal to eat it. The pastry was thin, transparent, golden, with its filling of caramelised onions, a sprinkle of thyme and scattering of olives. The green salad was beyond perfection. Mireille dressed it at the table: a tiny amount of mustard in a little bowl, a splash of best olive oil, and a clove of garlic grated on the tines of a fork.

'Don't crush it, don't chop it, don't use a grater. You won't get the same result,' she explained. 'No salt, no pepper, no lemon juice nor vinegar. Just oil, garlic and mustard.' When she poured the dressing, it glistened on the leaves of the salad, and tasted delicious beyond description. She was simply a brilliant cook and an enormously affectionate lady, but just too much for a reclusive and introverted widow to cope with. When she hid amongst the rhododendrons wearing a miniature yellow and blue umbrella on her head, leaping out waving her arms and yelling: 'Aiieeee', Princess Tippy Toes said she couldn't take any more, she'd have to move. Life here didn't work for her. One well-meaning Australian woman started a crusade to prepare her for remarriage.

'You'll have to get that thing removed from your neck and get something done about your eyelids. Then we'll be able to start circulating you in the right area,' she said encouragingly. However, the princess didn't want to circulate in the right area, or have things done to her neck or eyelids. She didn't want to get married again, so she sold up and went back to England.

Chapter Thirty-five

An elderly relative died and left us a small legacy. We decided to invest it in restoring two of our decaying buildings – the one which served as the garage, and the small dirt-floored one-up, one-down that flooded to a depth of nearly two feet during heavy rain.

Both had, far back in time, been dwelling houses and their original mantelpieces, in-built cupboards and stone sinks were still intact. Despite decades of neglect, both had managed to remain upright with shreds of dignity still clinging to them, interlaced with ivy, while their roofs sagged and their walls crumbled and cracked. Spiders, assorted insects and various birds lived in them, and shy plants thrived in their dark, damp corners. With each season that passed, the buildings visibly deteriorated, surely soon they would fall down, leaving tons of rubble. To make them habitable, our legacy was going to have to be managed with surgical precision, so we began our quest for that mythical being: a builder who could complete the project on time, to our specifications, within budget and for a price we could afford. Once they were renovated we would let these buildings out as holiday homes.

Some friends introduced an Englishman who was renovating his own house, quite artistically and apparently competently. It had swallowed up all his available budget and he needed to earn money to continue his project. We felt rather sorry for him because he was an oddball without any friends. Anyhow, he seemed to know what he was doing and was keen to start work, so when he asked if he could repair our roofs, we agreed.

The sun shone. I cooked three-course lunches for him daily, which was part of our agreement, and the roofs came along quite nicely. He asked what we planned to do about the remaining work, and whether we would be happy to let him carry on after winter had passed. We agreed that he would continue with the next phase of the work the following year, and he assured us that he could and would have both properties ready for our holiday guests by next July. In the meantime, he had his own house to work on and other jobs to keep him going over the winter.

It was all turning out rather well. The one cloud looming on the horizon was the state of Bill's property, and the effect it would have on would-be holidaymakers who came to stay. As well as the collection of mildewy caravans, there was an ice-cream trolley, several beach umbrellas, a heap of sacks of rock-hard cement, some ladders, old bed frames and decaying mattresses, half a car and a pile of old tyres, all discarded in his driveway. It was a worry, and we didn't know what we could do about it, but fairly soon something was going to happen to solve that problem for us.

Another Christmas was on the horizon. Gloria went to England leaving Bill dog-sitting. He appeared at our house one morning, grey-faced and almost in tears.

'She's had a heart attack. Gloria's in hospital.'

A few days later, I phoned her at the hospital, where she was her habitual perky self.

'Don't worry about me,' she chuckled, 'I'm not ready to pop my clogs just yet!' After several weeks of convalescence, she returned to France as bright and bubbly as ever.

During her absence, Bill had worked frantically to make their house habitable so that she wouldn't have to sleep in the damp caravan, which aggravated her asthma. By the time she returned, she had a cosy bedroom, a warm if rather dishevelled kitchen, and the beginnings of a living room. The outside had been tidied up too.

'He hasn't done badly,' she said, which coming from her was high praise.

***

In the middle of December my old *bête noire*, Michelle, reappeared. She phoned very late one night and asked if I would make a Christmas pudding for the schoolchildren she taught.

Instead of taking the sensible route and just saying no, I explained that even if I could and would, the pudding needed to be made very much earlier in the year and left for at least a few weeks to mature. However, I did happen to have one left from last Christmas, which she could have.

What kind of person was I to suggest giving seven-year-olds something to eat that was a year old? I explained that the alcohol content of the pudding meant that it would last two years or more, continuously improving. Now I was trying to corrupt young children with alcohol.

I withdrew my offer of the redundant pudding. She started again.

If she did agree to risk the health of the little children by feeding them this thing, she asked, how was it cooked?

Steaming for three hours is the traditional way, I explained.

Steamed for three hours, she shrieked. How could she steam anything for three hours in a classroom? I'd no idea, but blundered on to suggest a microwave oven, which would reheat the thing in seven minutes.

Where was she going to get a microwave oven?

Perhaps she could borrow one just for the morning?

Who did I think would lend her a microwave oven? How would she get it to the school?

My final suggestion was to reheat it in a pressure cooker. This idea she liked, as it would 'kill all the bacteria and destroy the alcohol', and she did own a pressure cooker.

What a relief.

Would she have to pay for the pudding, she wanted to know, or could she have it for nothing?

I'd happily have given it to anybody else but because I was fed up with her rudeness, I said she could have it for what it had cost, which was 40 francs.

She exploded. I didn't want it myself or I would have eaten it a year ago, so why was I exploiting her?

Calmly and very tiredly, I said if she wanted the pudding it was 40 francs, and if she didn't that was fine. So she said she would go to the shop that sold English products, some distance away, and try to find a fresher, less alcoholic, cheaper pudding. I put down the phone with relief.

The following evening she called again to say that the shop was very expensive and the people had been rude to her, so she would after all take my pudding, but I'd have to deliver it.

After long and fraught negotiations, I said I would leave the pudding in our letter box. She would collect it and leave 40 francs in the box.

I left the pudding in the box, where it sat uncollected until Christmas had long passed. When I retrieved it, it looked so inviting that I cooked it (pressure cooker method), and ate nearly half of it at one sitting. Gave me frightful indigestion.

197

January came around again – cold, wet and miserable. The log burner kept the living room reasonably warm, but consumed wood at a frightening rate, so I only lit it in the evenings. The rest of the house was arctic. Instead of sitting indoors all day shivering, swathed in clothes and flailing my arms around to keep the blood flowing, I started going for long brisk walks, and found I rather enjoyed them. Every day I walked for two hours, and one day the idea put itself into my head that I would have an adventure. I'd find a house-sitter to come and look after the animals, and I'd go for a *really* long walk. Back in the freezing house, I dug out a map of France and made up my mind to walk from la Rochelle on the Atlantic west coast, across the country to Lake Geneva in Switzerland, and to write a book about the venture.

With the help of Bill and Gloria who took me on forays to locate tents, boots and the other equipment I'd need, I started to prepare for the trek. They were supportive and encouraging, and Gloria joined me on my daily hikes. She had been told she must give up smoking and take a daily walk. She wasn't immediately enthusiastic, but soon she was waiting at her gate every day. With a tiny backpack containing her mobile phone and wearing a pair of high-heeled lace up boots, we tramped around the neighbourhood together. It was fun, once the weather improved. She couldn't walk as fast as me, nor as far, so after half an hour, we'd sit on the ground and put the world to rights.

I wore a backpack loaded with encyclopedias to get used to the weight I'd be carrying. The neighbours nodded and waved as I trundled past. If they thought it strange that I disappeared each day for several hours with a loaded pack that was still with me when I returned, they were too polite to ask why.

To measure the distance I covered each day, I wore a pedometer. The first time I walked twenty miles, it registered 43,680 footsteps. If the journey to Geneva covered 600 miles on foot, as it most likely would, that would mean a total of 1,310,400 steps. The thing about the pedometer was that to make it record each step I took, I had to put my right foot down with a slight stamp. I didn't know if I could keep that up over half a million times.

Chapter Thirty-six

In mid-March, Gloria returned to England for a medical check-up. While she was away Bill came around one Sunday morning.

'Could you come and help? There's a French couple here, but I can't understand what they're saying.'

They were a relaxed couple in their mid-thirties. I introduced myself and asked how I could help.

'We're looking for a house to buy in the country, and we understand this one is for sale.' They indicated the cottage between Bill and myself.

'Yes, that's right. I can give you the phone number of the owner, if you like.'

'We'd really like to have a look round the outside, if that's possible?'

The cottage had been advertised for sale for over two years, but the eyesore of Bill's place put off prospective buyers. I often saw people drive up, take one look and drive away again without even getting out of their car.

'Yes, I'll be happy to show you round,' I said, and led them over every inch of land, burbling about each tree, bush, bird and boundary, until they finally excused themselves and said they would ring the owner. They were pleasant and sociable, asking how long I'd been living here. Something they said made me realise that they thought I was Bill's wife.

'No,' I laughed, 'he's not my husband – we're neighbours.'

'Ah! Did you know each other before you moved here?'

No, I explained, it was just by coincidence that we came to be living next to each other. They asked whether I went back to England often, and whether Bill did, and whether I worked, and whether I enjoyed living here, and I thought what charming people they were.

When they'd gone, M. Meneteau called over the hedge. 'What did those people want?'

'They're interested in Madame Guillot's house. They're from Poitiers and want a weekend cottage.'

He wagged a finger. 'Be careful. They were parked here yesterday. Don't trust them! They aren't what you think they are.'

199

'How do you mean?'

'Just don't trust them!' he warned. I assumed he meant that they were potential burglars, but from their clothing, car and general manner, I thought it highly unlikely and that he was being rather melodramatic.

Bill and I went to town next morning, rummaging through second-hand shops and junk yards. I found a wood-burning oven which was too heavy to fit in the car.

'Don't worry,' Bill said. 'I'll go back and collect it this afternoon in the pick-up.'

Back home, I'd just finished lunch when the phone rang. It was Gloria.

'What's going on with Bill?' she snapped.

Well, for heaven's sake, I thought. What on earth is she talking about? She knows that Bill and I often go out together and that there is nothing at all between us apart from neighbourliness.

'Sorry, Glo, what do you mean?'

'I've just phoned him. He picked up the phone and said, 'The police have got me', then the phone was slammed down. I want to know what's going on.'

'OK. I'll go around and see if I can find out what's happening. Don't worry. I'll ring you back in a few minutes.'

I snatched up a cup and ambled around the corner humming nonchalantly. Outside Bill's front door stood two men in plain clothes.

'*Bonjour*,' I called cheerily and tried to glide past them.

'Stop, madame! You cannot go in there.'

'Of course I can. They're friends. I need some sugar.' I know it wasn't very original. I waved the cup at them and kept walking towards the door. They moved into the doorway, blocking it.

'You cannot go in there.'

'Why not?' I put on my most puzzled and innocent expression.

The door opened. Over the shoulders of a couple of uniformed policemen, I saw Bill's anxious face.

'Are you OK, Bill?'

'Do not talk to this man. Go back to your own house,' said one of the men in the doorway rudely.

'No, please wait a minute,' called one of the policemen. 'Are you the English lady who lives around the corner?'

'I am.'

'Well, we would like you to look after this gentleman's dogs for a couple of days.'

'Why? Where's he going?'

'It's nothing to worry about. He has to answer some questions. Will you look after the dogs?'

'Yes, of course I will, but I don't know where the food is kept, or what they have. Please can I just ask Mr Smith?'

'No, you cannot. You must find the food and decide for yourself how much to give them.'

They led Bill into one of the cars and sped off.

I phoned Gloria to tell her the news.

'That's great, isn't it? Here's me recovering from a heart attack, and he goes and gets himself arrested! Stupid bastard. I'll get the first train back.'

Seven months had passed since Bill's truck had been found with the cannabis aboard, and we had all assumed that nothing more was going to be heard about it.

At the police station the young 'house-hunters' were there, not house-hunters at all, but plain-clothes detectives. M. Meneteau had been quite right about them.

Word of Bill's arrest spread rapidly, and locally the debate about whether or not he was guilty, and what would happen to him, was the focus of conversation. Most people, it seemed, wanted him to be guilty, because that would be more exciting than if he wasn't. In hindsight, nearly everybody could remember something suspicious he had said or done, or might have said or done. The consensus was that he was getting what he justly deserved. Most people simply enjoyed the scandal. One or two people defended him wholeheartedly, while Fred was ecstatic, saying that he hoped Gloria would be arrested too.

Untidy and infuriatingly unreliable as he could be, Bill had plenty of good qualities. I was quite fond of him when he wasn't irritating me. I didn't want to think of him mouldering away for the rest of his life in an *oubliette* if he was innocent.

Two days passed.

Bill was charged with drug trafficking and remanded in prison.

Gloria arrived back and spent her days phoning solicitors in England, and the French solicitor who had been appointed by the court to represent Bill. As the French solicitor didn't speak English, nor Gloria

French, I interpreted these calls. Things weren't looking good for Bill.

Gloria had no money, she was recovering from a heart attack, Bill was in prison and there was no indication as to how long he was going to be there. She had to find enough to keep herself – and, more importantly to her, her dogs – fed. She sold off bits and pieces of furniture. Knowing her situation, people tried to beat her down. People who owed her money avoided her. People who didn't owe her money avoided her.

I started getting phone calls from people I knew.

'You want to watch yourself. You're getting a bad reputation,' one person told me.

'What do you mean?'

'Running around with that drug dealer's wife. You can imagine what people are saying about you.'

'No. I can't. What are they saying, exactly?'

'It's obvious, isn't it? You're in it with them.'

I was so angry.

'Well, I'm just giving you a friendly warning. Watch out before you find yourself in prison.'

A 'friend' rang. 'Oh, Susie, I'm so worried about you. You're going around with that woman. I'm terribly afraid you'll be arrested.'

'How can I be arrested for going shopping or having coffee with her?'

'Well, he's in prison for drug dealing. You'll be branded with them.'

'Can we put this straight? He's been charged. He has not been tried, nor found guilty. Gloria hasn't even been questioned. She isn't under suspicion. At this moment, she can use all the friends she can get. What's happened to you recently?'

The phone went dead.

I felt I learned a bit more about human nature during this episode, and not the nicer side of it, but nothing seemed to crush Gloria. She even came away laughing from a nearby English-owned restaurant (whose alcoholic beverages had been brought out from England by Bill to save them money, for which they owed him a considerable amount). They had also bought furniture from him for which they hadn't paid. I took Gloria there for lunch one day. She hadn't touched alcohol for years and declined the bottle of wine included with the meal, asking for a lemonade instead. There was one tiny alcoholic treat that she allowed herself – whisky trifle – which was one of the regular desserts at the restaurant, and her favourite. She'd looked forward to it and was disappointed that it wasn't on the menu. When she mentioned it, the owner of the restaurant said that he had a couple left over from the previous day, and she could have one of those if we paid extra for it. We also had to pay extra for the lemonade.

As we came out of the restaurant, she rolled her eyes and laughed. 'How about that – paying extra for leftovers! And not a mention of all the money they owe *me*.' She was her normal spirited, cheerful self. Nothing was going to crush her.

Her elderly computer was causing problems. 'One day,' she said, 'I'm going to get one of those Pantechnicon Two computers.'

'A what?'

'You know – the Pantechnicon.'

'Do you mean a Pentium?'

'Yes, that's right. That's what I said.'

It was bad enough when the computers went wrong. Trying to explain the problems to a French engineer was virtually impossible, as my French wasn't up to that. I saw a card advertising an English engineer and phoned him.

'Bring it over, and I'll have a look at it for you,' he said. Off we went and met a gorgeous, cuddly man named Keith, with a sweet wife called Beryl with bright blue, laughing eyes. Over the years, Keith patched up and repaired my computers more times than I could count.

'I don't know what you do to them, Susie,' he used to say as I turned up for the umpteenth time.

'I don't do anything to the damned things. They just keep misbehaving.'

'Never mind, let's have a look.'

If it hadn't been for Keith, I'd never have been able to write.

'Are you going to put me in your book?' he asked.

'You bet.' There you are, Keith, and thanks for everything.

***

Despite her bleak situation, Gloria wasn't going to miss an opportunity to have a bit of fun. She spotted a poster for a Country and Western evening in a nearby village hall.

'Shall we go?'

It was a rare chance for her to forget her problems for a few hours, so I agreed.

'What are you wearing?' she asked that afternoon.

'Oh, the usual, jeans and a sweater.'

'No, you can't! I thought we were going to dress up nicely.'

'People don't around here. Jeans and a sweater *is* dressed up.'

'Come on, let's give them something to look at. I'm getting myself dolled up. You put on something nice. Be a sport.'

I climbed into a mid-calf skirt with a short slit up the back, added a demure top, dabbed on some make-up and put on a pair of high heels.

Gloria was a sight to stop the traffic. Her long crimson skirt resembled a big tassel: almost down to her ankles, it was slit to the hip in eight places. She wore black fishnet stockings and black patent stiletto heels. Her freckled golden bosom pouted over a low-cut black top beneath a black leather fringed jacket. From her ears huge gold hoop earrings dangled to match a gold necklace, several chunky gold bracelets and a dozen rings. Her hair was piled in a bouffant blonde crown, with false eyelashes, startling turquoise eye shadow, scarlet lipstick. She was showing them all.

When we sashayed into the village hall, silence fell, jaws fell, and eyes blinked as we strolled casually over to a table. Two unsavoury characters grabbed four beers each and headed towards us.

'May we?' asked one, plopping onto a chair.

'Sure. Nice to have some company,' Gloria chirped, just as I opened my mouth to say no. The second chap, who looked like a cushion with a string tied round it, sat down next to me. I ignored him. Gloria chattered away brightly, fluttering her huge eyelashes and, kicking me under the table, indicated I should smile.

'So you've got a van!' Violent kick. 'We've got a stove to be collected from town' (the stove Bill had been going to collect for me before he was carted off to the pokey), 'and you two want to be shown around the second-hand shops. Well, we'll show you around if you bring the stove back. Won't we?' She kicked me again.

I smiled weakly and we arranged to meet the next day.

'May we invite you two ladies out for lunch on Sunday?' enquired one of our new friends.

'No,' I said.

'Yes, we'd be delighted!' said Gloria. Another kick. I scowled at her, but she babbled on. 'We'll go to the…' She named a local restaurant.

'It'll be Easter Sunday. Their menu is two hundred and twenty francs,' I told them. Cushion-body paled a bit, but his friend said, 'No problem. Two lovely ladies deserve the best.'

They went to restock with beers, another four bottles apiece, while I snapped at Gloria: 'Why on earth have you got us lumbered with this pair?'

'Look, Dearie,' she had started calling me Dearie, like Fred, because she knew I hated it. 'You need to collect that stove, don't you? How else are you going to get it back? You've got to be practical.'

The next morning, we called for our chauffeurs and found them still asleep. They were not at all enthusiastic about the stove project, but Gloria trilled and smiled and flashed her eyes, making them each a cup of tea while they got themselves ready, then succeeded in forcing them into the van, completely ignoring their obvious reluctance.

We kept to our part of the bargain by taking them on a guided tour of the second-hand shops, and got the stove back. After they had struggled to manoeuvre it into my house, we never saw them again. Easter Sunday came and went. 'Shame, really,' said Gloria ruefully. 'I'd have liked a good meal out.'

And forever after, whenever we reminisced about that evening, she would say, 'Hey, remember when we went out dressed like a couple of tarts?'

***

Because Terry had to work and couldn't stay here to look after the animals whilst I went walking across France, and I couldn't expect Gloria to do so, through an internet message board I found a lady called Jennifer Shields, from San Antonio, Texas. She agreed to come and hold the fort during my absence. Her ticket was booked, and it was too late to cancel the project, although I felt I shouldn't be going away with Gloria in such a sorry state and poor old Bill banged up behind bars. Until the last minute, I dithered with the idea of calling the whole thing off, but happily Jennifer and Gloria hit it off immediately. Abandoning them, my animals, and anybody who wanted anything at all, I set off on my solitary adventure, phoning home daily to keep up to date with events.

The day I reached Geneva, seven weeks after leaving home, I learned that Bill had been released from prison on bail.

Chapter Thirty-seven

Ever since I was a teenager, I had wanted to be a writer. I'd read many books about how to do it, and I had drawers and cupboards full of manuscripts that had quickly fizzled out for lack of inspiration and motivation. After my hike, I finally had those two ingredients as well as the material. I was ready to write. Nothing could stop me. With the reams of notes I had taken each day, a computer and a stack of paper, I could begin reliving the adventure and putting it down on paper. Working from home was more difficult than I'd anticipated. The only people who took me seriously were Bill and Gloria who agreed that we'd have coffee together mid-morning and, barring any emergencies, would see each other again in the evening. The rest of the day would be my 'sacred writing time'.

Nobody else respected this sacred writing time. A stream of strangers arrived at all hours, hooting, ringing the bell on the gate, or shouting to attract my attention.

A man arrived one day to say he was divorcing his wife and needed to contact the *notaire* to make sure she couldn't sell their house. It was imperative that he got to the *notaire* before she did, so would I get on the phone straight away to warn him. He did not know the name of the *notaire*, nor which town he was in, so it took me several hours and dozens of phone calls to find him. As my visitor couldn't speak French, he expected me to make an appointment to go with him to the *notaire*. He was quite unpleasant when I refused, and left without either thanking me or paying for the calls.

It was a rare fish who offered to pay for the calls, letters written and stamps purchased by me. A friend said she found the same thing, somebody else overheard our conversation and said they too were never reimbursed. One of them said: 'I think it's because people who come out from England imagine that because we live in France, we must be rich and won't mind buying their stamps and things for them. Nobody ever offers.'

I looked at the state of our house, the bare stone walls with bits missing, the empty window frames covered in plastic sheeting, and supposed such people thought I was a wealthy eccentric.

I put a notice at the gate, which read: 'Hi! I'm busy at present, but if you leave a message using the pen and paper in the letter box, I'll give you a call later on.'

Some read the message and actually came to the door tutting with sympathy. 'You poor thing! People are so inconsiderate. By the way, I've just had this letter from the tax office; you'll have to translate it for me. Then you can write your book later.'

I padlocked the gate with a heavy chain and stuck a mirror on a broom handle so that when the dogs barked, I could see who was at the gate from the office without being seen myself. If it was somebody I wanted to see, I could let them in; the rest I ignored. Most people gave up after five minutes, although those more determined tried to find a way in through the field and up the garden, but the geese usually scared them off.

There were peeved messages on the phone.

'Really, this is the fourth message we've left this week, and we've been around three times. We've got a problem with our electricity/gas/neighbours/car/cooker, and we can never get hold of you. Kindly phone back as soon as you get this message.'

With the dogs barking as people rattled the gate, the telephone ringing throughout the day and people screaming as they fled from the geese, I admitted defeat, writing only in the evening after 10.00pm.

***

Around the corner, Bill and Gloria's situation was worsening. He was out of prison awaiting trial and wasn't allowed to leave the country. He also wasn't allowed to work in France, so he was unable to earn a living. Every Tuesday, he had to report to the local *gendarmerie*. If he missed a week, they'd send him back to prison.

Whatever money they had was swallowed up by lawyers in England and France. Their truck containing the drugs was still held by customs in France; their trucks in England immobilised due to a dispute with customers. The lawyers still wanted paying to continue representing Bill until his trial, and there was no indication at all of when this might be — it could be years hence.

They started selling off bits and pieces, but it wasn't much more than a small drop in a large ocean. Gloria returned to England to try to sort out the problem with the immobilised trucks.

While she was away, Bill came across one afternoon looking more worried than usual.

'I haven't seen Horace since this morning,' he said. Horace was one of the two Great Danes.

'He's not been looking at all well. Would you come and help me find him?'

I knew what we were going to find, and so I think did Bill. We went to the old caravan where the dogs had their beds and found Horace there, curled up peacefully, in a ray of sunshine, as if he was asleep.

***

Bill kept working on their house, finally getting it into a habitable state. Outside it was still a jungle, but he'd tiled the floors, papered the walls and put in a staircase and a bathroom. He was very proud of his work, although the corner bath he installed made it impossible to open the bathroom door. Gloria dug out furniture from the Pandora's boxes in the barn. She hung curtains, dotted pot plants, plastic flowers and ornaments around, and if you could close your eyes to the desolation outside it had become quite homely.

Gloria was delighted. 'Now we can sell it!' Bill was angry and heartbroken that he was going to lose the home he loved and had worked so hard to build, but with no money and no means of earning any, there was nothing else he could do. Gloria contacted an estate agent and put the property up for sale.

***

I decided to have a go at decorating our living room, so I dug out a few pots of paint and a brush, pushed the furniture into the middle of the room and covered it with a load of old cloths, because I am notoriously messy when handling paint.

Terry did one of those impenetrably thoughtless things that husbands sometimes do. He phoned and said: 'Guess what? You're having a visitor!'

'How lovely,' I replied, as if I wasn't sick to death of uninvited visitors. 'Who is it?'

He named an old friend of his, Jim, whom I'd met a couple of times, the last time at least ten years previously.

'When is he coming?'

'Tomorrow.'

'Right, I'll organise something for lunch. How long will he be here for?'

'Six months.'

'What?'

'He's got a problem with the Inland Revenue and needs to disappear.'

'Where's he going to stay?'

'I said he could stay with you.'

'It'll be nice for you to have some company,' he said in response to my long silence. *Why did everybody think I wanted company?*

'Where's he going to sleep? You'll remember we only have one bedroom.'

'Well, surely you can sort out something for him. What about the living room?'

'I'm painting the living room. It's full of ladders, paint pots, brushes, splashes and cloths.'

'You'll sort something out,' he chuckled.

I stared around at the devastation, the makeshift kitchen, the half-finished bathroom and the sleeping space that didn't exist. I cursed and stamped my feet and shouted at the heavens, then picked up the phone and booked a room for my portending visitor at a local guest house.

When he arrived, I fed him and apologised that I had nowhere for him to stay. He said I shouldn't worry, he'd wait until I'd finished decorating and then he'd move in, although he was surprised at how primitive living conditions were. It wasn't what he'd expected, he said rather stuffily.

Once I'd finished the decorating, he moved in. I went to the pharmacy first thing next morning to buy the most effective ear plugs they sold, as he not only snored like nothing I had ever heard, he kept his radio playing all night. The noise jumped up through the ceiling into my bedroom and I got very little sleep. He took no notice when I mentioned that the radio kept me awake, so I very quickly began to hate him.

He'd been here a couple of weeks when he remarked that I spent too much time on the computer, when I should be out in the garden. I replied that I was writing a book.

'I wouldn't waste your time,' he advised. 'I don't think you'll find anybody will be interested in anything you write.'

***

Gloria dropped a bombshell.

'How much would it cost to have the house put in our name?' she asked.

'What house?'

'This one.' She waved her arm at their place.

'I'm sorry, I don't understand what you mean. Surely it's in your name already?'

'No, it isn't, because when Bill bought it he paid cash to the lady, and got a receipt, but he wouldn't go to the *notaire* to do the official paperwork, so it's still in the previous owner's name.'

I stared at her.

'Then legally the property still belongs to the previous owner. Why on earth didn't Bill go to the *notaire*?'

'That's Bill all over, isn't it? He paid, he got a receipt, it's his. That's how his mind works. He doesn't like anything official.'

Until then, I'd thought the biggest problem was the state of the garden; this news bleached that into insignificance. In the almost unimaginable event that somebody wanted to buy the place, the chances that they would do so if it was not in the name of the person selling it were practically non-existent.

'Does the estate agent know about this?' I asked.

'Oh yes, but he says it doesn't matter.'

Of course he would. Estate agents say things like that.

I didn't want to give Gloria any more worries. I knew that the paperwork to register the house in their name would cost at least a couple of thousand pounds, which I also knew they didn't have. So I said: 'Oh, well, that's OK then. Let's see what happens.'

The estate agent called them from time to time promising he was bringing 'an almost certain buyer', but nobody bought. Months passed. Their situation seemed hopeless, despite support from the French social services and regional authorities who were not unsympathetic. They did whatever they could to help financially within the framework of their system. There was still no news of Bill's trial, and as he was unable to earn a living, Gloria had to return to England. She found work with her usual cheerfulness, as a companion to wealthy elderly people. We joked about her 'going into service', and christened her 'Little Effie'. We spoke on the phone quite often. She said she was enjoying the work, it was easy and well paid, she was living in luxury and the people she was looking after were all kind and interesting. She was happy, but missing her dogs.

Fred Bear was still a regular visitor, and his first question was always whether there was any news of Bill being charged. I don't know why he was so malicious, because Bill had never done him any harm as far as I knew. He was trying to encourage some people he knew to buy Bill's house, as he needed a lot of storage space, which his own house didn't have. He confided that if his friends bought Bill's place, he'd get the use of the space for nothing. He'd told them Bill was so desperate to sell that they'd be able to 'steal' it. When the prospective purchasers made an offer, Bill was half pleased, half sad. He called Gloria and told her of the offer.

'Take it,' she said. So he did.

By the next day, the purchasers had thought it over and changed their minds. Bill was half pleased, half sad once more, deciding to double the asking price. Fred Bear was furious.

Jim, who had been living in my house, telling me not to bother writing, and keeping me awake for months, was spending more and more time with Bill.

'You know, I rather like that house,' he murmured one day.'I think I might buy it.'

It was a perfect solution. Bill and Gloria would sell their house, Jim could snore and play his radio all night without disturbing me. He would tidy the place up and we could stop worrying about the effect the current mess would have on our guests when our holiday cottages were ready.

I explained the situation regarding the ownership of the house to Jim, and introduced him to the lady who still legally owned the property. Bill often didn't have much luck, but he had this time, because the owner was honest and willing to do what was necessary so that the sale could take place.

Jim made an offer and told Bill he was a cash buyer, which is generally understood to mean you have all the necessary money and don't need a mortgage. Bill understood that Jim would pay him in crisp notes, and in return Bill would give Jim the keys and a receipt. Again, Bill was half sad, half happy. Gloria was ecstatic.

Jim asked me to arrange with the *notaire* to put the necessary paperwork together. I went to tell Bill that the legal owner and Jim were meeting the *notaire* to sign the preliminary agreement for the sale, and Bill was welcome to be present.

'I'm not selling through the *notaire*. Jim said he was paying cash.'

Through long hours, I tried to explain that exchanging a bag of money for a receipt didn't mean anything unless the legal paperwork had been completed.

Bill wouldn't listen. 'I bought this place cash. I paid cash, and I've a receipt to prove it. It's my house, and I can sell it any way I like.'

My short temper, which had stretched such a long way that I was proud of it, finally snapped. I said: 'It isn't your house. It doesn't matter how many receipts you have, whether they are carved in stone or written on tablets of gold, it isn't your house until you have a legal document saying so. As you haven't, you're more lucky than you'll ever know to have found a buyer.'

Later, Gloria rang from England. 'You just go ahead,' she said. 'It's a waste of time trying to reason with him. You sort it all out with the *notaire* for Jim and the owner.'

Bill didn't want to be involved in the meeting, so Gloria came back to France and together we met the owner at the *notaire's* office. I did the translating, and Jim paid the *notaire* the agreed deposit for the house.

Gloria was pleased that the wheels were in motion, but Bill was becoming more difficult by the day. 'You'd no business involving a *notaire*. This was meant to be a cash deal.'

There are times when you have to accept that you are never going to succeed in getting a point across to a particular person and this was one of them. When Bill made up his mind about something, there wasn't much you could do to change it.

The transaction would take almost three months to complete. Jim went off to England, and I began to catch up on all the sleep I'd lost, but now Bill really started getting difficult. Every day, he came to ask when Jim was returning. I couldn't tell him, because Jim wasn't answering my messages.

'I've seen no money from him yet.'

'I keep telling you, you won't. The deposit has been paid to the *notaire*, and the balance will be paid to him when the final papers are signed. He has to pay any outstanding taxes due, then he'll send a cheque to the legal owners, and they'll pay you. That's the way it works.'

'I'm not accepting that. I want cash. He said he'd pay cash, and now he's trying to cheat me.

I'm putting the price up. Doubling it.'

'OK, fine.'

'Or I might take it off the market completely.'

I began creeping down through our field and out of the back gate to go for long walks without having to pass Bill's house. Some days, I went off in the car with a book, drove somewhere and sat and read. The days passed infinitely slowly. Six weeks went by before Jim made contact and returned.

Two days before the signing of the final papers was due to take place, the *notaire's* secretary phoned to say he had decided to go on holiday, and the meeting was put back a fortnight. Everybody was furious. Bill was suspicious of everybody else and I was so frustrated I wished I could run away.

Then something else happened.

In between Bill's and M. Meneteau's was a tiny tumbledown cottage and a large barn. Bill had often talked in the past of buying the small house once 'his' house was sold, and M. Meneteau and I were curious as to whether or not he was going to do so. Bill had been playing his cards very close to his chest. We both liked him but we were fed up with the eyesore of his property. The prospect of the mess migrating twenty yards and being with us forever was not a happy one.

I had a phone call four days before the sale was due to be finalised. Gloria reported that Bill had had a row with somebody whom he had learned was trying to buy the little house from under his nose.

'He's fit to be tied!' she said. 'He's going to buy all the spare land in the village and turn it into a pig farm!'

That sounded like one of Bill's schemes.

Her call confirmed my worst fears – the junkyard wasn't going away, it was just planning to relocate. I picked up the phone and rang the owner of the little house, asking if he really was selling to Bill.

'If he has the money, yes. I'll sell to the first person who pays a deposit. Bill is bringing me the money as soon as he has sold his house.'

'If I can find another buyer for you before then, will you sell it to them?'

'Yes, of course. We'd like to sell to somebody who'll make the place look nice. We don't really want to sell to Bill, but if he has the money...'

I called Terry. 'We've got a problem. If Bill stays here, our guests will be demanding their money back when they arrive and see the state of the place. Do we know anybody who might buy the little house?'

Terry phoned back half an hour later. A friend of his would buy it.

I phoned the owner and put down a deposit the following morning. We shook hands, and the deal was struck.

The day before the completion of Bill's house sale, he came to see me. He was in high spirits. 'I've got a surprise for you!' he said gleefully.

'What is it?'

'You'll have to wait and see tomorrow. Maybe you'll be having a new neighbour that you didn't expect!'

He was beaming with delight and I hadn't felt so treacherous since I gave the cockerels to the neighbours to eat.

On the day of the signing, the air was as taut as a violin string. Bill blocked the lane so I couldn't get my car out.

'Bill, I have to be there. Somebody has to translate, and they don't have anybody but me.'

'How do I know I'm not going to be cheated?'

'Gloria's going to be there. She'll see what's happening and I'll translate what's being said. Please don't worry. Nobody is going to cheat you.'

'This should never have happened. He said he was paying cash.'

'Please, Bill, move your truck.'

He eventually let me out and I met Gloria, Jim and the lady who was the legal and registered owner of Bill's property.

The *notaire* read out the *Acte de Vente* – the final sale agreement, and I translated it into English for Jim and Gloria. When we reached the part where the money is handed over, Jim explained that he had agreed to pay the whole amount in cash to the lady who was still, legally, the owner. This is what he'd agreed with Bill. I'd already told them that it wouldn't be acceptable to the *notaire*.

'No.' The *notaire* shook his head. 'Payment has to be made to me, by cheque or international money order. I pay any taxes due, and then pay the rest by cheque to madame.'

My heart sank.

Jim was returning to England later that day, so he signed the documents, but the owner would only sign once the *notaire* had received the money.

Gloria was utterly crestfallen, and her mobile phone started ringing. She explained to Bill why the sale hadn't gone ahead. He yelled at her and she yelled back at him.

Jim returned to England to sort out the money transfer and to arrange shipment of his furniture.

Bill and Gloria had moved out, under much protest from Bill, into rented accommodation. When it seemed the drama would never end, the *notaire* telephoned to say Jim's money had arrived, the owner had signed and the house now belonged to Jim. The previous owner telephoned Bill to tell him they'd pay him as soon as they received the cheque from the *notaire*. Now everybody should be happy.

'Little Effie' had gone back to England to work, and Jim returned with a truck full of furniture. He telephoned Bill to ask him to bring the keys to the property. Bill said he'd be there in a few minutes. When an hour later there was no sign of him nor the keys, we phoned again. Bill said he was busy feeding his dogs. He'd come when he was ready.

Five hours later he arrived, and I can't recall ever seeing anybody in such a rage. He was glowing with fury. Having received payment for his house, he'd phoned the owner of the little cottage and learned that it had been sold to somebody else. He didn't yet know who.

'You stupid bastard,' he yelled at Jim. 'I've lost a damned good property because of you. It was meant to be a cash deal!'

I watched the two men waving their fists at each other and shouting, then thought back to our arrival and my dreams of a peaceful existence.

'Out!' I shouted. 'Enough. Go and sort yourselves out somewhere else.'

Bill stamped away, and that was the last I saw of him.

When Jim moved in, we wandered around the property, hacking at the brambles and nettles and pulling things out of the undergrowth. Amongst an extraordinary collection of objects, we found three car engines and two exhaust systems, an ice-cream trolley, a box containing somebody's family photographs, two King Edward cigars, a bundle of soft pornographic magazines, the cow-catcher from a Range Rover, a single rubber flipper, a mechanical fertiliser distributor, a damaged-but-complete sports car and an enormous lawn roller, the sort that a tractor pulls.

That evening I stood and looked at Bill's house for a while. It was a relief to know that the days of mess were over, yet I couldn't help feeling sad. It was the end of Bill's dream. However irritating he could be, and although we had fallen out from time to time, he was well-meaning. In many ways, I'd miss him.

Still, at least I had my own house back and would be able to sleep through the night once more.

I'd miss Gloria more than I could say. We were so different from each other: she was a bright bubbly extrovert, I was more of a hermit; she craved a bustling life in a busy place, I loved being far away from all that. What we had in common were a rather weird sense of humour and the fact that we both loved animals. I had great admiration for her strength under extreme pressure. We'd been through a lot together, and I'd miss her flashing smile and our ridiculous expeditions. The last time I saw her, I said: 'You'll come and say goodbye before you leave for good, won't you?'

She'd looked away for a moment and said: 'I don't like goodbyes, but I'll be in touch one of these days.' Then she drove away.

I'd only ever seen her weep twice. The first time was when one of her dogs had a monumental nose bleed, when she had sat with her head on her lap and her shoulders heaving. The other time was when she learned that Horace had died.

There was still no date set for Bill's trial. He slipped back to England and in his absence, he was tried and found not guilty.

Chapter Thirty-eight

Things were not going well with our 'builder'. He had returned after the winter, sullen and awkward. The people who had introduced him confided that he was a womaniser who was currently womanless and feeling bitter towards the female sex.

I felt as if he was directing his bitterness towards me, being as difficult as a person could be, arguing with everything I wanted done, complaining about the materials I had ordered at his request – 'bloody crap', he spat, kicking at the floorboards, 'junk' snarling at the windows.

The food I prepared wasn't good enough, the wine gave him heartburn. He needed to stop work every hour and stand indoors, drinking long cold drinks for fifteen minutes. He muttered darkly about hypertension.

He had taken on far more than he was capable of, and was clearly overwhelmed. From promising to have both properties ready for July, he said he would probably have one ready some time this year, but wouldn't start the other until the following year. The mess at the end of each day seemed disproportionate to the meagre progress. There were piles of rubble, sawdust, dirt, broken tiles and broken tools (ours), but almost no visible improvement. All the rubble had to be cleared away before the following morning: he wasn't going to work in a mess and risk injury. I staggered around with wheelbarrows loaded to the gunwales trying to dispose of the stuff.

A nice English lady whose husband was in poor health, and whose financial straits were dire, came to labour for him. She was a no-nonsense cheerful soul, glad to do anything to make ends meet, and set to with great energy, manhandling piles of rocks and climbing ladders with buckets of mortar. She seemed to achieve more than our 'builder' and she certainly worked with more enthusiasm.

'I can't say I fancy her,' he remarked one evening after she'd left. 'But if her old man pops off, I wouldn't mind marrying her. She's a damned good worker.'

After the first week, she didn't come back.

My weekly shopping bill increased as the 'builder' developed hyper-acidity which required a special diet, and could only eat organic produce. Each evening, I wandered around the site looking at the piles of debris and not finding any progress. I phoned Terry and said without more help, we would have to cancel our bookings.

He advertised a working holiday, and a couple of young men contacted him saying they would be delighted to come out to France. They were willing and happy to work a few hours each day in return for board, lodging and as much as they could drink.

When they arrived, one was thin and tanned with matted dreadlocks and a guitar; the other was plump and smiley with a small bundle of plumbing tools.

After dinner, they went into the garden where Dreadlocks twanged his guitar and the Plump One gazed at the stars. They drank five bottles of wine.

When I left to go shopping the following morning, Dreadlocks was up and about, taking instructions from our 'builder', who didn't seem very happy with his new workforce.

'I'm not at all sure about these two. I think you've got a problem there,' he forecast with manifest satisfaction. I had problems in several areas; one more wouldn't make that much difference.

The Plump One pleaded feeling unwell.

Dreadlocks mentioned that he and his friend weren't wine drinkers, they preferred beer. When I returned from shopping in the morning, Dreadlocks clamped his tanned fist over the two six-packs of beer in the boot of the car and disappeared with them. There was still no sign of the Plump One, but the daily rubble pile was building nicely, and a window was vaguely set in position, slightly off the perpendicular. A dozen empty beer bottles gleamed green in the sunlight.

Dreadlocks slaked his thirst with a few more beers. He didn't seem to be hungry. Mid-afternoon Dreadlocks announced that we were out of beer for that evening, so I went and bought another two dozen bottles.

The Plump One materialised blearily later in the day and downed a dozen or so bottles of beer, apologising for his non-showing but assuring me he would be up ahead of the larks the following morning, champing at the bit to start work. Between the two of them, they polished off some cold chicken and the rest of the beers. Then they opened a couple of bottles of wine which they took into the garden where they strummed and stargazed contentedly.

Dreadlocks surfaced for breakfast the next day and took a shower.

'How do you wash your dreadlocks?' I asked. 'How do you get them clean when the hair is all matted like that?'

'Oh, I don't wash them. Just wet them. I haven't washed them for three years. I never use any kind of soap on my body. It's bad for the skin.'

'How do you get clean then?'

'I just use water. That's all you need.'

The 'builder' didn't use deodorants, and several people had remarked that they felt it would be a good idea if he did, especially during the hot weather.

On the second morning of their stay, yet again the Plump One did not appear, and I asked Dreadlocks if he was unwell.

'Yeah. He's got a bit of a cold. Don't worry, he'll be OK soon.'

But he wasn't OK soon, and on the fourth day without any sign of life from him before 6.00pm, when he blundered from his sick-bed to guzzle quantities of beer, I said that he'd have to see a doctor if he wasn't fit the following day. The next morning, he appeared at breakfast with a wan smile. He didn't look well: his eyes were red-rimmed, his face was pale and shiny and he was a bit wobbly. However, he pronounced himself to be feeling much better. Shortly afterwards, he was working in the garden sorting out plumbing fittings, sipping from a bottle of beer. 'Kills the germs,' he explained sheepishly.

Dreadlocks joined him, so after an hour, we were once again out of beer. It didn't seem to affect them, and they were both working hard. If they preferred beer to food, that was fine with me. Off I went and came back with what I estimated should keep them happy for several days.

When I arrived home, the Plump One was nowhere to be seen. Happy little snoring sounds were coming from the spare bedroom and there was a pile of empty green bottles in the garden next to his abandoned plumbing tools. I felt slightly irritated.

'Doctor this afternoon!'

'No, don't do that!' Dreadlocks exclaimed. 'He'll be fine by tomorrow.'

'Our agreement was as much as you could eat and drink in return for a few hours' work a day. I've stuck to our part of the bargain, but I'm keeping two of you, and only one is doing any work. If he's ill, he needs treatment.'

'I'm doing the work for two. I'll keep on doing it, but don't call a doctor.'

'I think you'd better level with me,' I said. 'What exactly is his problem?'

'Heroin. He's an addict, and he's come here to go cold turkey. He's feeling really bad now, but if he sticks it out for another week or so he'll be OK. He really wants to come off the stuff.'

What was it about me? We'd already had one drug addict on our doorstep in the shape of Elsa's brother, now we had one actually staying under our roof.

'What about you? Are you on it?'

'No, of course not. I'm far too smart. Just stick to dope.'

'Have you got dope with you?'

'You bet! Half my backpack's stuffed with it!'

Great news! Our neighbour had not long before been implicated in drug smuggling. I was under a certain amount of suspicion, not only because I was English and his neighbour, and had been frequently out and about with him and his wife, but also because my surname was identical to that of the man who had been arrested driving Bill's truck with all the cannabis aboard. Now our house was full of drug fiends. Could things possibly get any worse?

I regard myself as extremely tolerant, and I'm a sucker for a sob story. The Plump One, despite being a self-confessed, feckless, good-for-nothing who had never done an honest day's work in his life, had a certain charm. He had a gentle nature and was endearingly honest about his wicked ways. He recounted strings of offences from stealing cars to assaulting policemen. As a registered drug addict, he was in the care of a social worker, and at every court appearance he had been discharged as a hopeless case.

He had a pharmaceutical encyclopaedia where he could find what kind of effect every drug would induce. When he found one that sounded fun, he looked up which ailment it was prescribed for, then researched the symptoms for that particular condition before trotting along to the doctor's surgery. There he would reel off a string of symptoms, suggesting to the doctor what the prescribed treatment was, coming away with the requisite prescription. His doctor, he said, was a very good sort. Generous state benefits ensured that the Plump One lived in comfort and enjoyed a self-indulgent lifestyle at the expense of the tax-payer.

I should have been shaking my head in dismay, but there was a child-like *innocence* about him, as if he really didn't believe he was doing anything wrong. I just couldn't dislike him.

'Where do you get the money to buy heroin?' I asked.

He smiled. 'Don't ask! There are ways if you know how. My sister's a lesbian, and she and her partner want a baby. If I make her partner pregnant, so the baby is like their own real biological baby, they're going to pay me five hundred pounds. But my mum's not very happy about the idea.'

'Oh,' I said. 'But now you've decided to quit the heroin?'

'Yeah. I know it's crazy, I've seen the error of my ways and I really want to get myself together. I'll leave if you want me to.'

He seemed so sincere. I agreed he could stay for as long as it took him to sort himself out, provided it didn't stretch into years, and he did something to help. For the next couple of days Dreadlocks worked, the Plump One went through the motions, and they drank beer, beer and more beer. We were going to need a skip to clear all the bottles. The 'builder' smirked and ate all the food.

Terry arrived for a visit, and as it was the weekend, we asked our helpers if they'd like to spend a day in town. We drove them to Poitiers, gave them each 500 francs to enjoy themselves, and arranged to collect them that evening from outside the *Hôtel de Ville* at 10.30pm.

It was a foregone conclusion that something would go wrong. At 10.30pm Dreadlocks was waiting, but there was no sign of the Plump One.

'I've been looking for him for hours. Checked out every bar in town. Heaven knows where he's got to,' said Dreadlocks.

What could we do? How did we go about finding one chubby person with a drugs problem on a Saturday evening in a town with a population of approximately ninety thousand? We drove around for an hour, peering into low dives and seamy bars, returning periodically to the appointed spot, where the Plump One still was not.

'There's not much more we can do, except go home and wait for him to call. He's got our phone number and address, hasn't he?'

Of course he hadn't.

Dreadlocks wasn't worried. 'He's always getting lost. He got robbed in Thailand and lost everything: passport, money, air ticket, all his clothes. But he sorted it out. He always does. Don't worry, he'll be back tomorrow.' He wasn't. While his friend spent the day sitting in the sunshine and working his way through the beers, we waited for news of our troublesome guest. When none came, we followed Dreadlocks' lead that evening and drowned our worries, then wobbled to bed hoping that our lost soul would eventually turn up.

The phone woke us at just after 2.00am.

'Madame Kelly?'

'*Oui.*'

'This is the *Hôtel de Police* in Poitiers. There is a young man here who is lost, and he thinks maybe he is staying with you. Will you speak to him, please?'

It was indeed our missing young man, and the nice policeman asked if we could come and collect him immediately. As the least inebriated driver, I had to drive there and walk into the police station to retrieve the prodigal who was, for the first time since he'd arrived, sober.

'I got lost,' he explained. 'Started going from bar to bar, and then found it was daylight. I didn't know where I was. I thought it was near Paris where your house was, so I followed the signs in that direction. I ended up in an industrial area, and I was really tired. I found my way to the police station. I wanted to phone my mum, but I didn't have any money.' He'd drunk all of the 500 francs.

'The police tried phoning her for me, but she'd gone out for the day and didn't get home until after midnight. So I sat around in the police station all day until they finally managed to speak to her. Luckily, she had your phone number.' Aren't mothers wonderful?

The following week unfolded much like the previous one: Dreadlocks dug trenches and drank quantities of beer; the Plump One did his best, which wasn't very much. On Thursday evening, we took them out to a restaurant where they ate and drank to their limit. We had also invited Jim, who took the two of them back to his house, plying them with further quantities of alcohol. We heard them staggering back in the very early hours, and weren't surprised when there was no sign of them the next morning, apart from loud snoring interrupted by guttural belches and spluttery farts. We left them to sleep it off until after lunch, when I shouted up that perhaps they could think about getting up.

'F off, stupid, it's Christmas,' was the cheery response from

Dreadlocks.

An hour later, I tried again. Same response, but now they were playing a noise on the cassette machine, at full volume.

I pulled the plug and asked them politely to come down, have something to eat and give us a hand. Nothing happened, so I went off shopping.

When I came back, our builder was looking pale and shaky. He waylaid me outside the house.

'Look, I wouldn't go in,' he said. 'There's a lot of shouting going on. I'm staying out of it until it's over.'

I didn't want to have to stay out of my own house. If there was shouting going on, I wanted to be part of it.

Terry and Dreadlocks were glaring at each other. Until then, Dreadlocks had been a pleasant, well-spoken and reasonable young man, who spent several months of the year, he said, making jewellery in Thailand, the summer season on a Greek island selling his wares and running a bar. Now, oozing alcohol from every pore and leaking at the seams, he had worked himself into a frenzy of resentment. Did we think they were slaves? How dare we buy them cheap beer, and take them to cheap restaurants! How dare we tell them when to get up! If we thought we were going to tell them what to do, we were very much mistaken.

He plugged the tape player back in, deafening us with some kind of noise that sounded like a battlefield. I pulled the plug out again. He turned to where the beer was kept, but we'd moved it out of sight. He stamped to the wine rack and took a couple of bottles.

'You're not having anything more to drink until you've sobered up.' We took the bottles from him with some difficulty, while he stood shouting and trying to get around me to plug the noise in again. The Plump One appeared and tried to take the wine.

'Not now. Once you've sobered up, but you've had enough for now.' He fell into some sort of fit: yelping, shaking, waving his hands in the air, gasping.

'Gotta have something to drink. Gotta have something to drink.'

He really was in a dreadful state, so we gave him a bottle and he clambered back to the bedroom.

Dreadlocks had totally lost it. The pleasant face he had worn for the previous ten days fell off. He shouted, yelled and whirled around in circles until I told him to get his things together because he was leaving

Still cursing, he started packing his bag. The Plump One appeared. 'Shut up,' he said to his friend. 'These people have treated us very well, and we've been pigs. They don't deserve this.'

He turned to us.

'I really am sorry. We'll go now. Thanks for putting up with us.'

And so they left, the Plump One full of apologies and promises to keep in touch, Dreadlocks muttering about exploitation and slavery.

'You people think I'm nothing. You think I'm just a beach bum. Well, you're wrong. Let me tell you, on the island' – he named a Greek one – 'I'm a big, big man. I'm the cannabis king. Everybody knows me. I make a fortune. I could buy this place ten times over if I wanted to.'

OK, your majesty, farewell. Go and buy yourself some decent beer. And some soap.

Terry drove them to the station and left them there.

***

Our 'builder' couldn't hide his delight at this turn of events, but at the same time he wanted to know how he was expected to continue working without helpers. I hated the sight of his car arriving later and later each morning, and leaving earlier and earlier each evening. He'd been with us for almost a year. All the money we'd inherited had gone, and we'd had to borrow more to complete the project. The work wasn't getting done. A window he put in had fallen out. He drove huge nails through the new floorboards, leaving the heads sticking up like small metallic mushrooms. With a month to go before our first guests were due to arrive, the cottage was still no more than a shell full of rubble. One day, I went out for several hours and came back to find a deckchair set up in the back garden, surrounded by half a dozen coffee cups. I was aware that he was also helping himself to materials.

I said: 'We have a problem. I know you're not happy, and neither am I. What are we going to do about it?'

'I don't want to be involved in this project any more. You're a laughing stock. You're wasting your money on this dump. Nobody's ever going to want to come here on holiday. You're living in a dream world. Everybody's talking about you and your crazy ideas. How could you think people on holiday would want to come to a place like this?'

'I understand. I'll pay you up until today and then you've finished here.'

'Hang on a minute! I can't leave just like that. What am I going to do for money?'

I had no idea. I paid him off and he marched to his car, shouting over his shoulder: 'You didn't expect me to work here, with all your f-ing animals around me, did you?'

Because of the way things had been going, and because the cottages had to be ready in time as our future guests had already paid for their holidays and we'd spent the money, I'd spoken to another builder a month earlier who was prepared to take over. He started the next day.

The two cottages were both finished in time for the holiday season – well, almost. When the first guests arrived, the varnish on their staircase was still sticky. Three hours before the arrival of our second guests, 12 cubic yards of crushed limestone we'd ordered for the courtyard was delivered in a great heap. It took me and two friends several fevered hours of raking and tramping to flatten it.

Wandering around the cottages looking at the neat tiled floors, the plastered walls, the double-glazed windows and the fitted kitchens, I was quite envious. We still had a very long way to go before our own house reached that standard. Despite the doubts expressed by our erstwhile builder, our guests fell under the charm of our little hamlet and enjoyed the company of our animals. They loved the peace and quiet, sipping wine in the sunshine, helping themselves to raspberries and herbs, watching the birds, and the fact that within a short distance they could reach several large towns for shopping, or the Atlantic port of La Rochelle. Seeing their pleasure, I soon forgot the anguish and aggravation of the building project: it had all been worthwhile.

Chapter Thirty-nine

The landscape changed dramatically with the seasons. In winter, the steel ploughshares churned the stubble left from the previous year into the upturned clods of crimson mud; then the tractors harrowed the clods into neat ridges of a fine crumbly tilth that bleached to a soft beige after a few hours of wind or sun. Soon a flush of green showed as the first tips of wheat and oilseed rape raced each other skywards. The wheat turned from green to fawn and rustled crisply in the spring breeze, becoming golden as it ripened under the summer sun. Sunflowers blazed briefly in their yellow glory and maize covered the land in rows of rustling green spears like Roman legions on the march. During late autumn, the withered sunflowers and the maize were harvested by machinery working around the clock, leaving the fields stark and empty, ready for the return of the plough and another cycle.

It was then you could see the rocks and flints that carpeted the earth, and you had to marvel at how things as fragile and vulnerable as new shoots could possibly force themselves up through the ground past these shoulder-to-shoulder chunks. Nature is extraordinary.

There seemed to be no pattern to the weather. We'd worn T-shirts and eaten in the garden in December, sunbathed during January and February and had to light the fire in August. We'd seen severe drought and endured torrential rain for days on end. Despite the fact that it didn't get cold here (remember the estate agent's assurance), we had recorded -18°C, and on summer afternoons the thermometer had more than once registered 50°C. There were days when violent winds rattled the shutters and window panes, the roof visibly moved, the trees were bowed almost double, the chickens were lifted off their feet and blown around like paper bags. The weather forecasters used terms like *détestable* and *catastrophique*.

Nothing could have prepared us for the weather that swept away the last days of the twentieth century. On 26 December 1999, parts of France, including Paris, were assaulted by a storm that seemingly caught the weather forecasters unawares. It lifted bus shelters from their moorings in the pavements, tossed park benches around like kites, and toppled construction cranes. On the coast, boats were lifted from the sea and dropped into the fields a mile away. That night, forecasters advised people not to travel the following day as more high winds were likely.

On the 27th, just as night was falling, the second storm approached, sweeping its way from the Atlantic across Europe. It came gently at first, a soft hissing, caressing almost, and the trees swayed languorously to its rhythm. The hissing turned to a howl, tearing across the land, bending the trees. It was exhilarating to listen to, even inviting to venture out into. The night sky was supernaturally, impenetrably dark. The dogs and cats crouched unhappily in corners, whimpering. We could comfort them, but we were anxious about Leila, alone out in the field. Cindy had been put to sleep at a great old age the previous summer. We dared not shut Leila in the barn in case it collapsed, but she sheltered each night beside a tall concrete post. We feared that this, the huge oak or the linden trees might fall on her, but we could do nothing except pray and rely on her to keep herself safe until the storm blew itself out.

As the violence of the storm increased, the whole house shook, the windows rattled, the tiles shifted on the roof, and outside we could hear constant crashing. The wind's howl had turned to a furious shriek, an ear-splitting banshee wail as it reached speeds of up to 120 miles an hour. The electricity died. The telephone lines went down. Crazy thoughts went through my mind: we were witnessing the end of the world. It was almost the last day of the twentieth century, and this was it, the end of everything.

Despite the fear, it was exciting. Terry and I had to fight an impulse to stand outside and feel the unleashed power hurtling past us. It was just as well we did, because four large sheets of corrugated iron which formed part of Jim's roof were torn off in their entirety, together with the huge oak ridge beam, and carried 80 yards to the bottom of the garden. Tiles billowed around like leaves.

We climbed into bed and lay with the animals all around us. The storm exhausted itself just before daybreak, crooning as it died, leaving behind a calm just like any other early morning.

I was afraid to look outside when daylight came. *What about Leila?*

'Will you look?' I asked Terry.

He went to the window, and turned to me, smiling.

'Leila's fine. She's standing by the fence with her ears pricked. But the walnut tree's down.'

Seeing Terry at the window she whinnied, and we went to the gate, taking her breakfast. I should have trusted her wisdom. She knew how to look after herself.

Our little hamlet and its ancient buildings had survived almost unscathed. The only structural damage was Jim's new corrugated iron roof and a few dozen broken roof tiles. The huge oak and lindens had survived, but the walnut tree was blown over on its side. Most, but not all of its roots were sticking up out of the ground, with one strong branch keeping it propped at an angle of about twenty-five degrees. We piled soil all around its exposed roots and it survived, quickly putting out new growth over the next year.

The surrounding landscape was devastated. There was not a single road that wasn't blocked by fallen trees. I wept to see them lying dead, their roots poking up at the sky in pathetic defiance. In a copse of poplars just down the road, every one had been snapped in half like a toothpick. At a nearby cemetery, three great pines had collapsed onto the wall and several of the gravestones, smashing them into fragments. Ninety-two people in France were killed as a result of the storm, and an estimated three hundred and sixty million trees destroyed. In some historic forests, not a single tree was left standing – the landscape resembled the aftermath of a tank battle. It was forecast that it would take a hundred and fifty years for the countryside to recover. In some parts of the country, it would be many months before the electricity supply was restored. Although our region took a terrible battering from the storm, we and our fragile property had survived.

***

Four days after the hurricane, just before midnight, Terry and I stood in front of the town hall in Poitiers, the beautiful historic city where Joan of Arc was questioned and Eleanor of Aquitaine had held court.

We mingled with tens of thousands of dancing, singing French people – all peaceful, happy, strangers hugging each other – and we felt we were now part of our adopted country. A toothless vagrant came and serenaded me in a fine voice that did not match his tattered clothing. Lasers projected messages of world peace onto the front of the splendiferous *Hôtel de Ville*, with recorded voices reading the messages aloud.

As midnight struck, the sky blazed with fireworks and the champagne corks flew into the twenty-first century. It was a supremely poignant moment.

It was four and a half years since we'd arrived. We'd been put to the test of starting new lives, coping with the unexpected, surviving crises and dealing with tragedies. Along the way, we had made many friends, had many laughs and learned many lessons. One lesson was that you never knew what was around the corner, so you'd better be ready for anything.

Many of our friends have moved elsewhere or returned to England, but Carole and Norrie, who helped us so much in the early days, are still here. They live not far away, and we see them regularly.

In the garden, little islands mark the resting places of our pets. Except for ours, all the English-owned properties in the hamlet have changed hands over the years. Madame Meneteau and Madame St Martin are still here, so is Jean-Luc, and so are the Roly Polys.

We have no plans to leave, although Brexit may force us to do so. At this time, nobody knows what will happen to those British who have chosen to make our lives in Europe.

2018

Photographs

Bathroom wall

Bathroom

First bathroom

Ladder to bedroom from future kitchen

Lavatory with view of cherry tree

Looking down to the kitchen

Second kitchen

Site of original kitchen

Acknowledgements

Diane Chandler, Janet Daykin and Carole Morrow were generous enough to give their time to read and offer their suggestions on the draft document, all of which were invaluable.

Andrew Ives used his eagle eye and editing skills to winkle out and crush the bugs that found their way into the final manuscript.

Stephanie at Blackbird Books has been, as always, a constant source of encouragement, as well as being infinitely patient.

The supremely talented David Lewis, whose client portfolio includes, amongst many other luminaries, myself and Her Majesty Queen Elizabeth II, created the enchanting cover art.

I am so grateful to them all.

This is the link to join my (very infrequent!) mailing list: http://eepurl.com/zyBFP (All email details securely managed at Mailchimp.com and never shared with third parties.)

More Susie Kelly Travel Books

I Wish I Could Say I Was Sorry
A US and Australian Amazon Top 40 Ranking Bestseller
'*A Child Called It* meets *Out Of Africa* in this stunning memoir of a woman's 1950s childhood in Kenya. Filled with candid humor and insights, this authentic tale captures one woman's incredible coming-of-age journey.' BookBub

Safari Ants, Baggy Pants & Elephants: A Kenyan Odyssey
The long-awaited sequel to *I Wish I Could Say I Was Sorry*. More than 40 years after leaving Kenya, Susie unexpectedly finds herself returning for a safari organised by an old friend. With her husband Terry, Susie sets off for a holiday touring the game reserves, but what she finds far exceeds her expectations.

Swallows & Robins: The Laughs & Tears Of A Holiday Home Owner
Finalist, The People's Book Prize 2016
'Laugh out loud funny. A must-read for anyone dreaming of the good life running gites in France.' *The Good Life France*

The Valley Of Heaven And Hell: Cycling In The Shadow of Marie-Antoinette
Novice cyclist Susie wobbles on her bike for 500 miles through Paris and Versailles, the battlefields of World War 1, the Champagne region and more.

Travels With Tinkerbelle: 6,000 Miles Around France In A Mechanical Wreck
Join Susie, Terry and 2 huge dogs on a 6,000-mile journey around the perimeter of France.

Best Foot Forward: A 500-Mile Walk Through Hidden France
When Susie decides, at the age of 50+, on a whim, to trek alone across France from La Rochelle to Lake Geneva in Switzerland, she entrusts her French farmhouse full of assorted animals to a total stranger from San Antonio, Texas.

The Lazy Cook (1) Quick & Easy Meatless Meals
The first of Susie's delightful round-ups of her favourite quick, simple, easy recipes, sprinkled with anecdote and humour.

The Lazy Cook (2) Quick & Easy Sweet Treats
'I like a dessert to make me feel slightly guilty about eating it, but not enough to make me stop.'

All of the above titles are also available in paperback on Amazon and can be ordered from good bookshops worldwide

La Vie En Rose
A pick from some of the best bits of the popular travel author's blog diaries reveal the minutiae of expat day to day life in rural France. A must-read for Susie Kelly fans and anybody thinking of, or dreaming of, moving to France. *Kindle only*

Blackbird Digital Books
The #authorpower publishing company
Discovering outstanding authors
www.blackbird-books.com
@Blackbird_Bks

Blackbird